Understanding THE *Prophets* AND THEIR *Books*

VINCENT P. BRANICK

D1596516

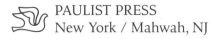
PAULIST PRESS
New York / Mahwah, NJ

The scripture quotations contained herein are translations by the author.

Cover photo: Monument to Gospel Authors, Kiev City, courtesy of Sergey Kamshylin/Shutterstock.com

Cover and book design by Lynn Else

All the charts and maps in this book are by the author.

Citations from *Ancient Near Eastern Texts Relating to the Old Testament—Third Edition with Supplement*, edited by James B. Pritchard, copyright © 1950, 1955, 1969, renewed 1978 by Princeton University Press. Reprinted by permission of Princeton University Press.

Library of Congress Cataloging-in-Publication Data

Branick, Vincent P.
    Understanding the prophets and their books / Vincent P. Branick.
       p. cm.
    Includes index.
    ISBN 978-0-8091-4763-2 (alk. paper) — ISBN 978-1-61643-138-9 1. Bible. O.T.
Prophets—Criticism, interpretation, etc. I. Title.
    BS1505.52.B73 2012
    224'.06—dc23
                                                                2012002143

Published by Paulist Press
997 Macarthur Boulevard
Mahwah, New Jersey 07430

www.paulistpress.com

Printed and bound in the
United States of America

Contents

Contents

Part II:
THE PROPHETS OF THE SEVENTH CENTURY
AND OF THE PERIOD OF THE EXILE

Contents

Contents

Contents

Dedicated to the memory of
Lawrence Boadt, CSP

Preface

This is a study of the sixteen books attributed to prophets now found in Jewish and Christian Bibles. It is a study of the faith of Israel, the faith implied in the preaching of these prophets and then expressed by Israel in the writing, collecting, and canonizing of this preaching.

This study, therefore, proposes both a historical and a theological understanding of these texts. For religious people of the Jewish or Christian faith, these texts are supposed to nourish faith, to provide insight into God's ways, to mediate the word of God for the contemporary readers, to speak of divine realities to people today.

This theological effort, however, is not the same as simply allowing religious and inspiring thoughts to enter our minds while reading the Old Testament texts. It is also not the same as simply repeating the words of the biblical texts. Rather, real theological understanding is an attempt to understand the authors—that collectivity of storytellers, writers, and editors—with their historical intentions and contexts as saying something to us today.

Such a theological and historical grasp of ancient documents is difficult. It involves letting the truth of the texts grasp us, yet these texts were not written for us. A huge cultural and temporal gap separates us from the writers and editors of these texts, and we must respect that gap. As religious scholars, however, our expectation is to find a connection between the faith of these historical writers and our faith.

That continuity with the present appears especially in the historical faith that directed the writings and in the religious themes that often link the writings together. Whether it is the importance of care for the poor, the link between sin and death, or the evil of hypocritical religion, a theme arises from repeated clusters of stories and images and summons people to decisions.

The faith expressed by a theme touches structures of life that reach beyond ancient historical contexts and embrace also our day, allowing the ancient text to speak to us now.

I consider this study as one of "biblical theology." However, I do not want to simply "distill" the images, stories, and injunctions in the biblical texts into ideas. Therefore, I have selected the format of biblical commentary on select **Significant Passages**. The theological themes will be summarized in the **Message** section of each chapter, but only after study of the texts and with constant reference back to those texts.

By no means is this study meant to substitute or even distract from the reading of the biblical texts of scripture and the effort to gain a thorough familiarity with those texts. The commentaries provided for each of the **Significant Passages** are meant to be read after a reading of the actual biblical text. I strongly suggest, therefore, the reader have two books open at once, a Bible and this book.

The English translations of the Hebrew and Aramaic are mine. I would suggest reading the full biblical texts either with the New Revised Standard Version (NRSV) or the New American Bible (NAB), two excellent translations. No translation, however, can at once capture the artistic elegance of the original language, express the precise idea of the text, and read well in English. I chose to give priority to the precise idea. The differences among the versions can dramatize the possibilities of the text.

This book was in progress and accepted for publication during the final months of Father Lawrence Boadt's work as editor at Paulist Press. Larry was a friend. We studied together. We met at professional conferences. He did much to support and encourage me, especially in his work at Paulist Press. I was saddened by his death in 2010, and I hope that this work will testify to his efforts to evangelize through the printed—and electronic—word.

I want also to thank my wife, Arlene, for her painstaking efforts to proof the typed copy of this book despite her own busy schedule of work for the Community of Apostolic Christians and the Dayton Art Institute.

Thanks also to my colleagues at the University of Dayton who gave me the sabbatical to finish this study.

Dayton, Ohio, 2011

Preliminaries

1
Historical and Literary Background of Biblical Prophecy

I. The Historical and Cultural Background of Prophecy

A. IN ANCIENT ISRAEL

Prophecy was alive and well in Israel long before Amos barked his condemnation of Israel in the mid-eighth century BC. The ancient story of Deborah in Judges speaks of her as a "prophetess" (Judg 4:4). First Samuel narrates the leadership role of Samuel as not only "judge" but also as "prophet" (1 Sam 3:20). The books of Kings narrate the activity of Nathan, Elijah, and Elisha, among many others who spoke in Yahweh's name, advising and even threatening kings, calling the nation back to the traditional faith of Israel. Common to all these prophets was their role as extraordinary preachers who preach dramatically on subjects of fundamental importance at times of religious crisis. (For a more detailed study of these preliterary prophets, see my study, *Understanding the Historical Books of the Old Testament* [Mahwah, NJ: Paulist Press, 2011].)

The Hebrew Old Testament generally names such a person a *nabi'*. Greek translators chose the word *prophêtês*, the cognate of our English word *prophet*. The Hebrew word, *nabi'*, by itself seemed to connote the idea of a spokesperson. We see this in the commission to Aaron as Moses' mouthpiece: "See, I make you a god to Pharaoh, and your brother Aaron shall serve as your *nabi'*" (Exod 7:1). We see this defining function of the spokesperson for God also in the messenger formulas used by so many of the literary prophets such as, "Thus says Yahweh" or "The word of Yahweh."

Within the narratives of the Old Testament, the word *prophet*, however, is a broad term. We see, for instance, references to groups, like the "band of prophets" (1 Sam 10:5), "sons of the prophets" (2 Kgs 2:3), "prophets of Yahweh" (1 Kgs 18:4), or "prophets of Ba'al" (1 Kgs 18:19). These "prophets" often appear in a mantic state, where they appear to lose conscious self-possession (l Sam 19:24). On the other hand, we also see rugged individuals, like Elijah and Elisha, reputed to be prophets by the people or claiming to be prophets. Their prophecy appears more as a conscious argumentation with others.

The high esteem of prophecy at this time appears also in the way the stories of many of the past patriarchs and leaders of Israel were formed to portray them as prophets. A tradition of storytelling identified by modern scholars as that of "the Elohist" (E) developed at the time of the monarchy. In that tradition, Abraham is explicitly called a prophet (Gen 20:7). In another tradition identified today as that of "the Deuteronomist" (D), Moses becomes the paradigm of prophecy (Deut 18:15–18). The activity of these earlier leaders that attracted the title "prophet" was that of speaking in God's name, publicly declaring a message derived, not from themselves, but from God.

Contrary to a common misunderstanding today, the principal concern of the prophet was not the future but rather their current situation, the events, vicissitudes, and challenges to the religious faith of their contemporaries. When the prophets spoke about the future and made true predictions, they did so only as that future related to events contemporary to themselves and their audience. In fact, their predictions tended to be so vague that they did not give any real control over the future in the manner of a fortune-teller. Their words were directed to the audience in front of them, not to an unknown people of a future era. Separating the word of God spoken by the prophets from the historical setting addressed by that word, therefore, inevitably entails a loss of meaning.

B. OUTSIDE ISRAEL

Historical evidence suggests Israel probably derived both the very concept of a prophet as well as many prophetic literary forms from non-Israelite prophetism. Ancient extrabiblical documents suggest that prophetism flourished outside of Israel (see Appendix 1a). Even the Old Testament itself presupposes a recognition of non-Israelite prophecy. This recognition appears in the story of Balaam, a Moabite prophet, who blesses Israel instead of cursing this enemy, to the chagrin of his employer (Num 22—24). The story hinges on the accepted existence of prophecy outside of Israel. The same acceptance appears also in the story of the prophets of Ba'al (1 Kgs 18). These prophets were not "false prophets" in the sense of pretending to be something they were not. Their problem was that they were not prophets of Yahweh, as was Elijah.

When considered in this larger historical context, prophetism appears to center around the image of an official "messenger." Even after the advent of writing in the ancient Near East around 4000 BC, communication in oral form took place over distances with accuracy and authenticity. Messengers memorized the message of the sender, physically crossed the distance between the sender and the addressee, and ultimately delivered the message orally to the addressee. The messenger served as the ambassador of the sender and when delivering the message would use "messenger formulas" such as, "The king...has sent me," "The word of the king," or "I, the king, say to you...." The messages from the king often developed from a meeting with his advisers, in Hebrew known as the *sôd* or "council" of the king.

When the theological storytellers of this time attempted to visualize the life of the gods, they patterned the gods' way of life after the way of life among kings. They pictured a high god meeting with his council, or *sôd*, and then sending "living letters" to other gods (see Appendix 1b).

C. THE ADAPTATION OF PROPHECY WITHIN ISRAEL

When Israel's storytellers and writers described Yahweh and his dealings with human beings, they used and adapted this language. This adaptation is graphic in the prophet Micaiah's description of the court and *sôd* of Yahweh (1 Kgs 22:1923), in Isaiah's description of his inaugural vision (Isa 6:1–12), and in Job's description of the *sôd* of Yahweh (Job 1—2). The plural in Genesis 1:26, "Let *us* make man in *our* image and likeness," may well reflect this same situation.

Israelite theologians reformed the myths by replacing the non-Israelite gods with the one God of Israel. In Israel's conception of Yahweh meeting with his council or *sôd*, no other gods are present. The lesser gods of the myths become—in the language of Israel's writers—*bᵉne 'elohim*, "sons of God," or *mal'achim*, the Hebrew word for "messengers," which we also translate "angels." Israelite prophetism fits into this picture of Yahweh transmitting his decisions through messengers. Now human beings instead of angels serve as Yahweh's messengers or "living letters" to his covenanted people, Israel.

The uniqueness of prophecy within Israel lies also in the manner of the exercise of that prophecy. We find no parallel to the story of Nathan's accusation of King David (2 Sam 11—12) or Elijah's opposition to the northern monarchs (1 Kgs 18—2 Kgs 1). We find nothing that parallels the prophets' oracles of woe against their own nation. Such action would be absolutely unheard of in Egypt or Mesopotamia. Only in a political and social context where loyalty to God outweighs loyalty to one's nation and king, only in the context of Israel's faith, does the exercise of prophecy as we see it in the Old Testament make sense. Israel may have inherited the concept of "the prophet" from neighboring cultures, but that concept began a radical transformation when it made contact with Israel's faith.

D. THE PROPHETIC BOOKS

The prophets of our study, the "literary prophets," begin to appear in the last years of the northern kingdom. Unlike the earlier "preaching prophets," who preached but left no writings, the literary prophets not only preached but somehow left behind writings for the benefit of posterity. In the Old Testament we generally identify fifteen literary prophets. The three major prophets are

Isaiah, Jeremiah, and Ezekiel. The twelve minor prophets are Hosea, Joel, Amos, Obadiah, Jonah, Micah, Nahum, Habakkuk, Zephaniah, Haggai, Zechariah, and Mal'aki. The Book of Jonah, however, stands apart as very different from the other prophetic books and will be treated separately. In the Greek Bible, the translation made around the second century BC (a translation usually indicated by the Roman numerals LXX) for Diaspora Jews, the Book of Daniel was also grouped among the prophets, as it is in most Christian Bibles. Again, this sixteenth book also needs to be treated separately.

For understanding the literary formation or writing of the prophetic books, we have very little data. Isaiah 8:16–20 mentions the writing of a record to be kept by Isaiah's disciples. Jeremiah 36 speaks of a scroll that Baruch, the prophet's disciple, wrote and rewrote at the dictation of Jeremiah. These writings, it would appear, form the nucleus around which the books of Isaiah and Jeremiah developed.

On the other hand, the activities and personalities of these prophets do not appear like those of professional writers or scribes. Like Moses in the desert, these firebrands looked much too busy to spend long stretches with quill and papyrus. Moreover, the "books" now named for these prophets do not appear as unified compositions, but rather like collections of short speeches, sometimes without much order.

Some accounts, like the "confessions" of Jeremiah (Jer 11:18—12:6; 15:10–21; 17:12–18; 18:18–23; 20:7–18) appear so personal that they may not initially have been intended for publication. They may very well have been integrated into the book, not by the prophet himself, but by disciples remembering these confidential communications.

All this suggests that the books that we have of the prophets are actually written not by the prophets themselves but by their disciples who gathered notes taken from the sermons of the prophets. This hypothesis would explain why the books now appear like hodgepodge collections of small units. If the books began with disciples copying snatches of the prophets' speeches, collecting these notes, then arranging them into larger collections, we can understand how topics can shift suddenly, for instance, from prophesies of woe to those of salvation. The books do not appear as unified literary works, but rather as anthologies of spoken sermons interspersed with narratives explaining their historical contexts.

In this view, the difference between the early "preaching" prophets and the later "literary" prophets would therefore not lie in the medium of delivery—one preaching the other writing. Rather, the difference seems to lie in the preservation of their instructions. The words of the early nonliterary prophets have now been lost except for the brief summaries in the books of Samuel and Kings. Those of the literary prophets have been preserved in the notes and collections made by their disciples.

E. THE PROPHETS AND THE TORAH

The usual approach to the study of the prophets is to begin with the Torah, the first five books of the Old Testament, known also from the Greek as the Pentateuch, considered even today in the Jewish faith the heart of the Bible. The books of the prophets as they now appear in our Bibles then function as a canonical interpretation of the Torah, just as the letters of Paul in the New Testament are often read as a privileged interpretation of the gospels.

Although the history of the writing of the Torah remains a matter of scholarly controversy, the portrayal of God dictating these writings to Moses in the middle of the twelfth century BC appears to most scholars as a literary fiction, simplifying a much more complicated history of multiple oral and written traditions—J, E, P, and D—gradually developing and coalescing into our present collection of the five books of Moses. The more or less final form of this collection appears to date from the fifth century BC as an effort to reestablish the identity of Israel after the Babylonian Exile (587–538 BC).

The books of the prophets—like the letters of Paul in the New Testament—are thus witnesses to an earlier stage in the development of faith. In fact, the writings of the prophets, especially the pre-exilic prophets, provide an extraordinary window into the development of this Torah. In the **Overview** sections of our treatment of each prophetic writing, we will attempt to glean whatever information we can about that particular prophet's understanding of what we today see in our Pentateuch.

II. Literary Analysis

For a modern reader, understanding the writings of the prophets can be a real challenge. Instead of an interesting narration, we find a collage of images and warnings, often disjointed. The thought jumps from portraits of disaster to calls for hope and joy. Nothing is really resolved. Hardly any plot appears, except for the "superplot" of God dealing with his rebellious people.

Like a large and detailed tapestry, the books of the prophets require not one but several approaches, including moving up close with a magnifying glass and then stepping back for general impressions. A real understanding of these writings might well involve five important steps.

A. UNDERSTANDING THE PARTS AND DIVISIONS OF THE PROPHETIC BOOKS.

First, we need to understand the distinguishable parts of the prophetic books. The collection of sermons and narrations that form the whole of our prophetic books appears somewhat artificial. As mentioned above, the books are probably the anthology of diverse notes contributed by followers. Rarely is there any narrative thread to follow. In some ways, then, the sum of the parts of these books is more than the whole. Any attempt to read these books simply from start to finish would most likely lead to a discouraging bewilderment. For instance, the Book of Jeremiah looks like the collection of at least three accounts of the prophet's preaching and life, assembled one after the other without clear indications of beginnings and ends. Someone reading this book from start to finish would be thrown back and forth in the temporal sequence.

The chapter divisions in these books, as well as in the rest of the Bible, came in during the Middle Ages and as many times as not disregard the more significant divisions. On the other hand, repeated superscripts or other formulas in the text often give us a better sense of the real divisions of the book. Sometimes the editors seemed to have a clear organizing theme as they grouped material, such as Amos's visions of destruction (Amos 7—9) or the "oracles against nations" found together in many of the longer books.

Furthermore, within the major parts of the biblical books, we find smaller literary units each with its structure and theme, each developed perhaps for different audiences and purposes, some apparently combined by followers and editors. The units, sometimes only a few verses long, contain insights that require leisurely gazes. We therefore need to know when to pause.

In the **Overview** to each prophet, this study will suggest a major division that seems to work well. The **appendices** of this book will also include more detailed outlines of the biblical books. In the **Significant Passages** section of each book, the grouping of verses will attempt to follow the smaller literary units.

Remembering the outline of each prophetic book may be one of the most important tools for understanding this literature. The outline provides a broad overview for the book, allows us to situate important passages, and helps us remember where these passages are.

B. Understanding the Forms of Prophetic Speech

Second, a tool for dividing the biblical book into the smaller literary units is the work of classifying the forms of prophetic speech. These forms often had an elaborate structure that helps us see beginnings and ends. The forms also help us understand the intention of the prophet as he seemed to follow those forms—or sometimes deliberately distort them. This will become clearer as we study the texts. Much study has gone into the identification of these forms. Here is a sketch of the more accepted results.

1. The Messenger Formula

The major part of prophetic literature appears to have developed around the fundamental literary form used by the most ancient messenger-prophets, namely, the messenger formula, often in the context of a divine judgment against an individual or against the nation. In its full form, the messenger formula contained the following structure:

> a. *The commissioning* of the messenger: "Go out to meet Ahaz...and say to him..." (Isa 7:3–4); see also "Start down to meet Ahab....This is what you shall tell him" (2 Kgs 21:17–18)
> b. *The accusation* in the form of either an accusing question or a direct statement, with a causal connection expressed by the words, "because you," or the equivalent
> c. *The messenger formula*: "Yahweh says..."
> d. *The judgment*, introduced often by "therefore"

From this basic structure for literary form, other forms develop.

2. The Inaugural Vision

The inaugural vision is an outgrowth of the first part of the messenger formula, the commission of the prophet by Yahweh. Its significance hinges on the importance of the prophet convincing his audience that he is an authentic messenger from the *sôd* of the covenant king. The best examples of inaugural visions are in Isaiah 6, Jeremiah 1, Ezekiel 1—3, and Isaiah 40:1–8. Amos does not properly describe an inaugural vision, but his words in 3:3–8 and 7:14–15 serve the same purpose.

In addition to authenticating the prophet as Yahweh's messenger, the inaugural visions of Isaiah, Jeremiah, Ezekiel, and Deutero-Isaiah often serve as a summary of the prophet's message. In Isaiah 6 the prophet claims that he has been admitted to stand before the *sôd* of Yahweh and that Yahweh has decided to send Isaiah with a message of judgment against Israel.

3. The Rîb or Lawsuit

The *rîb*, often translated "lawsuit" or "controversy," is connected with the second and third parts of the basic forms of prophetic speech, the accusations and announcement of judgment. As a rhetorical device, the *rîb* is an adaptation of Israel's trial procedures, dramatizing the accusations and judgments of Yahweh against the unfaithful vassal, Israel.

Ezekiel 17:11–21 provides an example of a secular *rîb*, a suzerainty-pact lawsuit between a human king and his vassal. We find here the "lawsuit" between Nebuchadnezzar, the suzerain king of the Babylonian Empire, and King Zedekiah, the vassal king of Judah. In this *rîb*, Judah is found guilty of infidelity to Nebuchadnezzar, who had made a suzerainty pact with Judah following the siege and fall of Jerusalem in 598 BC.

The first chapter of Isaiah illustrates the use of the *rîb* to describe Israel haled into court to account for her crimes against the covenant and to be judged guilty by Yahweh. In Isaiah 1:1–31, Isaiah presents himself as Yahweh's messenger who has been sent out from the court of Yahweh following the judgment that has been enacted in the *sôd* of the covenant king. In this passage we see the commissioning of the messenger, the accusation, the judgment, all part of the *rîb* giving form to the prophetic speech. The forensic vocabulary is unmistakable.

v. 2a:	Summoning of *witnesses* against Israel (the heavens and the earth)
vv. 2b–3:	The covenant king's complaint in the form of an *accusation*
vv. 4–9, 10–14:	Further *accusations, interrogations,* and threats
vv. 16–20:	An *appeal* from the covenant judge
vv. 21–23:	A final *complaint*
vv. 24–31:	The covenant king's announcement of *judgment*

The *rîb* lent itself to many forms and variations. Isaiah's "Song of the Vineyard Owner" (Isa 5:1–7) is a *rîb* in poetic form. Here Yahweh complains that Israel, his vineyard, has produced only "wild grapes." The most elaborate use of the *rîb* as a literary device is found in the Book of Job where it is used as background for the book as a whole.

We see echoes of the *rîb* in the New Testament. Forensic vocabulary fills the Fourth Gospel. The Advocate is promised who will condemn the world and declare Jesus as innocent, while scripture and John the Baptist are witnesses at this great trial.

4. The Dirge or Funeral Lament

To describe the certainty of divine punishment, a punishment unto death, the prophets on occasion draw on the literary form by which one mourned a beloved dead person. This was the dirge or funeral lament. Amos laments Israel as dead: "She is fallen to rise no more, the virgin Israel....Therefore in every square there shall be lamentation (*qînah*)" (Amos 5:2, 16). Micah mourns over the mortal wound of Judah as a result of Sennacherib's invasion: "Because of this I lament and wail...for her wound is incurable" (Mic 1:8–9). Deutero-Zechariah describes the funeral lament over "one who was pierced through...as one mourns for an only son" (Zech 12:10).

5. Parables and Allegories

When Isaiah wanted to depict the disappointment of God in Israel, he told the story of a vineyard owner who expended great energy in his field yet received only "wild grapes" at the harvest. As Isaiah then explains, the vineyard represented Israel, and the whole story was meant to illustrate one idea, the destructive disappointment of God in his people (Isa 5:1–7). This story is a classic parable.

Ezekiel also used imaginative narration to point his messages. His stories, like that of the eagle and the great tree, however, incorporated details that had distinct symbolic value. The great eagle represented the king of Babylon. The crest of the cedar represented Jehoiachin (Ezek 17:1–10). By this detailed symbolism within the story, this narration moves into the category of allegory.

C. Appreciating the Poetry of the Writing

Third, understanding the prophets means understanding the poetic character of their writings. We need to look for intense images rather than clear and precise concepts. For Amos, God is a roaring lion (Amos 3:8). According to Hosea, Israel is a faithless prostitute (Hos 9:1). For Micah, Zion shall be plowed like a field (Mic 4:1). For Isaiah, God's salvation will sprout like a living shoot from a tree stump (Isa 11:1).

In reading this poetry, the first step is to identify the image as such and then speculate about the evocative power of that image. Why would the prophet use it here? What did the image suggest for him? What does it suggest for us? The task is above all to understand how that image fits into the message of the poet-prophet and then eventually to understand how that image could fit into our world.

Like all good poetry, the thought is dense, at times even to the point of obscurity. Isaiah's sign to assist King Ahaz in an extremely complex international decision is simply this: "The young woman will be pregnant and bear a son and will name him Immanuel" (Isa 7:14). That is basically it! How is that supposed to advise Ahaz on diplomacy at a time of war?

What the obscure density forces us to do is to stop and look. What background or context could make this thought apply to the situation at hand? What deeper meaning is implied? The obscurity also becomes the way of evoking a wider vision. Much is left to the audience or reader, which explains the wide range of applications of the prophetic texts, including Matthew's use of this text to explain the conception of Jesus (Matt 1:22–23).

Some poetic images appear with a certain consistency throughout the various prophets, like the images of the disappointing vine, the faithless spouse, the city of Jerusalem, the desert, the sprout or bud, the day of Yahweh, and the human heart as either hard and resistant to God or as transformed. In the **Message** section of our study of each prophet, we will attempt to inventory the most striking images.

D. FINDING MEANING IN THE ASSOCIATIONS OF WORDS AND IMAGES

The images also often come in patterns and connections. One image is associated with another. It is in these associations that we can understand the particular nuances intended by the author. At times one image clearly explains another.

Therefore, as a fourth step, we need to find a mediating thought that bridges the two images. For example, Isaiah 40:6 describes the prophet hesitant to cry out: "What shall I cry out?" The next image is "All humanity is grass." What is the connection of this expression with the preceding? Is this a divine response to the prophet telling him what to cry out or is it perhaps the reason given by the prophet why he does not know what to cry out? We cannot be sure what the author intended, but reading this second image as in the mouth of a reluctant prophet fits the general pattern in other prophets and sets up the counterargument two verses later: "The word of our God stands forever" (40:9). Finding an association of images and ideas consistent with the general message and historical context of the author is thus the key to understanding these texts.

The identifiable structures of ancient Hebrew poetry are powerful tools for our grasp of the associations. The basic structure of the poetry of the prophets and of the Bible in general is parallelism. In Hebrew poetry, intensity is developed by repeating the same thought with different words and images. Amos states:

> The lion roars—who will not be afraid!
> Yahweh God speaks—who will not prophesy! (3:8)

Because parallelism associates one image with another, recognizing the structure is a basic tool for grasping the evocative power of the image and the overall point of the prophet. In the example here we can therefore associate not only "the lion" with "Yahweh God," but also God's speaking with roaring, and prophecy with being afraid. The point seems to be to portray God as dangerous and compelling. Any sense of a gentle, soothing God is wiped out by this parallelism. Any sense of the prophet wanting "to think about" the job is eliminated.

In larger units, that association of images and ideas can be quite complex. At first no obvious connection appears, and we must speculate about the pattern that brought those images and ideas together in the mind of the author. That pattern could be a historical event, a story or liturgy, an idea or theme. For instance, the text of Isaiah 1:5–8 combines the images of a severely wounded person, of cities burnt, and of a shed in a melon patch. The reference to "daughter Zion" (5:8) suggests the background pattern is an attack on Jerusalem. The siege of Jerusalem by Sennacherib in 701 BC allows all of these images to cohere in a mournful lament over the destruction left by the Assyrians. We cannot be sure about this background pattern because the prophet does not explicitly identify it, but as long as it works to bring meaning to the text, we can justifiably use it as a working hypothesis until a better suggestion turns up.

E. Understanding the Texts as Exhortation

Fifth, and as a corollary to what we said about the poetic nature of the texts, we need constantly to keep in mind the practical intention and tone of the prophets. When they preached, the prophets intended to move their audience not only to believe but to live their belief. To this end, they used all the customary rhetorical techniques employed by preachers. They exhorted, rebuked, threatened, cajoled, enticed. They stormed the will by appealing to the imagination, employing all the persuasive power of concrete words, similes, metaphors, parables, allegories, paradoxes, and even puns.

Above all, they exaggerated. To describe the peace and justice of the reign of "Immanuel," Isaiah speaks of the wolf and the lamb, the leopard and the kid, the calf and the lion, the baby and the cobra as playing together (Isa 11:1–9)! Zephaniah gets the attention of his audience by proclaiming, "I will completely sweep away all things from the face of the earth, says Yahweh" (Zeph 1:2). Yet the book concludes with God's promise, "I will leave in your midst a people humble and lowly…the remnant of Israel" (3:12). The prophet was not a legislator, a sociologist, or a scientist who needed to speak with precision. He was a prophet, a preacher with a mission to make God's will and plan for his people ring in their ears and resonate in their hearts. To this end he is more concerned about the intensity and passion of his words than their precision and clarity.

2
Reading the Prophets for Their Theology and Message

There comes a point in reading scripture when we must step back from examining the text and let the text question us. We read scripture to find guidance and clarity of purpose. We listen to scripture in church to guide our prayers. The canon of scripture, the list of books to be included in the Bible, was chosen so that believers of all times could have a criterion of faith. The books of the prophets, along with the rest of scripture, are therefore supposed to be authoritative texts. How do we find this authority?

The choice by the Jewish people and then by the early church of the biblical canon was a recognition that truth was expressed by these texts. A text describing someone's perception of things can be ignored. A text describing the way things truly are makes us take a position. Truth has its own power over the person who understands it. How do we find this truth?

This may be the easiest and the most difficult part of the study. In some ways it may be easy to grasp the truth of scripture. Simple people have done it for centuries. Over and over again, people recount reading a text of the prophets or any other part of the Bible and being touched by the message without any great effort on their part. And this can happen without much knowledge of the history around the text or the literary forms within the text.

On the other hand, we have probably all heard horrendous interpretations of a text leading people to unspeakable actions. Illusions swarm the world of religion. Problems occur when imaginative interpretations lose continuity with the original historical meaning intended by the authors and editors. Hence, the need in a community of believers for rigorous study, employing as much scientific history and literary analysis as possible, looking for some evidence for an interpretation, some objective data that others can see even if they come with other values and desires. Of course, theology like art, literature, and the other humanities cannot be absorbed into any scientific method. The difficult part is to balance the scientific and analytic approach, on the one hand, with the intuitive and global, on the other.

I suggest a series of steps to work at that balance. These steps in fact guide the development of this whole study.

I. Respecting the Historical Context

The first step is to respect the historical context of the writing. If we really accept the authority of the biblical text, then we must respect the text for what it is. It was not originally written for us. It arose and took its meaning from a historical context very different from ours. The truth of the text was originally generated by a combination of ancient writers and editors. In order to grasp the authors' original intention, we need to situate each of the writings in their historical context.

The prophets spoke and wrote for the people of their times. Because what they said was written down, their words can now be overheard by people of all times. Yet, the meaning of the prophets' statements begins with and forever remains anchored in the needs and people they addressed. If we are in any way to grasp the historical intentions of the authors of these biblical books, we must try to see what the prophets were trying to address, to look at that reality through their eyes. Then we can try to see the prophetic perspective and presuppositions that could speak to us today. Without this historical anchor, our interpretations can easily drift into self-confirming mirrors of our own positions.

The opening line or superscript of most of the prophet books situates the prophet at the time of specific kings. We can cross-reference the text with the accounts of those kings in First and Second Kings or Ezra and Nehemiah to recall the circumstances of that time. Often we can receive help from archeology and extrabiblical sources. (I again refer to my earlier work, *Understanding the Historical Books of the Old Testament* [Mahwah, NJ: Paulist Press, 2011].) At times, the prophetic books themselves will intersperse narratives relating this historical context, as does Isaiah 7 or Jeremiah 26.

Many of these times were times of crisis. Isaiah, Jeremiah, and Ezekiel preached in times of war. Hosea spoke out while he watched political disintegration. By all appearance, Amos preached at a time of prosperity and tranquility, but he saw the social rot about to ulcer onto the surface of Israel. If we are to understand what the prophets meant, we must understand their historical settings.

We have grouped the prophets by historical epoch into the major **Parts** of this book. Each of the first three parts will open with a chapter sketching the historical background of the period. The chapter or subchapter that deals with each individual prophet will begin with an **Overview** section, where we will add what we can about the times of that particular prophet.

II. Moving from First to Second Order Theological Themes

A theological theme—also known as a motif—is an idea or complex picture that appears repeatedly in an author, expressing the values that govern his or her writing. When the prophet makes an important statement or point, when we see that point frequently repeated, or when we find points recurring in different prophets, we can identify a prophetic theme. These themes are expressions of the author's faith. They guide their thought.

Much of what Hosea wrote develops the theme of Ba'alism as a form of harlotry. Isaiah frequently reassured the king of God's protection of Jerusalem. Ezekiel developed the theme of God's mobility. Running through many prophets is the theme of the Davidic dynasty as the carrier of Israel's hope. Such themes are more complex and often a bit more abstract than the poetic images, although they are often articulated in images.

These themes are what I would call *first order themes*. They are rooted in the historical setting of the authors. They can be examined and verified by observing the wording of the text. Identifying a theological theme requires a bit of abstraction from the concrete statements and images, but for the most part the process takes place on an empirical level. We examine the evidence and make our conclusions.

Working with the first order themes is the key to maintaining continuity with the historical context of the text. It is here that respecting the historical context is critical. This means not reading our own concerns into the statements of the ancient writers. Many times the themes do not really address our concerns. This semblance of foreignness should not push us to distort the text. We are not approaching these themes from a totally neutral point of view, but we are observers who need enough quiet and patience to let the prophet speak for himself.

Other themes move quickly into our world and speak to us. In Amos, we have an overriding theme of the importance of not oppressing the poor. In Hosea, we see the theme of God's love of Israel as his unfaithful spouse. In Isaiah, we note the importance of calm, patient waiting for God's help. These themes address all peoples. They are first understood in the historical context of the authors, but once we express them as themes, they radiate a truth that immediately expands beyond those historical limits. These are the themes we need to find to discover the prophet's message for today. Often, however, the themes in the text need further work to get to this applicable stage. Hence, I would call these applicable, message-filled themes *second order themes*.

As we try to identify a second order theme, we move generally away from a scientific method. The grasp of the theme is far more intuitive and global, like the appreciation of fine literature or art. This is the method in the study of the humanities.

We hear Hosea speak of God as the destroyer (first order theme) and perhaps we can understand this in terms of a link between sin and disaster as well as a sense of God as a power we cannot manipulate (second order themes). Analogies sometimes help. Most of us are appalled at how the human degradation of nature is leading to terrible disasters. In our attempt to exploit nature for the sake of our comfort, in our refusal to respect and reverence a power that envelops us, we pay for the terrible consequences of our sins. We are not identifying nature with the God of Amos, but we now have an analogy that moves us toward an involved understanding of Amos's first order theme. God is a power we cannot exploit to our comfort. God is a force who must be reverenced and worshiped. All else depends on this attitude.

Applying this method we can move from first order theme to the same idea expressed as a second order theme. Hosea may have intended to speak of Ba'alism as a form of prostitution. However, embedded in his statements is the idea of God's passionate love for his people, a love that brings intense demands. Isaiah's teaching about the eleventh-hour rescue of Jerusalem may have had to be undone by Jeremiah a century later, but the Isaian theme contains the idea of God's fidelity to his people, the idea of God as the stable rock of security in time of danger, the idea of good prevailing over evil in "the end." The theme in Ezekiel of God's glory moving out of the Temple and migrating to Babylon leads to the second order theme of God's transcendence over any religion and the silliness of thinking that we can domesticate God in our temples.

The articulation of first order themes is an attempt to see things *as* the prophets and editors saw them. The articulation of second order themes is an attempt to see *what* the writers saw. If we can follow the first order themes, we will find links that connect the texts and books with each other and give us insight into the faith of Israel. We will see the common presuppositions and perspectives from which the prophets understood their experience. If we can nudge these presuppositions and perspectives into second order themes, we can then grasp the message of the prophets, individually and as a whole, for all peoples. The process consists of enlarging the context so that the theme can speak to us without losing the basic structure or form of the theme.

At the level of second order themes, we can move beyond the historical context of the prophet and touch the reality of God and human life. On this level, we are still attempting to look through the eyes of the prophets to see the reality that they intended and whose summons they accepted. In a faith-filled reading today, we can touch that same reality and experience its summons.

In this study, we will strive first to observe how the ancient prophet developed the theme. As we study the **Significant Passages**, a principal concern will be to point out these first order themes. The passages are chosen with this in mind. The details that contribute to such a theme are the focus of the commentary. We will then try to list these themes in the **Message** sections of the study, as we start with a **Review of Images and Themes**.

As we proceed into the **Theology** of the prophet in the **Message** sections, we will attempt to bridge the theme of the prophet to our own questions. Without that bridge, the statement of the prophet is not interesting—and perhaps not even intelligible. However, if we insist on limiting the text to what is interesting to us, we do not let the prophet speak to us. All this involves a delicate task, recognizing the prophet's view in its own right, yet perhaps nudging the prophet's theme toward the vocabulary of our concerns. In one of the final chapters of this study, we will try to further articulate these second order themes as we reflect on the **Message of the Prophets** in general.

III. Evaluating Presuppositions and Perspectives

Developing a second order theme in biblical theology may often mean recognizing a controlling presupposition or perspective in the first order theme of the prophet, a presupposition or perspective that may well need to be discarded if we are to express the second order theme, the theme that can speak to our world.

As an illustration of this situation, one of the most common presuppositions and perspectives from Genesis to Zechariah deals with the universe. These writers generally presupposed that the world was a flat surface, supported by pillars, and protected by a hemisphere or dome that held out the waters of chaos lying above, around, and below the world. This perspective may have been the only one the writers could have used in their time. If we are to understand the statements of these writers and their first order themes, we must recognize and discard this presupposition. This presupposition and the perspective out of which this presupposition arises are all part of the historical context of the biblical texts, but if the statements of these writers are to speak to our world, this perspective on the universe must be set aside. Only in this way can we develop second order themes.

The matter gets more delicate when these controlling presuppositions and perspectives involve a constellation of values and morals. Prophets like Nahum and Ezekiel clearly see matters in the perspective of a patriarchal society that at times encouraged the abuse of women. Both prophets speak of divine punishment of evildoers in terms of the disgusting abuse of a prostitute (see Nah 3:5–7; Ezek 16:35–40). This perspective may have been unconsciously inherited and perhaps was the only basis from which they could view the matter. We need to recognize and understand this presupposition and then discard it. In fact, we need to denounce it as sinful.

How can we do this? Are we standing in judgment on the word of God? Actually, the text of John 8:1–11 gives us the perspective from which we can denounce the earlier presuppositions. Jesus treats the sinful woman with great respect, while not approving her sin. In effect we are using the Bible *as a whole* to recognize when God's word is at times under a layer of human sinfulness. "Canonical criticism" is theology, the intuitive and heartfelt attempt to "pull it all together." It proceeds more like the study of art in the humanities than the study of sociology in the sciences. It is a complement, not a substitute for historical critical biblical study. Historical criticism recognizes what is in the text and the framework or perspective out of which the text arises. Canonical criticism, or theology, recognizes and evaluates the summoning power of the text on us.

The task of recognizing and evaluating such controlling presuppositions and perspectives is enormous. This task requires moving beyond the scientific method of searching for empirical evidence to a more intuitive humanistic method, requiring a sense of the whole picture and a sense of the continuity as the reader moves from one perspective to the other. This procedure requires an understanding rooted more in the "heart" than in the analytic mind. The Old Testament is filled with such challenges, which, in my opinion, cannot be dealt with by any one person however scholarly. This is the role for a community of scholars and a community of believers contemplating the matter in good-will perhaps over a long time.

IV. Focusing on the Overarching Theme of God

For all their metaphorical and exaggerated imagery, these prophetic texts intended to speak of God as an awesome force that first breaks into the life of the prophet and threatens the earthly and human realities around the prophet. For the prophets, God is not the divinization of some earthly reality—like prosperity and fertility, the temple, or the state. This God is not even a representation of some divine dimension of human prayers and rituals. Rather, this God seems to break in as from a great abyss ready to swallow the false gods that human beings create to comfort themselves, the earthly illusions of security that fill human lives. The day of Yahweh is a day of doom.

The vocabulary of "abyss" is a dominant theme of modern literature and reflection. The term (*tᵉhom, abyssos*) can also be found in the vocabulary of some of the prophets (see Amos 7:4; Hab 3:10; Isa 51:10; Ezek 26:19) as well as in the psalms and other parts of the Old Testament, describing the mysterious and frightful "depths" over which the Earth is perched. In modern literature, the term appears in struggles with "the meaning of life," "the suffering of humanity," or "the basic absurdity of things," often an expression of a pervasive desperation found in serious thinkers today. These issues are probes into the ultimate context in which we live our lives, the context we must face when we stop playing our distracting games. That context is outside our control, one that therefore often appears dark and terrifying to us.

For the prophets, however, the darkness of the abyss was not that of absurdity and despair, but rather that of the obscurity of a reality beyond human reach, the obscurity of what is totally other than our world and at times threatening our world. This abyss is a divine abyss, an enormous chasm of reality that seems empty because it cannot be controlled, always beyond human grasp and human understanding. For the prophets, this great divine abyss shines at times with "holiness" and calls human beings to "justice." From this dark abyss also come the words, "You are my people....I love you." At times of human despair, it commands the prophet, "Comfort my people."

Thus the biblical texts can address the modern anguish of life that at times appears as a gaping, apparently meaningless abyss—once the superficial illusions of wealth and power are removed. The biblical texts address our fundamental questions, "Who is this God?" "Where is this God?" I offer the suggestion that these texts locate God precisely in this abyss.

V. Understanding the Relationship between the Prophets and the New Testament

Finally, reading the prophets from a Christian perspective leads us to search for the connections between the prophetic images and the Jesus of the New Testament. We are led this way because the New Testament writers describe such connections. We have no indication that the prophets or those that wrote out their preachings had any conscious intention to speak about Jesus. To the contrary, they appeared to be absorbed in the difficulties of their contemporaries.

Likewise the New Testament usage of the prophets is an indication of the faith of the New Testament authors, which often operated in disregard for the historical intention of the ancient Jewish writers. Yet the New Testament authors at times in fact touched the faith presuppositions of the Old Testament. They saw connections and patterns that both give us insight into the theology of the New Testament writers and at the same time suggest an aspect of the mysterious reality envisioned by the Old Testament writers.

A key to understanding the New Testament's use of prophetic texts along with some later Jewish reinterpretations of these texts lies in the exaggerations or the excesses found in the prophets' messages of hope. The exaggeration or excess appears in the comparison with the realizations of what actually happened in the time of the prophets. The lamb and the lion never did lie down together in peace. The dynasty of David in fact died out. The return from Babylonian Exile did not replace the Egyptian Exodus as the saving event. Around the limited realizations of the prophetic messages, the unrealized excesses cast a type of shadow figure on the future. These shadows of a return to paradise, a new David, or a new exodus become the patterns of biblical hope.

Convinced of the unity of God's plan of salvation, the New Testament writers seized on these shadows to describe God's salvation through Jesus. The result is an overlay of Christian meaning on the Old Testament texts. This superimposition expresses the faith of the Christian writers. It is an enrichment to the text, but it should not distract us from seeking the historical meaning centered on a historical intention, evidenced by the historical context and literary forms of the prophets. Often this historical meaning provides deeper insight into the New Testament's use of the prophets. At the same time, the overlay suggests a pattern of divine salvation, which could provide deeper insight into the Old Testament text, allowing us to approach the prophets with a new sensitivity and new questions.

As we analyze the historical meaning of the **Significant Passages**, we will briefly sketch the use of their texts by authors of the New Testament.

PART I

The Classic Prophets of the Eighth Century

3
Historical Background

To follow the Old Testament prophets of the eighth century, we need to know of the critical historical events of that time. This investigation takes us on a dizzying view of not only the kingdom of Israel in the north and that of Judah in the south, but also of the Assyrian Empire in Mesopotamia. A synoptic chart of the kingdoms of Israel and Judah helps keep track of the kings in each realm and of the international events affecting each one.

I. A Synoptic View

The attempt to coordinate the kings of Judah and Israel in a synoptic history has long baffled many biblical scholars. However, the biblical data for the most part can be followed if we allow for two important factors. First and most important, coregencies allowed the reigns of fathers and sons to overlap. We in fact read about the coregency of Uzziah and Jotham (2 Kgs 15:5). I would suggest this system of father and son ruling together also for Jehoash and Jeroboam II in the north as well as for Amaziah and Uzziah, Ahaz and Hezekiah in the south. In the Book of Kings *the length of the rule of a king* usually, but not always, extends into his coregency, while *the date when he "became king,"* indicated in terms of the rival king's year of reign, is determined in general by the year when the king became sole ruler.

The second factor that allows us to use the biblical data in the synchronization of the kings is the way the southern kingdom tended to "postdate" the accession of the king, counting the number of years in a reign only from the first New Year's enthronement ceremony, not counting the first partial year of the

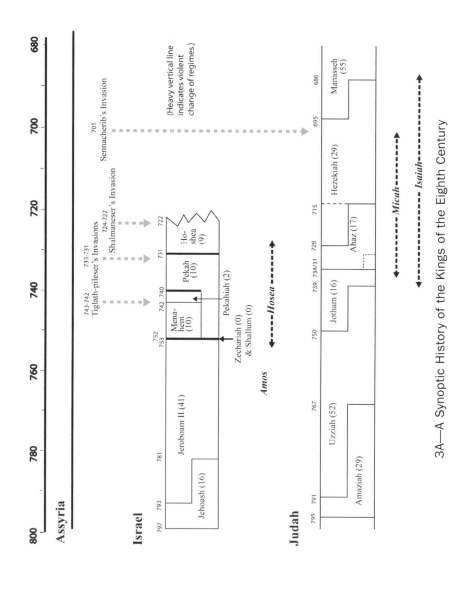

3A—A Synoptic History of the Kings of the Eighth Century

reign. The northern kingdom, on the other hand, seemed to count the first partial year of a reign. Furthermore, the unit of the year was measured at times from fall to fall; at other times, from spring to spring. Many difficulties remain; however, by using these factors we can employ almost all the chronological indications in Kings to make the following synoptic history of the kings of the eighth century BC (see diagram 3A; see also Appendix 2 for a synopsis of the whole monarchy period).

II. In Israel

In the north, the century begins roughly with the rein of King Jehoash (797–781; see 2 Kgs 13:10–19). He is followed by his son Jeroboam, known to modern historians as Jeroboam II (793–753; see 2 Kgs 14:23–29). Apparently he ruled as coregent with his father for seventeen years. During the long and peaceful reign of Jeroboam II, commerce flourished. The rich amassed great wealth. The archeology of Samaria has uncovered the relics of opulent villas, some with carved ivory furnishings. From the preaching of Amos, however, we know that not all benefited from this prosperity. The power that wealth brought to the rich became an instrument for oppressing the poor.

Four well-known prophets were sent to the northern kingdom. The Deuteronomist history reported on Elijah and Elisha (see 1 Kgs 17—19; 21:17–29; 2 Kgs 1:3—8:15; 9:1–3; 13:14–21). Amos, the next in time but not mentioned in the books of Kings, is the first prophet who left us a record of his preaching, as did Hosea. Elijah and Elisha had succeeded in staving off the Phoenician spearhead led by Jezebel, yet the people continued to turn away from Yahweh in the succeeding years (see 2 Kgs 13:1–2,10–12; 14:23–24). The preaching of Amos and Hosea likewise appeared to be of little avail.

Six months after Jeroboam's death, his son Zechariah (753) was assassinated (2 Kgs 15:8) and the dynasty of Jehu came to an end. With the death of Zechariah, the northern kingdom enters a period of anarchy (15:8–31). Shallum (752), the assassin of Zechariah, is himself assassinated after a one month reign by

Menahem (752–742), who suffers the first Assyrian assault led by Tiglath-pileser III (named Pul in the text) sometime between 745 and 742 (15:19–20). Menahem was forced to give Tiglath-pileser a thousand talents of silver. Menahem's son, Pekahiah, reigned two years (742–740), before being assassinated by Pekah ben Remaliah (752–731), who then counts the length of his reign back to the death of Zechariah (15:27–28).

Around 734 Pekah attempted to arrange an anti-Assyrian alliance with Rezin, king of Damascus (Aram). Such an alliance would succeed only if closely coordinated with Egypt, the other superpower of the day. King Ahaz of Judah, however, somehow stood in the way. The ensuing Syro-Ephraim attack to unseat Ahaz was thwarted when Ahaz appealed to Tiglath-pileser for help. The Assyrian army moved west and swept through Israel in 734, deporting to Assyria many of the inhabitants of northern Israel, particularly those in the area around the Sea of Galilee (see Map 3B; 2 Kgs 15:29; Isa 8:23). Only the assassination of Pekah by Hoshea ben Elah (not to be confused with the prophet Hosea ben Beʿeri, although their names in Hebrew are spelled the same) saved Israel from complete destruction. After destroying Damascus and executing Rezin in 732 (2 Kgs 16:9; see Isa 17), Tiglath-pileser confirmed Hoshea as king of Israel in Samaria (2 Kgs 15:30–31).

About eleven years later, 722, Hoshea revolted against Assyria. The disaster that followed entailed the destruction of Samaria and the deportation of the Israelites to the Gozan region in northern Assyria (17:1–6; see Map 3D). This disaster was

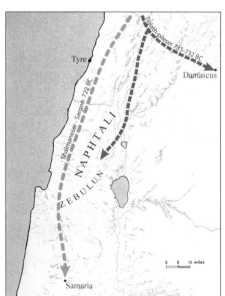

3B—The Invasions of
Tiglath-pileser and Shalmaneser V

later interpreted as a punishment by God for failure to listen to the prophets and follow the commandments of Yahweh (17:7–41).

III. Meanwhile in Judah

The authors of 2 Kings describe the events in Judah that parallel this disaster in Israel. Kings Amaziah (795–767) and Azariah (also called Uzziah; 791–739) parallel the period of Jehoash and Jeroboam II in the north (2 Kgs 14:1–22; 15:1–7). Azariah apparently became coregent during the captivity of his father. Then when he contracted leprosy, Azariah appointed his son Jotham as coregent (750–734; see 15:5).

Jotham's son Ahaz (734–715) came to the throne to face the Syro-Ephraim attack of Pekah and Rezin (2 Kgs 16:1–20). Ahaz called on Tiglath-pileser for help. As a result, Ahaz's enemies are destroyed, but Judah became at this time a vassal state of the Assyrian Empire. Apparently such a status required the worship of Assyrian gods in the Jerusalem Temple. Such cultic irregularities are hinted at by 2 Kings 16:10–18.

According to 2 Kings 18:1, Ahaz's son, Hezekiah, became king in the third year of Hoshea, king of Israel. The year would be roughly 728. The length of Ahaz's reign, however, is described as sixteen years (16:2). This would take his reign down to 715 (presuming that the "official" beginning of Ahaz might have been displaced some two years until confirmation by Tiglath-pileser). If we are to accept these numbers from 2 Kings, Hezekiah would have been coregent with his father for some thirteen years.

The naming of Hezekiah as coregent may have occurred just four or five years after his birth (making Hezekiah around nineteen years old at his accession to the throne in 715, not twenty-five years old as indicated in 2 Kgs 18:2). The accession to the throne of a child is not unparalleled in Judah (see Jehoash of 2 Kgs 12:1 and Josiah of 22:1) and was perhaps provoked by the prophecies of Isaiah.

Around 715 Ahaz died and was succeeded by Hezekiah as sole regent, who then rules as the best-intentioned king of Judah since David. Invited at the very outset of his reign to join with

Philistia and Egypt in their revolt against Assyria, Hezekiah, probably under the urging of Isaiah (see Isa 14:28–32; 20), resisted the temptation and was spared the crushing suppression by Assyrian forces in 711. Instead of engaging in anti-Assyrian revolts, Hezekiah organized a vigorous religious reform, sweeping away the non-Israelite cults introduced by Ahaz (2 Kgs 18:2–6; 2 Chr 29—31).

The year 715, the year of Hezekiah's reign as sole king, is based on 2 Kings 18:13, describing the invasion of Sennacherib in 701 as occurring "in the fourteenth year of King Hezekiah," understood as measuring his sole regency from 715 to 686. By strange exception, then, the twenty-nine year length of Hezekiah's reign (18:2) would refer only to his governance after the death of his father, Ahaz. These calculations are important for the study of Isaiah and the possibility that Immanuel (Isa 7:14) or the "child born to us" (Isa 9:5) could be Hezekiah.

To understand the invasion of Sennacherib, we must back up to around 703, a year or two after Sargon II of Assyria died. At this time Hezekiah decided to refuse the hegemony of Assyria. The revolt was probably fomented by Egypt in the southwest and Babylonia in the east. It was also joined by a number of small states in the west. The result was an attack around 701 by Sennacherib, Sargon's successor, to put down the revolt (see Map 3C).

Sennacherib's attack against Jerusalem is described in detail by 2 Kings 18:13-19:37 and in annals of Sennacherib (see Appendix 3c). We apparently have multiple accounts of this event in 2 Kings, one of which conforms to the Assyrian account, describing a siege that ends by a heavy tribute given to Assyria (18:13–16). A second describes "a certain report," perhaps of a rebellion back home, that required the Assyrians retreat (18:17—19:7). The third describes a miraculous intervention of "the angel of Yahweh" who kills a large part of the Assyrian army (19:8–37). In these second and third accounts in the Book of Kings we see the appearance of the prophet Isaiah (19:2–7, 20–34), the only reference in the whole Deuteronomist history to one of our literary prophets. The Book of Isaiah also reproduces the second and third accounts of Sennacherib's siege of Jerusalem (Isa 36—37).

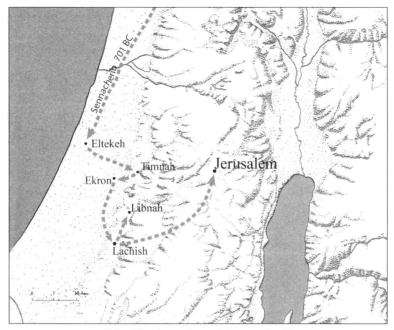

3C—The Invasion of Sennacherib

Second Kings 20 then describes the illness of Hezekiah and a visit of Babylonian envoys from Merodach-baladan, a visit that probably preceded Judah's revolt against Assyrian domination—although in both Kings and Isaiah, it is recounted as if following Sennacherib's siege (2 Kgs 18—19; see Isa 36—39). In this story of Kings, Isaiah also appears as a counselor to the king.

We will see more details of the conflicts between Judah and Assyria as we study the Book of Isaiah.

IV. Meanwhile in Assyria

Assyria began to assert hegemony in Mesopotamia in the thirteenth century and by the ninth century was ruling most of the former Babylonian Empire. The capital of the nation was Nineveh on the Tigris River. For the most part, Assyria took her culture from the old Babylonian Empire of the great Hammurabi. During the eighth century under Tiglath-pileser III, Shalmaneser

V, Sargon II, and Sennacherib, Assyria exerted a crushing pressure on Judah and Israel (see Map 3D).

Because of her geographical position in north-central Mesopotamia (modern Iraq) without natural frontiers and surrounded by enemies on every side, Assyria developed naturally into a nation of warriors. By the beginning of the ninth century she had become the first predominantly military empire in history. In her march to power she dealt summarily with her enemies, giving them a choice of surrender or destruction. Those who surrendered retained a nominal independence but paid a heavy annual tribute. Nations that resisted were invaded, their cities destroyed, their citizens tortured and killed. Future resistance was forestalled by deporting all influential citizens to distant parts of the empire. The ferocity and cruelty of her armies made her name a synonym for terror.

Stopped temporarily at Qarqar in 854 (see Map 3D) in a battle to which Ahab of Israel brought ten thousand foot soldiers and two thousand chariots (James B. Pritchard, ed., *Ancient Near Eastern Texts [ANET]*, Princeton, NJ: Princeton University Press, 1969, 278–79), Assyria was nevertheless able by 842 to reduce most of the Palestinian states, including Israel under King Jehu, to the condition of tributary satellites. Internal troubles kept her armies at home during the first half of the eighth century, but during the second half, under Tiglath-pileser III (745–727), the Assyrian army again moved west. Between 738 and 732, Tiglath-pileser conquered most of Syria and Palestine. When in 735–732 Damascus and Israel warred against Judah, Tiglath-pileser came at the call of Ahaz of Judah. He destroyed Damascus and reduced both Israel and Judah to vassalage (Appendix 3a; 2 Kgs 16; 2 Chr 28:16–27; see Isa 7—8).

Shalmaneser V succeeded Tiglath-pileser in 727. When the northern kingdom rebelled again in 724, his armies besieged Samaria. Apparently he died in 722 and was succeeded by Sargon II (722–705), who completed the siege, destroyed Samaria, and deported the northern tribes to the Gozan region in northern Assyria, thus bringing that dissident kingdom to a disastrous end (see Map 3D; 2 Kgs 17—18). At this time however, Babylon under Merodach-baladan rebelled and remained independent from 721 to 710. Hamath, Damascus, Gaza, and Egypt also rebelled. Sargon's armies again moved west in 720 and defeated the Syrian kings at Qarqar and the Philistines and Egyptians at Raphia (see Appendix 3b).

When Sargon died in 705, ambitious satellites in Palestine, including Judah under King Hezekiah, saw a chance to throw off the Assyrian yoke. This revolt was probably fomented by the Babylonian leader Merodach-baladan. In 702 the Assyrian armies crushed Merodach-baladan's forces. In 701 Sennacherib appeared with his armies at the Mediterranean and captured Tyre. Many of the rebel states then hastened to switch their allegiance back to Assyria, isolating Philistia, Egypt, and Judah. Sennacherib attacked and defeated the Philistine city-states, paused briefly to defeat an Egyptian army at Eltekeh (near Ekron), and then proceeded to besiege and devastate one Judean city after another, including Timnah, Lachish, Libnah, as he moved around to the south of Jerusalem (see Map 3C). In 701 he besieged Jerusalem, exacted a heavy tribute, but did not destroy the city. The story of the failure of this revolt is recounted in 2 Kings 18—19; Isaiah 36—38; and 2 Chronicles 32 (see Appendix 3).

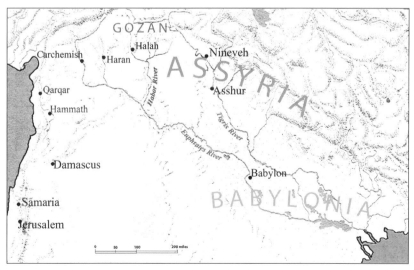

3D—Map of Eighth-Century BC Middle East

4
Amos

I. Overview—Read 2 Kings 14:23—15:7

A. THE PROPHET

What we know about Amos, we know only from his book of sermons. The inscription (1:1) tells us he was a shepherd from Tekoa, a small town about ten miles south of Jerusalem in the hill country (see Map 4A). He was thus a Judean, not an Israelite. The incident related in chapter 7:10–17 tells us he was not only a shepherd but a "dresser of sycamore trees." It tells us further that Amos preached at Bethel, in one of the two temples founded by Jeroboam I (1 Kgs 12:29) to keep Israelites from journeying south to the Temple of Jerusalem. There he faced opposition from Amaziah, the high priest of Bethel, the opposition that probably ended his career as a prophet.

The "inscription," or opening lines of the book, gives us the historical background of Amos's preaching: "the days of Uzziah, king of Judah, [called Azariah in 2 Kings; 791–739 BC] and in the days of Jeroboam, son of Jehoash, king of Israel, two years before the earthquake." Jeroboam II's reign (793–753) was a time of great material prosperity and of corresponding social exploitation and other forms of corruption. A major earthquake occurred in the region around 760. That would put his mission around 762.

Amos's powerful, colorful, and forthright sermons with their passionate concern for the oppressed poor have earned him the title, the "prophet of social justice." Expressing intense reproach, threatening punishment, proclaiming doom, the prophet basically declares God's judgment against the kingdom. Not even the religion of Israel escapes Amos's criticism. Such a messenger would probably not have been very popular anywhere.

B. THE BOOK

It is hard to know how the preaching of Amos became the Book of Amos. The present text of Amos shows extraordinary literary skills in the use of number-sayings, funeral laments, comparisons, and metaphors, even descriptions of visions. If in fact Amos penned much of this book, he was an educated farmer. The scattered refer-

4A—Cities and Places of Amos

ences to Judah, Jerusalem, or David (1:2; 2:4–5; 9:11–15) are probably later editorial additions to apply Amos's preaching to the south.

The book of his sermons falls clearly divided into three main parts:

Amos 1—2:   Indictments of the surrounding nations and Israel for their crimes
Amos 3—6:   "Hear the word" and "Alas" sermons
Amos 7—9:   Five visions of destruction

(See Appendix 4a for a more detailed outline of Amos.)

C. TORAH TRADITIONS IN AMOS

If we can in any way sift through the later additions to the Book of Amos to the material dating perhaps back to the eighth century BC, we can catch glimpses of ancient traditions that eventually come together to form our Pentateuch or Torah. The reference to Sodom and Gomorrah (4:11), for instance, shows his familiarity with at least this patriarchal tradition (see Gen 18—19). Creation traditions show up in Amos (4:13; 5:8–9; 9:5–6), but they show little or no connection to the accounts we now have in Genesis 1—2.

Several times, Amos appeals to the Exodus traditions to underline the particular culpability of Israel (2:9–10; 3:1–2; 5:25). When Amos, however, denies any sacrificial practices associated with the wilderness traditions (5:25), he clearly does not know of anything like our present Torah or Pentateuch, which of course could have been used to refute his accusation (for example, Exod 24:3–8; 30:7–10; 34:26–30; and so on). The allusion to some battle against Amorite giants (2:9), may refer to some early form of the Elohist stories now found in Numbers describing either the threat of a race of giants in the promised land (the *Anakim*; Num 13:25–33) or the battle against Sihon, king of the Amorites (21:21–35).

Amos is also familiar with the Sabbath requirement of not doing business (8:5; see Exod 21:8–11) and the stipulation about clothing "taken in pledge" (*chabal*; Amos 2:8; see Exod 22:25). However, the one explicit reference to "the law (*torah*) of Yahweh" appears in one of the generally recognized editorial additions (2:4). Amos himself does not appeal to the law or any book of the law as the basis of his message or position.

All this suggests that oral Torah traditions circulated in eighth-century Israel, but that no collection had been written down as we know it. The Torah did not come ready made from the time of Moses but developed gradually.

II. Significant Passages in Amos

A. Amos 1—2 / Oracles against the Nations

The book opens with oracles against the nations (Amos 1—2) as "Yahweh roars" (1:2). Evoking the power of God's word, the expression is a keynote in Amos. After an oracle against Damascus in 1:3–5, Amos then roars God's displeasure against Philistia,

Phoenicia, Edom, Ammon and Moab—the neighboring enemies of Israel (1:6—2:3; see Map 4B).

Then in the same breath, the roar is turned against Israel herself in a devastating indictment (2:6–16). The oracle against Judah (2:4–5) appears to have been added much later, to broaden the message.

In each oracle, a set formula is followed:

4B—Nations around Israel

a. *messenger formula*: "Thus says Yahweh…"
b. *announcement of judgment*: "For the three transgressions… I will not revoke my word."
c. *indictment*: "Because they have (for example, threshed Gilead)…"
d. *punishing judgment*: "I will send a fire…"

The oracles imply that God is ruler of all nations. Wherever it is, moral evil is rebellion against a suzerain ruler, and this ruler punishes this evil wherever he finds it. The crimes of the outside nations cited here mostly deal with extreme brutality in warfare. The oracles against the nations become a typical stock-in-trade type of sermon for subsequent biblical prophets (see Isa 13—23; Jer 46—51; Ezek 24—32; Nah 1—3; Zeph 2; Hab 1—2).

2:6–16 *Oracle against Israel*

Amos, however, does the appalling thing and turns such threats against his own people with a much longer list of sins (2:6b–12). If the Israelites cheered the terrible judgments of God on their enemies, they all the more would have felt a shock in hearing how they themselves fall under the same judgment.

Amos singles out crimes especially against social justice: enslaving the poor (2:6), oppressing the weak (2:7). Oppression of the poor by the rich must have been widespread in the prosperous reign of Jeroboam II. We hear also a hint of the legal corruption of the day in the expressions "selling the just one," that is, enslaving the innocent, and "forcing the lowly out of the way (*derek*)," probably "the way" of justice. The description of the rich enjoying the forfeitures of the poor in a religious context emphasizes the same perversion (2:8). Amos returns consistently to this same theme (see 4:1; 5:11–12; 8:4–6).

By way of contrast, the indictment includes a description of God's past saving activity, the description that the Israelites delighted in, the one that gave them an intense sense of hope for the future. The saving deeds of God are rooted in the rescue from Egypt and the conquest of Canaan (2:9–10) and include the "raising up" of prophets and nazirites, whom Israel rejects and corrupts (2:11–12). The reference to the Exodus tradition here appears to be one of the earliest written testimonies we have to that story (see also 3:1–2; 5:25).

In the middle of the sermon (2:10), Amos shifts from the third person to the second ("you"). What his audience has, it has from God. Thus Amos stresses how the sins of God's chosen ones, the ones Amos is speaking to, involve greater culpability. Because of its intimacy with God, Israel's failures in regard to the norms of justice become opposition to God himself.

The prophet insists (*hinneh*: "behold") on a threat of God himself coming to destroy Israel like roadkill (2:13). God will crush Israel as a heavy truck crushes anything under its wheels. With words that should have shocked the audience, God describes himself as the destroyer. The story of God's salvation will now become the story of God's destruction. The text then continues with a description of total military collapse (2:14–16).

B. Amos 3—6 / "Hear This Word" and "Alas" Sermons

3:1–2 *The first "hear this word"*
In an address to the "children of Israel," Amos summons the group to listen to a divine proclamation. The prophet speaks in the first person, but this person is God himself. Another allusion to the Exodus traditions sets up the basis of Israel's special culpability. God has cared for and rescued (literally "has known") Israel in a way not done for any other nation. His audience probably knew and accepted this, but Amos throws this privilege back in their faces. "Therefore" (*'al-ken*) special punishment attaches to her crimes— not actually mentioned here. The theological principle for the rest of the book is now set up. The grace of God is a dangerous grace.

3:3–8 *Amos must prophesy*
The next six verses form a poetic unit. Amos piles up a series of rhetorical questions drawn from images of the countryside and the city, including an allusion to the lion. The first four call for a resounding "of course not" (3:3–5); the next two, for an emphatic "yes" (3:6).

Verse 7 expresses the nature of prophecy. Amos is a prophet because God reveals his *sôd* to him. The Hebrew word *sôd* means at once a "council of advisers" and a "plan." In the Greek it was also translated as *mysterion*, which we translate as "mystery," a word used to describe the mysterious plan of God (see Dan 2:19; Col 1:26).

With poetic parallelism, verse 8 expresses the compulsion of prophecy. Whether the audience approves of the message or not, God like a lion has roared. Amos must prophesy.

4:1–3 *The second "hear this word"*
Amos turns to the wealthy women of Samaria ("cows of Bashan"; see Map 4A) who insist on being served and thus participate in the social oppression that supports their luxuries. Amos predicts deportation for them. It will happen. God has sworn.

4:6–12 *"Yet you returned not to me"*

In a section that stands out by reason of the plaintive refrain, "Yet you returned not to me," Amos recounts the attempts of God to discipline his unruly people. Amos refers to a series of historical disasters and interprets them as God's own deeds dealing with Israel. "To return" (*shûb*) is the Hebrew word for repentance. It refers literally to a 180 degree turn and a retracing of one's steps back to a starting point. It involves a humbling recognition that one has been on the wrong path.

Israel is unwilling to return to God. "Therefore" (*laken*) she will meet him as a destroyer.

4:13 *Yahweh the Creator*

Appearing like a "lump" in the text is a short hymn to Yahweh as Creator. This text, along with 5:8–9 and 9:5–6, appears to be among the oldest professions of faith in God, the Creator of heaven and earth. It is hard to judge whether Amos spoke these hymns or whether they were added by the later editor. Their place in the text is to reinforce the seriousness of any command of God. To sin against God is to offend the very ground of the universe.

5:1–17 *The third "hear this word"*

If we temporarily set aside the creation hymn fragment in 5:8–9, this section forms an interesting structure of inverted symmetry—A , B, C, B', A'—what scholars today call a "chiasm," from the inverted symmetry of the Greek letter *chi* ("X"). The associated pairs explain and develop each other. The central element is often the key to the whole.

> A—A' Amos 5:1–3 and 5:16–17 are written in the form of a dirge (*qînah*). This literary form taken from funerals appears frequently in the prophets to describe the grief associated with God's coming punishment. In some mysterious way, the grief here depicts also God's own emotion, now felt by Amos. The prophet conveys not only God's thoughts and words but also his feelings.
>
> B—B' Amos 5:4–6 and 5:14–15 develops the theme of true and false religion (see also 4:4–5). "Seek me…do not

seek Bethel" (5:4–5). Jeroboam I set up temples at Bethel and Dan to compete with the Temple of Jerusalem (see 1 Kgs 12:26–32). However, in Amos the contrast is not between the sanctuaries in the north and the one in Jerusalem. The contrast is between "seeking" Yahweh and "seeking" any sanctuary. "Seek Yahweh" (B) is equivalent to "seek good" (B'), explained further as "hate evil and love good, and let justice prevail" (5:14–15). The sanctuary at Gilgal was probably located just outside Jericho by the Jordan River. Beersheba is a town at the southern extreme of Judah. Apparently shrines existed in these places before the later Deuteronomistic centralization of cult in Jerusalem.

For Amos, worshiping God at such sanctuaries is vain, given the moral condition of the people. True religion demands a moral life. "Seek good not evil....Hate evil and love good, and let justice prevail at the gate" (5:14–15). The gates of the city were the places where trials were held, the equivalent of law courts, the place where the weak and vulnerable were supposed to be protected.

The imperatives here, "Seek Yahweh," "Seek good," imply maybe there is still a chance. Israel's destiny is still in her hands. The future is not determined by some impersonal fate but by a God who can change his mind (see 7:3, 6).

C   Amos 5:7, 10–13 is the heart of the sermon. This is the word of God condemning oppression of the weak and the poor for the sake of personal gain. What God expects from Israel is above all is *mishpat* ("fair judgment") and *tz^edaqah* ("justice"). *Mishpat* literally means "judgment" in the legal sense of the word. In the biblical usage it is what leaders or judges (*shophtim*) are supposed to do in favor of the weak and injured. Therefore, it is not any old judgment, but always a "fair judgment." *Tz^edaqah* (or *tzedeq*) describes first of all the rightness of God, his fidelity to his covenant, in that sense, his "justice." As describing the norm for human behavior under God, the two words essentially belong together and express one reality, the righteousness and fairness that reflects the will of God. Amos gives concrete examples of their absence.

5:18–20 *The first "alas"*

In a sermon that begins with the sorrowful exclamation, "Alas!" (*Hoi*), Amos calls attention to the stupidity of those who yearn for the "day of Yahweh." Religious expectations of the time apparently looked forward to a day when God would vanquish Israel's enemies and establish her in power. A day of holy military victory over wicked enemies may have been the earliest meanings of "the day of Yahweh" (see "the day of Midian," Isa 9:3). But Israel's prayer for the punishment of the wicked turns out to be a prayer for her own punishment. Without repentance, encountering God means destruction and doom.

Although Amos did not coin this expression, this prophet begins the sense of "the day of Yahweh," or "the day of the Lord," as the great "day" when God will realize his plan of salvation, with "fair judgment and justice." The expression takes on eschatological overtones in Isaiah and Jeremiah and in later apocalyptic literature. In the New Testament, Paul and the first Christians adapt it to their hope for the return of Jesus (1 Thess 5:2).

5:21–24 *False religion*

The following verses return to a condemnation of hypocritical religion. God is infuriated when people try to substitute religion for justice. The prophet provides a line that could well be engraved at the entrance to any church or synagogue: If you would offer holocausts, "then let fair judgment (*mishpat*) surge like water and justice (*tz^e^dakah*) like an unfailing stream" (5:23–24).

C. AMOS 7—9 / VISIONS OF DESTRUCTION

7:1–6 *Destruction averted*

Part three of Amos begins with two visions of destruction, one of locusts, another of fire. In both we see the same sequence: a clearly destructive action of God, an intercessory prayer by the prophet, and a statement of God's change of mind. The visions are vivid descriptions of an often overlooked aspect of the prophet's vocation, intercessory prayer for his people (see Moses in Exod 32:11–14). God listens to the prayer of the prophet. He relents.

7:7–17 *The third vision and the episode in Bethel*

The third vision begins in the same way, that of an object, a plumb line, that now by a divine interpretation (7:8–9) is understood as a symbol of destruction. Before intercessory prayer can occur, however, the vision is broken off by the story of Amaziah's opposition to Amos. Ironically, the priest of Bethel forbids the prophet to function. God no longer relents.

In the short narrative of Amos at Bethel, we hear briefly of the prophet's call by God: "Yahweh took me from following the flock, and Yahweh said to me, 'Go, prophesy to my people Israel'" (7:15). We also hear of the prophet's strange rejection of the title "prophet" (7:14). This line could be translated, "I was no prophet" or "I am no prophet." More than likely, Amos is rejecting any identification with the professional prophets ("sons of prophets") hired to utter "religiously correct" prophecies. The description of Amos as "a shepherd and a dresser of sycamores" underlines the place of the prophet outside the power structures of the day. Whatever authority he has to speak, he has from God. From such a place the prophet can freely speak the word of God, even an oracle of judgment to the priest of the royal shrine (7:17).

8:1–14 *The fourth vision*

The fourth vision like the third is that of a symbolic reality, which is given a divine interpretation. The expression "a basket of ripe fruit" plays on the words *qayits* (ripe) and *qaets* (end). As summer fruit comes to maturity and is ripe, so Israel has come to her end, ripe for punishment.

Verses 4–6 seem to interrupt the series of visions, like the Amaziah story. As placed here, however, this oracle of judgment describes again the reason for Israel's punishment, oppression of the poor (see 2:6–8; 5:11–12). Using one of his favorite literary devices, that of direct quotation, Amos has the powerful merchants condemn themselves with their own words. They in fact seem to respect the religious holidays, but their hearts are set on making money by any means, even by cheating and selling the waste, "the refuse of the wheat" (8:5–6).

9:1–4 *The fifth vision*

The fifth vision describes Yahweh presiding over the destruction of the temple at Bethel and all of Samaria. The prophet sees Yahweh in the sanctuary, but here is no dialogue between Yahweh and the prophet, only images of destruction. The shaking of the large stone thresholds may allude to an earthquake (see 1:1). The sword is an image of war. There will be no escape. God himself will hunt down his adversaries.

9:8b–15 *Future salvation*

The section here with its reference to David appears to be a later addition to the collection of Amos's sermons. The sudden shift to images of salvation suggests that these verses were added by later Judean editors, who may have also added the prophecy against Judah in chapter 2:4–5. The pebble in the sieve may be an image of hope. Verses 11–15 are clearly prophecies of salvation. The images of fabulous material prosperity become stereotypical of salvation and eventually of the messianic age (see Hos 2:21–21; Isa 11:6; 54:1–12; 60; Joel 4:18; Rev 22:2). "On that day" (v.11) along with the expression "the days are coming when…" (v. 13) becomes a way of pointing to a hopeful future. When the past is a disaster and the present disappointing, the prophets point to the future.

"The fallen hut of David" (9:11) would refer to the collapse of the house of David in the Exile of 587 BC. Here we have a promise of restoration connected with a reference to "all the nations" bearing God's name. Luke cites this text, with some variations, and places these words in the mouth of James, the brother of Jesus, to describe the Jewish Christian acceptance of the Gentile nations (Act 15:15–18).

III. The Message of Amos

A. Review of Images and Themes

In Amos's poetry we find the following striking images: the day [of Yahweh] (2:16; 5:18; 8:9, 13; 9:11); God's plan or council (*sôd*; 3:7); the lion (1:2; 3:4, 8); cows of Bashan (4:1). These are the signature images of the prophet.

Amos's interest revolves around several more involved religious themes:

- The sin of oppression of the poor (2:6–7; 4:1; 5:7–13; 8:4–7)
- The Exodus and conquest of the land (2:9–10; 5:25)
- God as destroyer (2:13–16; 4:12; 5:17; 8:9–11; 9:1–4)
- The divine call of the prophet (3:7; 7:14–15)
- The worthlessness of hypocritical religion (4:4–5; 5:4–6; 5:21–25)
- The call to return to God (*shûb*) (4:6–11)
- Yahweh the Creator (4:13; 5:8–9; 9:5–6)
- Prophetic intercession (7:1–6)
- Human opposition to the prophet (7:10–12)
- The restoration of Israel (9:11–15)

B. The Theology of Amos

Amos's understanding of the reality of God and his intervention in human history appears to form around several of these themes as hinges for the rest. Among those cardinal themes are the following:

1. *God of all creation*. From the first chapters of this book, this concept becomes clear. God is not the national God of Israel, one who guaranteed prosperity and national success. Amos preached just the opposite. For Amos, Yahweh was the Creator, who "strides upon the heights of the earth" (4:13) and "summons the waters of the sea" (5:8). As such he stands therefore as judge over all nations and intervenes far beyond the limits of Israel. This God cannot be controlled by Israel's worship. This God could

destroy Israel and remain God. Israel was called to listen to this God's demands for justice.

2. *God as destroyer*. The message of Amos drew form from the presence of this powerful divine dimension that threatened all worldly objects and the illusions they created, leaving nothing in their place except devastation. For Amos to listen to this message of justice was to stand on the brink of doom. This was the abyss of the incredibly destructive anger of God. Amos did not flinch as he stared into it.

The message of Amos thus includes an implied theology of suffering. Sin brings destruction. As a common theme in the following prophets, the link between these two elements is forged by the portrayal of an angry God who judges evildoers. God punishes sin. This is certain. "Never will I forget a thing they have done!" (8:7). Moreover, the sin of the individual entails more than the destruction of that individual. It spills out to the nation. The sin of the individual has vast social consequences.

Some forty years after Amos, in 722 BC, the Assyrian army invaded Israel, destroyed the city of Samaria, and deported the "lost tribes of Israel." Amos understood, however, that the invasion was really that of God like a heavy truck crushing everything under its wheels (2:13).

Amos probably saw this angry, destructive God much like the vengeful despots of his time who would lash out at those who insulted them. This image seems to function as a controlling presupposition and perspective. Amos may not have been able to picture this destructive God in any other way. That the word of God could enter our world constrained by such limits hints at the great mystery of the incarnation that would come to light some eight hundred years later.

Canonical criticism shows us a different image of God. From the perspective of the whole of biblical revelation, we can reject this controlling presupposition of Amos. God is not like a vengeful despot. Yet the truth of the matter lies in the link between destruction and sin. Today we might more easily understand that link with the images of global warming and the other forms of "natural" disasters provoked by human sinfulness. With other presuppositions and perspectives, we can see how our actions extend beyond our lives to affect the very basis of life and existence.

In any case, the picture of God in Amos is a picture of God "out of control"—out of human control. The theological truth for all generations was simple. God cannot be controlled by us. The picture of the angry God is one that tells us to duck. He is dangerous, and his grace is dangerous. The angry God is the God of power and might—not the great pain reliever in the sky whom we approach when we have a headache. This God is not the domesticated deity of the nation. He is God, not some power that can be manipulated, not even by observance of religious practices, prayers, or rituals. This image of God appears behind related themes in Amos.

3. *The day.* Amos's mission was to preach to the rich and complacent about a "day of Yahweh" (5:18), a day that would explode in utter disaster for the north. The lion roared, and the summit of Carmel withered (1:2). Amos is thinking neither of the day of victory in holy war nor of the eschatological end of time, but of a day coming in God's time when evil will be punished. "On that day" God will deal with sin (8:3, 9, 13). This is certain— even if hidden in the unseen future, hidden in God's time.

4. *Opposition to the prophet.* Amos was drawn away from his animals and lands by the word of Yahweh. This word was an angry word, like the roar of a lion that broke into Amos's perhaps comfortable world. God revealed his "plan" to him, a plan of divine chaos.

In his time as in most times, it was easy to ignore Amos's message, to ignore "that day" which was unseen and hidden in God. The forty years between Amos's preaching and the Assyrian disaster is a long time in any particular human life. Riches and comfort provide addictive illusions. It would take years of historical retrospection to see the truth of Amos's predictions.

It was easy to be fooled by the hiddenness of God's word in the prophet. At the time of Amos, God did not manifest himself in any dramatic way to the people, no theophanies, no miracles like those of Elisha. God, who communicates with his people by sending messengers, sends Amos without any imposing credentials. He has no social status to back up his authority and credibility. For this Amos can only say that Yahweh took him and sent him to prophesy and then expect authorities to believe him (7:15).

It would seem that God set his prophet up to fail. Like Elijah, Amos faces opposition. Amos's opposition, however, is not from the Ba'alist authorities, it is from the priest of Yahweh. This opposition successfully silences the work of Amos. Thus the book describes the failure of the prophet and the failure of God: "Yet you returned not to me, says Yahweh" (4:6, 9, 10, 11). The apparent refusal of God to back up his prophet with miraculous protection and to neutralize the opposition remains one of the darkest of divine mysteries—down to the crucifixion of Jesus.

5. *Justice and judgment.* God's anger, however, is not capricious. It is directed against sin, especially the sin of injustice. God demands *mishpat* ("fair judgment") and *tz^edaqah* ("justice"). Out of the abyss, we hear the call for justice. Offences against justice are offences against God himself.

For Amos, perhaps more intensely than for any other prophet, this justice is manifested by fair treatment of the poor. Amos preaches during a time of prosperity and affluence, a time when earthly illusion abounds. This prosperity was not equitably distributed. The gulf separating rich and poor yawned. However, oppression of the poor is an attack on the ultimate ground of creation.

Amos offers no advice on restructuring the economic system of his day. He simply denounces the unjust treatment of the poor. This is not "business is business." On the contrary, God—the source and founder of the universe—will not tolerate this action, and no attempt to silence the prophet will change this. God is an attentive and powerful ruler of all nations and deals with sin. Because God is who he is, human beings must be moral and ethical. Sin is serious, and God inevitably deals with sin.

6. *Restoration.* A later editor was convinced that failure and the ensuing destruction could not be God's last word. That editor did not change the words of Amos but added an epilogue: "On that day I will raise up the fallen hut of David…" (9:11). God is just and demanding, but God is also good. Crucifixion and death are the inevitable consequences of sin. However, God is capable of raising the crucified from the dead.

5
Hosea

I. Overview—Read 2 Kings 14:23—15:31

A. THE TIMES

The end prophesied by Amos for Israel began in the days of
Hosea, his contemporary. The opening line or superscription cor-
relates Hosea's work with several kings of the south and one in
the north (1:1). The period from Uzziah to Hezekiah in Judah
would stretch at least twelve years, from before 739 to after 728.
The period of Jeroboam II in Israel would extend back another
fourteen years to a time before 753 (see A Synoptic History of the
Kings of the Eighth Century, Illustration 3A). Nothing is said
about the kings after Jeroboam in the north down to 728.

Thus Hosea preached at a time during the last chaotic years
of Israel's independence, a time of national and religious disintegration. Wealth increased; justice and fidelity decreased. Hosea
repeatedly denounces the making of idols ('azabim; 4:17; 8:4; 13:2;
14:9). He refers to "the calf ('egel) of Samaria" (8:5–6; see 10:5; 13:2)
in what appears to be an echo of the Deuteronomistic history's
way of ridiculing the northern shrines (2 Kgs 12:28). In their single-
minded concern for the good life in disregard for Yahweh, the
people also became deaf to the approaching tramp of Assyrian
troops under the command of the new and vigorous king, Tiglath-
pileser III (744–727).

B. THE PROPHET

Of Hosea, son of Beeri, we know nothing beyond what is
told us in the biographical section of his book (chapters 1–3) and

in the editor's superscription (1:1). From the prophet's focus on the northern shrines like Bethel, disparagingly called Beth-aven (house of wickedness), Gilgal, and Shechem (4:15; 5:8 6:9; 9:15; 10:5) along with his accusations against Gilead and Ephraim (6:9; 7:8), we can conclude that Hosea like Amos preached in the northern kingdom, perhaps a born Israelite. This northern location would explain his battle with Ba'alism and his opposition to the kings (8:4).

Hosea is called the prophet of divine love. Himself profound and passionate, the prophet describes God as a lover deeply upset at the infidelity of his beloved.

To render God's disappointed love visible, Hosea lived out his own unhappy marriage with Gomer. At some point in the marriage, Gomer apparently leaves Hosea and becomes a prostitute, probably a sacred prostitute at one of the Ba'al shrines (see Num 25:1–5; Deut 23:18–19). Thus Hosea considers divorce (Hos 2:4). Instructed by God, Hosea instead takes Gomer back and sees in this wounded relationship the parallel of God's experience with Israel. A double description of this parallel is found in chapters 1–3. Of the two accounts of Hosea's marriage to Gomer, the first is biographical (1:2–8); the second, autobiographical (3:1–3). Here Hosea represents God; Gomer, Israel. The lovers are the Ba'als with whom Israel was committing adultery. The hire of the harlot describes the material blessings that Israel ascribed to the Ba'als.

5A—Cities and Places in Hosea

C. The Book

A poorly preserved text, in addition to Hosea's frugal yet passionately emotional style, make the book difficult reading.

Modern translations do not agree on the versification. We will follow the present Hebrew verse numbering (followed also by the NAB with confusing rearrangements). Other versifications will be shown in brackets.

Attempts to divide and subdivide the book vary. Except for the distinctive form of chapters 1–3, we find no clear basis for identifying subsections other than the small pronouncements that average about ten verses. The bulk of this book seems to be made up of a hodgepodge collection of these pronouncements. At the very least, the book appears in two clearly distinguished parts:

Hosea 1—3:   The marriage and family of Hosea
Hosea 4—14:   Sermons

(See Appendix 4b for a more detailed outline of Hosea.)

D. TORAH TRADITIONS IN HOSEA

As we search through the oldest material of the Book of Hosea, we catch several glimpses of Pentateuchal or Torah traditions. The preaching of Hosea makes several explicit references to the Exodus tradition, mostly by citing simply the action of "coming up," "being called," or "being brought up" from the land of Egypt (2:17; 11:1; 12:13–14). These references are without the narrative details we have in our Pentateuch, although mention is made of "the desert" as the place of Israel's youth (2:16–17). The allusion to Moses (without naming him) as prophet (12:13) echoes Deuteronomist traditions (see Deut 18:15–20). A reference to the sinful rites of Ba'al-peor by the Hebrews at Moab (Hos 9:10) reflects the story now in Numbers 25:1–5.

This preaching also makes several references to the patriarch traditions now found in the Book of Genesis. The patriarch Jacob appears by name (12:13; see also 12:4). An allusion is made to a story of Abraham without naming him (2:1; see Gen 15:5; 22:17).

Unlike the Book of Amos, this book refers to God's law or laws (*torah, torot*) in sections that have no clear earmarks of being added later. This law is mentioned as violated by Israel's worshiping other gods and by its social crimes (4:6; 8:1, 12). God's law appears in clear parallelism with God's covenant (*berit*; 8:1 see also 6:7). It is described as written (8:12). Hosea's list of sins in 4:2 in fact parallels "the Ten Commandments" of Exodus 20:13–16, and Hosea 13:4 is in part the commandment of Exodus 20:2–3 verbatim. All this suggests that Hosea, when he uses the term *torah* is thinking of specific written covenantal regulations, perhaps something like the "tablets" of the law (*luchot*; Exod 24:12; 31:18), not the Pentateuch as we know it. Nevertheless, it would seem that the Exodus traditions and the Sinai (Horeb) covenant traditions are coming together in Hosea.

II. Significant Passages in Hosea

A. HOSEA 1—3 / THE MARRIAGE AND FAMILY OF HOSEA

1:2–3 *Hosea and Gomer*

The description of Yahweh beginning to speak to Hosea (1:2a) is as close to a call narrative as we get in this book. God commands the prophet to marry a prostitute. The message is in the action. The explanation, marked by the word *for* (*ki*), makes the prophetic act more understandable: "For the land has committed intense harlotry" (1:2b). The real issue is not Hosea's personal life, but Israel's relationship with Yahweh, as it deviated from its covenant with Yahweh to engage in the sexual fertility cults of Ba'al. In his painful encounter with infidelity, Hosea understands the failure of his marriage to be a vivid representation of Israel's sin against Yahweh.

Hosea's symbolic use of marriage will reecho in later prophets (see Jer 2:1–2, 20–21; 3:1–5; Ezek 16:23; Isa 54:4–6; 61:10–11; 62:4–5). In the New Testament, Jesus is identified as "the bridegroom" (Mark 2:19–20 and parallels; John 3:29). In the New Testament, however, the symbolism shifts from a negative example of the infidelity of the wife to the positive image of her faithful love (see Eph 5:25–33; Rev 21).

1:4–9 *The children*

Three children are born of the marriage and given ominous names. "Jezreel," the name of the firstborn son, is also the name of a valley in northern Israel marked by wars and bloodshed, as the text reminds us (see also 2 Kgs 9–10). "Lo-ruhama," the name of the daughter, is a Hebrew expression, "not pitied." "Lo-ammi," the second son, is named by another Hebrew expression, "not my people," a name that appears to negate any covenant between God and Israel (see Exod 6:7; Deut 26:18).

Isaiah will follow Hosea in giving his children symbolic names (see Isa 7:3.14; 8:4; 9:5). The children of the prophet thus become living prophecies.

2:1–3 [1:10–2:1] *Salvation*

These verses shift suddenly to thoughts of salvation. Two of Hosea's children will be renamed with positive names. Israel will be named "sons of the living God" (*b*ᵉ*ne 'el-chay*; 2:1). This is the first time in prophetic literature when divine sonship is attributed to Israel (see 11:1; Isa 1:2; Exod 4:22; Deut 1:31). The verses are a description about the future. Perhaps these lines were spoken by the prophet at a much later date but placed here by editors to create the jolting alternation between condemnation and blessing. (The NAB translation relocates these verses to the end of chapter 3.). St. Paul will freely cite this text when writing about the eventual salvation of all Israel (Rom 9:26; 11:26).

2:4–15 [2:2–13] *The divorce*

Representing God as if in court indicting Israel and divorcing Israel ("she is not my wife and I am not her husband"), Hosea dramatizes Israel's history of infidelity from the time of her first encounter with Ba'alism (Num 25), down through the days of Jezebel (1 Kgs 17–21), to his own day when her apostasy to Ba'alism had become general and irreversible. The prophet's allusions to the crops (2:7, 10–11) and his mention of "lovers" (2:7, 12, 14–15, 19) are references to the Ba'alist fertility cults. In a daring comparison, Yahweh appears as the true source of fertility: "She has not known that it was I who gave her the grain, the wine, and the oil" (2:10). Repeatedly beginning with the dreadful "therefore" (*laken*), the oracle describes the punishment—the end of material prosperity (2:8–9, 11–14).

2:16–25 [2:14–23] *The reconciliation*

Suddenly and without motivation, the text shifts to a promise of salvation to take place "on that day" (2:18, 20, 23), some mysterious future day when Yahweh acts decisively. Hosea recalls Israel's happy beginnings, making repeated allusions to the rescue from Egypt, past prosperity, and a future covenant.

The rebirth of love comes with a return to beginnings in the desert (2:16). The desert, normally a place of demons and deprivation, becomes an image of purification and intimacy with God, an image that will have a powerful force in Christian spirituality (see Jesus' preparation in the desert, Matt 4:1–11 and parallels).

Verse 20 introduces the promise "on that day" of a future covenant. This covenant involves all of nature and human society, giving security from the scourge of war. Verses 21–22 indicate the six aspects of a future "covenant" (*bᵉrit*) considered as a betrothal. This covenant will be in "justice" (*tzedeq*), "fair judgment" (*mishpat*), "kindness" (*chesed*), "mercy" (*rachᵃmim*), and "fidelity" (*'ᵉmûnah*). Each aspect is rooted in the faith of Israel and describes the qualifications of intimacy with God. The result of the covenant will be that "you will know Yahweh" (*yada'at YHWH*).

With the promise of this future covenant, Hosea begins to give a glimmer of hope that will be picked up by future prophets. Ezekiel will predict a "covenant of peace" (Ezek 34:25), and Jeremiah will foresee a "new covenant" written in the heart (Jer 31:31). Eventually Paul will see the whole saving work of Jesus in terms of this "new covenant" constituted by the Spirit of God (2 Cor 3:6).

3:1–5 *Hosea and Gomer again*

Chapter 3 retells the story of Hosea's marriage to Gomer, this time in the first person. The relationship between Hosea and his wife parallels that between God and Israel: "Give your love to a woman…even as Yahweh loves the people of Israel" (3:1). Perhaps for the first time chronologically in biblical literature, God is described explicitly and emphatically as *loving* Israel (see also Hos 11:1). Deuteronomy will later pick up this theme (Deut 7:8, 13; 10:15; 23:5).

B. HOSEA 4—14 / SERMONS

4:1–3 *The divine indictment*

These verses form a solemn proclamation ("Hear the word") of God's indictment (*rîb*) of Israel. The accusation catalogues the crimes of Israel: no fidelity (*'emet*), no kindness (*chesed*), and no knowledge (*da'at*) of God. From the parallelism here we have a clear indication of what the word *knowledge* connotes for Hosea. It is not something mostly intellectual and speculative, but rather something moral and practical. For Hosea to know God is to love him, to acknowledge one's relationship to God by doing his will (see 2:22; 6:6).

Echoing several of the "Ten Commandments" (Exod 20:13–16; see also Hos 13:4), Hosea connects failure to know God with social disorder and violence: "Bloodshed follows bloodshed" (4:2). This text may be one of the earliest texts documenting the Sinai (Horeb) covenant tradition. Hosea speaks of "transgressing the covenant" also in 6:7.

Verse 3 begins with the word *therefore* (*'al ken*), introducing the sentence of punishment. Here Hosea points out how human sin then spills out into nature, which loses its life-giving power. The land and the animals that dwell there are deeply harmed. What begins as a sin against God leads to sins against human beings and eventually to sins against nature. Suffering spills out as a necessary consequence beyond those responsible for the sin.

The Yahwist (J) tradition of the Torah saw the way in which human sinfulness affects nature (Gen 3:18; 6:11–13). In the New Testament, St. Paul will also insist on the solidarity of humanity and nature in both sin and salvation (Rom 8:19–21).

4:4–11 *Unworthy priests*

Hosea attacks the leaders of Israel for not fulfilling their duty to teach the people the "knowledge of God," which here is placed in parallel with God's Law (*torah*; 4:6). The first mentioned are the priests who abet the sins of the people (4:8) in order to increase for themselves the portions of the sacrifices for sin ordinarily given to them. Perhaps the setting for this accusation is Bethel, where Amos was silenced by the priest Amaziah (Amos 7:10–17). Similar accusations against priests will be taken up by later prophets (see Isa 28:7; Mic 3:11; Jer 2:8; 6:13; Zeph 3:4; Mal 1:6—2:9).

5:15 *God's absence*

In a verse that stands apart from any context, Hosea describes God as leaving Israel and returning to his "place." We are not told where this place is. The emphasis is simply on the departure. The resulting absence of God remains until two conditions are met: the people of Israel pay for or experience their guilt, and they "seek" God's face—the negative and positive sides of real conversion. Sin must be exposed for what it is, and Israel must experience its destructive power. Only then can she turn to God and seek him in wholehearted submission.

6:1–3 *Healing on the third day*

The next passage picks up the theme of conversion. Hosea describes the people proclaiming its intention to "return" (*shûb*) to Yahweh. They are confident—perhaps a bit too confident— that he will heal them and "raise us up on the third day" (6:2). Whether intended to illustrate sham or sincerity, this reference to "the third day" as a day of resurrection begins a quiet tradition that will surface with dramatic intensity in the New Testament (see 1 Cor 15:4; Mark 8:31; 9:31; 10:34 and parallels).

6:4–6 *Religious formalism*

Like Amos, Hosea then assails Israel for putting its confidence in external religious rites divorced from internal dispositions of love and obedience. The oracle begins with God speaking like a caring parent to a rebellious child, "What can I do with you?" (6:4) Verse six then drives home the point: "It is love [*chesed*] that I desire, not sacrifice; knowledge of God [*da'at 'elohim*], rather than holocausts" (6:6). The parallelism here between *love* and *knowledge* shows the basic equivalence of the two terms.

Hebrew idiom often expresses emphasis or preference by stating something and then denying the opposite: "This, not that." (See 1 Cor 1:17, "Christ sent me not to baptize but to preach," and Mal 1:3, "I loved Jacob and hated Esau.") The words of Hosea therefore should not necessarily be taken as a blanket rejection of sacrifice and holocausts, but more likely as a stress on love and religious knowledge over religious ritual. God is rejecting external acts of religion not accompanied by internal sentiments. He is rejecting outward gestures that do not engage the whole person in their relationship to God.

This judgment against religious formalism is a fundamental theme of the prophets. Hosea's warnings against formalism are renewed repeatedly in the Old Testament (see Amos 5:21–25; Isa 1:10–17; Mic 6:7–8; Jer 7:3–11; Ps 50:8–13; Sir 34:8–19). In the Gospel of Matthew, Jesus insists on the interior (Mat 5:21–30), criticizing the Pharisees for their arrogant sense of superiority based on external observances (23:1–36). Twice Matthew cites Hosea 6:6, "For I desire mercy not sacrifice" (9:13; 12:7).

7:8–12 *Foreign alliances*

King Menahem (752–742) offered tribute to the king of Assyria, Tiglath-pileser, and thus set up an alliance (see 2 Kgs 15:19). King Pekah then broke the agreement and developed an anti-Assyrian alliance, presumably with the support of Egypt. Later King Hoshea (731–722) will begin his reign as a vassal of Assyria (see 2 Kgs 17:3; Hos 5:13; 8:9). The prophet Hosea attacks such foreign alliances because they signal a lack of faith and confidence in God who has promised to watch over his people. We can imagine Hosea delivering this prophecy in the royal court of Samaria, comparing it to a "half-baked loaf of bread" (7:8) or a "silly dove" (7:11).

10:1 *Israel the vine*

In prophetic literature the vine is a frequent image of Israel. Here the image underlines Israel's infidelity. Its abundant fruit leads to corruption. This image of disappointment, often associated with destruction, appears again in Isaiah (5:1–7), Jeremiah (2:21; 6:9; 12:10), and Ezekiel (15:1–8; 17:3–10; 19:10–14). Psalm 80 laments Israel as a vine transplanted from Egypt, which at one time prospered but now is devastated.

In the Synoptic Gospels, Jesus picks up the same image, with its elements of disappointment and judgment, to describe Israel's rejection of his mission (Matt 21:33–41 and parallels). In the Fourth Gospel, the image drops its negative elements to become a description of Jesus himself and the shared life he offers those who believe in him (John 15:1–8).

11:1–7 *Israel, God's beloved son*
The image of God's care for Israel shifts to that of a parent's tender love for a young child (*na'ar*). The poignant image of a parent's love for a child recalls the symbolism of Hosea's children in chapters 1 and 2.

Here the idea of Israel as God's son is connected with the Exodus tradition, with a remarkable similarity to the story in the Book of Exodus where God instructs Moses to tell Pharaoh, "Israel is my son, my firstborn….Let my son go that he may serve me" (Exod 4:22; see Deut 1:31). In the New Testament, Mathew will connect Jesus as God's son also with a type of Exodus experience (Matt 2:15).

In Hosea the image of divine sonship is used to describe Israel's failure (see also Isa 1:2). The child who received such tender care and love is an ungrateful child. Thus Hosea shifts to the theme of judgment and punishment.

11:8–9 *Divine pathos*
In his love and justice, God is caught up in a maelstrom of emotions, described here as a veritable revulsion of feeling. Like a just judge, God has passed judgment on his people. But like a prodigal father, he draws back from complete rupture. The just anger of the loving parent turns into excruciating pain: "My heart is overwhelmed" (Hos 11:8). The parent must suffer the punishment of the beloved child.

In his own life, the prophet communicates this divine pathos to Israel by his life, just as he communicates the divine word by his speech. Hosea can speak the word of God to Israel, but he must live this pathos. The prophet is caught up in the divine suffering, as we see in the description of his unhappy marriage.

13:1—14:1 [13:1–16] *Punishment for ingratitude*

In this passage Hosea makes it clear that God's love cannot be scorned with impunity. Nowhere else in the Old Testament is the anger of God described in such savage terms. Like a wild lion or bear, God will rip Israel apart (13:7–8).

Reference to an indictment occurred earlier in 12:3. Now in 13:12 the sentence appears final. The description of a guilt "wrapped up" and "stored away" probably refers to the court record of the sentence folded and tied with cords then covered with a seal. The sentence is death: "Ephraim has died" (13:1). In 722 BC the Assyrian armies destroyed the city of Samaria, deported the bulk of the population, and brought the kingdom of Israel to an end.

14:2–10 [14:1–9] *A call to repentance*

Despite the bleakness of the preceding texts, the collection of Hosea's sermons ends with a positive note. The prophet first issues a call to conversion: "Return (*shûb*), O Israel, to Yahweh your God" (14:2). This conversion involves a petition for forgiveness of sin, a sacrificial offering (14:3), a renunciation of foreign alliances ("Assyria"), of military action ("riding on horses"), and idolatry ("saying 'our god' to the work of our hands"; 14:4).

In the second part of this text, Hosea speaks God's word of salvation. God promises to heal his people and love them freely (14:5–9). If divine anger uncovers and manifests the sin, divine love heals it. With a series of images drawn from nature, God promises true fertility. "Because of me, you will bear fruit" (14:9). In Yahweh alone can one find life.

III. The Message of Hosea

A. REVIEW OF IMAGES AND THEMES

When we think of Hosea, the major poetic images that come to mind are those of his wife, Gomer, the prostitute (1:2; 3:1), his children with the weird names (1:4, 6, 9; 2:1–3, 25), and that of fertility in general (2:10; 14:9). Testifying to the richness of his imagery, this prophet also includes a number of other images such as the desert (2:16), the vine (10:1), God as a lion (11:10; 13:7; see Amos 3:8), and even the death of Israel (13:1). Amos also uses a series of ambivalent images, at times to describe a blessing and then to describe a threat. Egypt appears in reference to an Exodus tradition (2:17; 12:14; 13:4) and a threat of exile (8:13; 9:3; 11:5). Hosea speaks also of a divine covenant, either as one transgressed in the past (6:7; 8:1) or one coming in the future (2:20). "That day" in Hosea is a day of salvation (2:18, 20, 23), whereas in Amos it was a day of disaster (Amos 2:16; 5:18; 8:9, 13; 9:11).

Using these and other images, Hosea develops a central theme of God's love that comes in two forms:

- The love of God for Israel as his wife (2:21–22)
- God's love for Israel as his beloved son or little child (2:1; 11:1–4)

As a counterpoint, Hosea develops the themes of sin and punishment:

- Israel's sin as adultery with Ba'al, Israel's illegitimate lover (2:7, 12; 4:12–15; 13:1)
- God's suffering as a result of Israel's sin (11:8)
- The consequences of sin as the degradation of the land (2:11–14; 4:3) and the destruction of society (4:1–2)
- The error of thinking of religion as a substitute for morality (6:6)

Hosea, however, balances these themes of sin and punishment with those of hope:

- A future recovery and salvation (2:1–3, 16–24; 11:8–11; 14:5–9)
- The importance of "returning to God" (2:9; 3:5; 5:4; 6:1; 12:7; 14:2–3)

- The desert, a place of intimacy with God (2:16) and a place of a new espousal (2:21–22)

B. THE THEOLOGY OF HOSEA

At times, the voice of God in Hosea roars like Amos's lion. At other times, God's voice sounds more the sorrowful lament of a wounded lover. God does not break into Hosea's life only as the awful abyss. He also appears in a broken marriage relationship and in the pain of parental disappointment. God appears here more like the gentle abyss of love, calling human beings away from their infidelities.

1. *God's love for Israel.* Like Amos, Hosea insists on "fair judgment" (*mishpat*) and "justice" (*tzedeq*) as defining the relationship between God and his people (2:21). But Hosea adds to the list the qualities of "kindness" (*chesed*), "mercy" (*rachamim*), and "fidelity" (*'emunah*). These are the qualities that bind persons together in love. It is Hosea who first explicitly states that God "loves" Israel (3:1; 11:1). Whatever we are to think of the punishing anger of God, we are to understand this action as motivated by love.

In the New Testament, Paul will insist on this primacy of divine love: "God proves his love for us in that while we are still sinners Christ died for us" (Rom 5:8). The suffering and death of Jesus—or Israel—is not an appeasement of God, but in a mysterious way an expression of love. Hosea brings together the images of anger and love by means of the mediating images of a disappointed spouse and a frustrated parent.

2. *The suffering of God.* The images used by Hosea dramatically express a wide range of divine emotions. The prophet clearly draws from a long tradition portraying the deity exploding with vengeful anger like a threatened human despot. His description of God as a wild beast is unparalleled in the Bible (Hos 13:7–8). Yet Hosea introduces another form of divine anger in which God also suffers deeply, an anger that is more distress than desire for vengeance. This distress is clearest in the portrayals of God as parent of a rebellious child (11:1–4). God's heart is "overwhelmed" (11:8). A parent is inevitably drawn into the evil produced or suffered by his or her child. A parent cannot simply

walk away from it. Love will not allow that. A parent must deal with it. Similarly, the image of God as married to an unfaithful spouse implies a sense of intense suffering (chapters 1–3). By portraying God in this light, Hosea adds an extraordinary new dimension to the biblical theology of suffering.

The intensity of divine pathos described here has no parallel any place in the Bible, although the theme will reappear in later prophets. We call such descriptions highly anthropomorphic, yet any image of a placid Unmoved Mover fails to express the intensity of God's love for his people. Whether parental or conjugal, love renders a person vulnerable. We cannot think of love without this aspect of vulnerability. Our imagery is certainly inadequate to fully grasp God, but disregarding this imagery of love and suffering moves us further from the truth. Love makes one vulnerable. God is no exception. Much later the Christian theology of an incarnate God rejected and crucified will give us tools to see this mystery of divine suffering in even more realistic terms.

3. *Human suffering.* As in Amos, the link between sin and human suffering in Hosea is clear. God punishes sin. However, by his portrayal of divine suffering, Hosea adds an important perspective. God is drawn into the destructive force of human sinfulness. God is vulnerable to this destruction.

Not only by the prophet's words but also by his life does Hosea proclaim this vulnerable God of love. We know of divine suffering through the prophet's own family. The prophet is drawn into this suffering by his love of the faithless spouse. In this way Hosea manifests the suffering of God. The prophet's own misery becomes a manifestation of God. The manifestation of God here is not by way of awesome theophany and miracle but by way of suffering. Although Hosea never expressed the idea of redemptive suffering, perhaps he saw something redemptive in that manifestation to the world of divine suffering by the medium of the prophet's life.

4. *Nature involved.* Hosea insists on the way God communicates his suffering also to nature: "Therefore, the land mourns, and everything that dwells in it languishes" (4:3). Hosea was drawn to this perspective in his polemic against the cults of Ba'al. In many ways the prophet accepts the link between religion and nature.

What he rails against is any attempt to control God and nature by the fertility cults, certainly not by the idolatry and sexual excesses associated with that cult. Concern for nature must be shown by acknowledging Yahweh, the ultimate source of vitality.

Again Paul will insist that all of creation that was made subject to corruption because of the sins of humans is now waiting to "be set free from slavery to corruption and share in the glorious freedom of the children of God" (Rom 8:21). The sins of humanity degrade nature. That degradation manifests the evil of sin. Yet God's love is greater than sin. In the end, all material creation will be redeemed. This is God's work. The human part of this picture is responsible love and moral justice, exercised in intense hope.

5. *Salvation and reconciliation.* Hosea reminds us of this hope in God's saving power. Unlike Amos, this prophet includes oracles of salvation, words that promise a restoration of God's covenant of love. These words can come unexpectedly, often after dire judgments of death. Again this alternation might be the logic of love. The parent becomes angry but also cajoles. Anger alternates with expressions of love. So God deals with sin. He does not ignore the problem, nor does he use the ultimate option of total annihilation. He becomes angry and threatens. But like that of the parent of the rebellious adolescent, God's anger ends with love.

Like the efforts of a wounded spouse intent on reconciliation, God calls Israel back to the beginnings of the love affair: "I will call her; I will lead her into the desert and speak to her heart....She will respond there as in the days of her youth when she came up from the land of Egypt" (2:16–17). Instead of a place of punishment, the desert becomes a place of intimacy with God, a place where love began between a husband and a bride and where love can begin again.

The greatest manifestation of God's love and redemptive vulnerability is found in the New Testament descriptions of the incarnation and crucifixion, where God directly suffers from the sins of his people. But the Old Testament also knows God very clearly as a God of love as well as of justice.

6
Isaiah 1—39

I. Overview—Read 2 Kings 15:32—20:21; 2 Chronicles 27—32

A. THE PROPHET

When we think of Old Testament prophets, the name Isaiah is usually the first to come to mind. His book leads off the series of the literary prophets in all Bibles. His hymn to the holiness of God (Isa 6:3) is one of the most familiar passages of the Old Testament. His Immanuel prophecies (chapters 7–12) are echoed over and over in the New Testament and in Christian churches at Christmastime.

Isaiah was born during the prosperous reign of King Uzziah (791–739 BC). He was a contemporary of Amos and Hosea in the northern kingdom and of Micah in Judah. He preached during the reigns of kings Jotham, Ahaz, and Hezekiah (1:1), apparently mostly in Jerusalem. His position as counselor to Ahaz (7:3–17) and Hezekiah (39:1–8), his knowledge of political affairs, his poetic language and exquisite Hebrew style, all indicate a cultured nobleman of high rank in the royal court. His wife was known simply as "the prophetess" (8:3). Their two sons were given prophetic names, Sh^{e}ar-yashub (7:3), whose name is a Hebrew sentence, "A remnant will return," and Maher-shalal-chash-baz (8:3), whose name means, "Hurry! Plunder! Booty hastens."

According to Jewish legend of the second century BC (see *The Martyrdom and Ascension of Isaiah* in *The Old Testament Pseudo-epigrapha*, ed. J. Charlesworth [2 vols.; New York: Doubleday, 1985], II, 163), he died a martyr around 687 BC, when, by order of the infamous King Manasseh, he was sawed in half.

Much of the narrative setting in Isaiah takes place in the city of Jerusalem. Isaiah spends much of his ministry advising two kings, Ahaz (734–715 BC) and Hezekiah (728/715–686 BC). For both, the water-supply system was a critical matter in these times of war. The conduit of Shiloah is mentioned in Isaiah in dealing with Ahaz. The underground tunnel con-structed by Hezekiah (2 Kgs 20:20; 2 Chron 32:30) does not appear in Isaiah, but would have functioned prominently during the siege of Sennacherib (see diagram 6A).

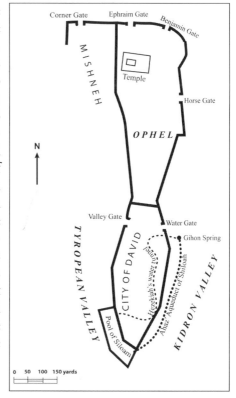

B. His Focus

6A—Jerusalem at the Time of Isaiah

Isaiah shares with Amos a deep concern for social justice. With Hosea he expresses God's love for Israel. What distin-guishes this portrayal is his insistence on God's holiness, that awesome characteristic of God which focuses on all that sepa-rates the transcendent God from this profane world. For Isaiah, God is "the Holy One of Israel" (*Qᵉdôsh Yisrael*; 1:4; 5:19, 24; 10:17, 20). His emphasis on holiness can be traced to his inaugural vision in which he hears the seraphim chant, "Holy, holy, holy is Yahweh of hosts! All the earth is filled with his glory" (6:3).

Dominated by the overwhelming realization of this holiness of God, Isaiah is filled with dismay at the corruption of his people. The nation called to be holy failed miserably in fulfilling her purpose of imitating the all-holy God. Therefore, Isaiah came to realize the necessity and inevitability of punishment to purge away Judah's corruption. Assyria will be the instrument used by God to punish his people (10:5–9). Judah will be chastised by the very nation with whom she betrayed her trust in God. However, because the divine promises are without recall, her chastisement will not be to the death. Out of destruction (6:9–13) will come a "remnant" (sh^e'ar; 10:20; see 6:13) from which will eventually come a Davidic king (9:6–7; 11:1–5; 11:10) and the nucleus of a holy and faithful people (2:1–4; 4:2–6; 9:7; 11:6–9).

C. THE BOOK

The Book of Isaiah as we know it is an anthology, the work of a compiler sometime after the Exile. Part I (chapters 1–39) is mostly the preaching of the eighth-century prophet. Part II (chapters 40–55) is the work of an unknown prophet who preached during the Babylonian Exile, whom scholars today refer to as "Deutero-Isaiah." Part III (chapters 56–66), frequently called "Trito-Isaiah," dates from the years immediately following the return of the Jews to Jerusalem after the Babylonian Exile. The fact that writers centuries later would collect prophecies and add them to the Book of Isaiah suggests something of an Isaian "school," a group of disciples studying the work of the master and attributing to him the best of their own inspirations.

Since we will examine Deutero-Isaiah and Trito-Isaiah after Ezekiel in the context of the Babylonian Exile and of the return to Jerusalem of the repatriated exiles, we will limit our study in this chapter to Isaiah 1—39. As with the preceding prophets, we situate ourselves in the eighth century BC. Now, however, we move to the kingdom of Judah.

Chapters 1–39 fall into nine parts, often marked by introductory comments about chronology or the prophecies of Isaiah:

Isaiah 1:	The introduction to the collection
Isaiah 2—5:	The indictment of Judah and Jerusalem, possibly from the time of Jotham and perhaps Ahaz before the Syro-Ephraimite war
Isaiah 6:	The call of Isaiah

Isaiah 7—12:   The Immanuel prophecies, during the
reign of Ahaz in the context of the
Syro-Ephraimite war
Isaiah 13—23: Oracles against the nations
Isaiah 24—27: "The apocalypse of Isaiah," probably the
work of a disciple in the postexilic period
Isaiah 28—33: Prophecies against foreign alliances, against
the background of King Hezekiah's anti-
Assyrian policies to which Isaiah was
strongly opposed
Isaiah 34—35: An oracle against Edom, probably the work
of a later disciple, added around the time of
the Nabataean destruction of Edom in the
fifth century BC
Isaiah 36—39: A historical appendix, a copy of 2 Kings
18—20 plus an account of Judah's collusion
with emissaries from Babylon, obviously
added by the later editor of the book

(See Appendix 4c for a more detailed outline of First Isaiah.)

Our study will attempt a somewhat chronological order
starting with the call of Isaiah (chapter 6), returning then to the
introduction (chapter 1) and proceeding through the early prophecies under Jotham and Ahaz (chapters 2–5), then the Immanuel
prophecies under Ahaz (chapters 7–12). Finally we will look at the
later prophecies under Hezekiah (chapters 28–33).

D. TORAH TRADITIONS IN ISAIAH

In the chapters attributed to the eighth-century prophet, we
see some traces of the ancient traditions that eventually will
become our Pentateuch. Jacob and Abraham are named in Isaiah
29:22, and Abraham stories echo in 1:10 and 10:22.

A brief mention of God "lifting his staff over the sea on the
road of Egypt" (10:26) seems to allude to the story of Moses at the
sea (Exod 14:15–30), although there are some indications of this
text being added later. A stronger argument could be used to

show the secondary character of Isaiah 11:16 where an explicit reference is made to the Exodus.

There is no mention of "the book of the Law." The Hebrew term *torah* in fact does appear frequently in this book but in the sense of specific divine instruction. Instead of being presented as some fundamental covenantal law connected with the Exodus or Sinai, the term *torah* in Isaiah appears in parallel with a word of God issued from the prophet (1:10; probably 5:24) or from Jerusalem (2:3) or described as a spurned prophetic instruction (8:16). For Isaiah, refusing to obey the *torat YHWH* is telling the prophets to stop their prophesying (30:9).

A reference to "laws" and "statutes" as well as to "the ancient covenant" (24:5) appears in the "apocalypse of Isaiah" (Isa 24—27), a section of this book generally considered to be a later addition.

II. Significant Passages in Isaiah

A. ISAIAH 6 / THE CALL OF ISAIAH

1:1 *The superscript*

The opening verse of the book describes Isaiah's call as "a vision" (*chazon*; see also 2:1), although most of this book will recount the word of God. The mention of Jerusalem and the list of Judean kings situate the mission of Isaiah geographically and temporally.

6:1–13 *The prophet's call*

The story of Isaiah's call by God now introduces the collection of Immanuel prophecies (chapters 7–12). However, the event is dated from the death of King Uzziah in 739 BC. The narration may well be an account of the first prophetic experience of Isaiah, before the coming of the Assyrians, when Judah lived in peace and prosperity.

The chapter describes Isaiah's vision of God, his prophetic call, and his mission. The chapter in fact serves as a compendium of Isaiah's theology. The scene is "the Holies" (*ha-hekal*) of the

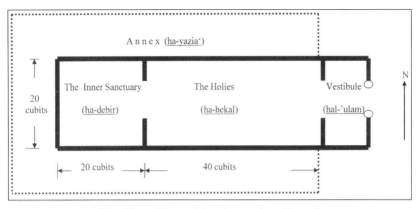

6B—Floor Plan of the Jerusalem Temple

Temple (see diagram 6B). Yahweh is above the Temple, but "the train of his garment" fills the Temple. The divine transcendence is reinforced by the heavenly beings, the *seraphim* (literally, the "burners"), proclaiming God's holiness but veiling their own eyes from looking on God. The "danger" of this holiness shows up in Isaiah's reaction. After his purification by fire, Isaiah volunteers for the mission, standing out among the prophets for his willingness to accept the divine call (6:8). Others before him and after him express reluctance, like Moses (Exod 1—3) or Jeremiah (Jer 1), or intense compulsion, like Amos (Amos 3:8).

What follows is an allusion to the mystery of human sinfulness as part of God's plan (6:9–10), a plan leading to disaster, willed by God (see also Exod 4:21; 1 Kgs 22:13–23; Judg 9:23). The sin here is a sluggish heart, a lack of understanding (see Isa 1:2–3). God's judgment is already decreed, and Isaiah's job is to realize this judgment in his prophetic proclamation. Instead of enlightening and converting the listeners, the goal of this proclamation is rather to dull their eyes, close their ears, and harden their hearts. The very proclamation of the prophet is to bring this judgment about.

Mark's Gospel uses this text of Isaiah to explain the inability of "outsiders" to understand Jesus and his teachings (Mark 4:10–12). At stake here is the same mystery of human sinfulness that will lead to the crucifixion, a disaster that becomes God's means of salvation.

In a prayer parallel to Amos's intercessions (Amos 7:2, 5), Isaiah protests, "How long, O Lord?" (Isa 6:11). The blindness cannot be the only message. The divine response seems to confirm the impending disaster. Just a fallen trunk (*mazebeth*) will remain (6:11–13). A positive element, however, lies mysteriously in the obscure last words of verse 13: "Her trunk [*mazabtah*] is holy seed [*zera' qodesh*]." After devastation, the trunk still contains life. A hidden seed promises new vitality. Behind divine anger and destruction remains a glimmer of God's patience and love.

B. ISAIAH 1 / INTRODUCTION

1:2–31 *An overture*

In this opening chapter to the Book of Isaiah, we see a proclamation, focused on the city of Jerusalem ("Zion"). It is in the form of a divine "lawsuit" against Israel, although the term *rîb*, does not appear here.

The chapter in fact looks like a summary of Isaiah's theology, perhaps assembled by the editors of Isaiah 1—39. We find mention of religious blindness (1:2–4), God as the Holy One of Israel (1:4), God's punishing judgment (1:5–9), the remnant (1:9), the evil of cult not accompanied by a moral life (1:10–15), the call to social justice (1:16–17), and hope of salvation based on God's power to forgive a person even of the most heinous sins (1:18–31). Like an overture to the book, this chapter introduces themes that will be developed at length in the remaining chapters.

C. ISAIAH 2—5 / SERMONS OF ISAIAH DURING THE TIME OF JOTHAM AND AHAZ

2:1–5 *The exaltation of Mount Zion*

The heading in 2:1 indicates that chapters 2–5 probably at one time constituted a separate collection. The oracle concerning the prominent place of Jerusalem and the house of God in the world of the Gentiles is shared with Micah (4:1–4). We have no indication of who is borrowing from whom or when it was added to the text. It is an oracle of great hope for Jerusalem and remarkable openness to all nations, proclaiming that world peace can come and eventually will come under the justice and judgments of God.

2:6–22 *An indictment of Judah for materialism and idolatry*

With a jarring break from the previous text, Isaiah condemns the people and warns of "that day" (2:11–12, 17). The accusation describes a country in great prosperity, "full of silver and gold" (2:7), well armed for war, "full of horses and...chariots" (2:7), and abandoning Yahweh for manufactured religion, "full of idols...the work of their hands" (2:8). In the next chapter, Isaiah will also focus on the way the rich oppress the poor (3:13–15). The accusation would fit well in the early career of Isaiah under King Jotham, when economic prosperity marked both the northern and southern kingdoms.

Isaiah warns of the destructive presence of Yahweh, when God will appear in "glorious majesty" (2:10). For the sinful human being, the presence of Yahweh is itself destructive. Thus Isaiah describes "that day" (2:11, 17). It will be as a day that levels any earthly object that boasts of arrogant power (2:11–17). Human beings will feel the need to hide from Yahweh, like Adam and Eve, even if that means hiding in the dust and rocks. The image of hiding among the rocks and caves also suggests the way Moses had to protect himself from the presence of God's face (Exod 33:18—34:9). This image also echoes in the New Testament (Luke 23:6; Rev 6:16).

5:1–7 *The song of the vineyard*

In a classic parable, Isaiah likens ungrateful and unresponsive Israel to a carefully tended but inexplicably unfruitful vineyard. This image of Israel as a vine is a favorite of the prophets, usually to express failure and disappointment (Hos 10:1; Jer 2:21; 5:10). The parable puts the listeners on the spot: "You be the judge!" (5:3–4). The normal consequence of such unfruitfulness is destruction (5:5–6).

The interpretation of the parable is given in verse 7, where God describes his desire to have from Israel and Judah "fair judgment" (*mishpat*) and "justice" (*tz^{e}daqah*). In place of those fruits came "bloodshed" (*mispach*) and "outcry" (*tz^e'aqah*).

In the New Testament, Jesus uses the imagery of Isaiah with a shift from the vine to the workers in the vineyard (Mark 12:1–12). In John's Gospel, the vine is an image of Jesus himself, "the true vine" (John 15:1–10), incorporating in his person the true Israel.

5:8–25 *The indictment of the unjust*

This oracle against Judah is an example of Isaiah's use of the rhetorical technique known as chiasm. It consists of a tightly structured poem that appears to have lost a strophe (A'), one however that now can probably be found at 10:1–4. The poem consists of seven "alas" (*hoi*) statements in a chiastic order:

> A Alas to those amassing wealth by depriving the poor (5:8–10)
> > B Alas to those inflamed and blinded by wine and neglecting the work of Yahweh (5:11–16)
> > > C Alas to sinners who complacently await God's intervention (5:18–19)
> > > > D Alas to those "who call evil good, and good, evil" (5:20)
> > > C' Alas to those who complacently think themselves wise (5:21)
> > B' Alas to those blinded by wine and perverting justice (5:22–23)
> [A' Alas to those who oppress the poor (10:1–4)]

The outermost stanzas (A–A') clearly denounce the sin of oppressing the poor. The next concentric development (B–B') introduces the rich lifestyle with its excessive consumption of wine. In this paired section we see the correspondence of "taking no note of the plan of Yahweh" (v. 12) and "withholding justice for him who is in the right" (v. 23). The next level in (C–C') condemns the overconfident attitude of these oppressive rich people. In the middle of the chiasm (D) may be the fundamental evil, the refusal to distinguish good and evil.

D. ISAIAH 7—12 /PROPHECIES OF ISAIAH DURING THE REIGN OF AHAZ

Isaiah 7—12 includes probably the best-known texts of this biblical book, at least in Christian circles. They are known as the Immanuel prophecies from the name given to a promised child described in 7:14, who apparently appears again in 9:5–6 and 11:1–9 as a saving Davidic leader.

The scene opens with the Syro-Ephraimite war breaking out in 734 BC. Attacking Jerusalem, Rezin, the king of Damascus, and Pekah ben Remaliah, king of Israel, made it clear that they would not only force the reluctant Judah into the coalition against Assyria but would also depose Ahaz and inaugurate a new line of kings in Jerusalem (Isa 7:6; see Map 6C). To make things worse, Ahaz seems to have turned to the Canaanite practice of sacrificing his infant son (2 Kgs 16:3). Without a successor to Ahaz, the nation and the Davidic dynasty were in serious peril.

Against the pleading of Isaiah, Ahaz calls for help from Tiglath-pileser. This king of Assyria then ravaged Damascus, executing Rezin, and destroyed the northern parts of Israel, deporting many of the citizens, but left Hoshea on the throne of Israel in Samaria (see Map 3B above).

In Judah the results of the intervention of Tiglath-pileser were mixed. The nation and the dynasty were saved, but Ahaz was forced to pay a huge price in money (2 Kgs 16:8–9) and apparently to introduce some form of Assyrian worship into the Temple of Jerusalem

6C—The Attack of Rezin and Pekah

(2 Kgs 16:10–18). As is clear from the description of religious syncretism practiced by Ahaz in 2 Kings 16:2–4, Ahaz was a man of little or no faith in the God of Israel. Against this background, the Immanuel prophecies (Isa 7—12) appear.

7:1–9 *The threat of war and the call to faith*

As the war breaks out, Isaiah intervenes directly in the affairs of state. He tries to stop the alliance of Ahaz with Tiglath-pileser. With his son, Sh^ear-jashub, he goes to meet the king, apparently by the Gihon Spring at the beginning of the Shiloah aqueduct (see diagram 6A). The contrast here is that between the fear gripping the king who "trembled as the trees of the forest tremble in the wind" (7:2) and the faith resolve described by Isaiah, "Take care and remain calm; do not fear and do not lose heart" (7:4).

The oracle culminates in the line, "Unless you believe, you shall not be firm" (7:9). The full meaning of the line is lost in English translation. The Hebrew word for "to believe" is *he'^emin*, the causative or hiphil form of *'aman*, "to be firm." In Hebrew to "believe" in God is to declare God to be firm. Isaiah is telling Ahaz that his security lies in God as his rock, not in any alliance with Tiglath-pileser. Acting in faith is in direct opposition to acting out of fear. Ahaz must not act out of fear of Rezin and Pekah. He must trust in God to deal with them.

7:10–16 *The sign of Immanuel*

Ahaz refuses a reassuring sign from God. In the second oracle, probably at a different time or place than the preceding, Isaiah nevertheless offers the sign of Immanuel, the sign of a young woman (*'almah*) who is now pregnant and who is bearing a son and will call him "Immanuel." The name "Immanuel" is a symbolic description. *'immanu* is the Hebrew preposition "with" connected with a suffix indicating "us." *'El* means "God." The name implies a saving intervention of God. This sign is apparently offered at first to reassure the king of God's presence with his people and therefore of his protection (see Ps 46:8, 12).

What would Isaiah have meant by the sign of a pregnant young woman and the birth of a son who would symbolize God's presence with his people at the time of Ahaz? The mention in 2 Kings 16:3 of Ahaz's earlier sacrifice of his son may in fact indicate that the Davidic line had no successor at the beginning of the Syro-Ephraimite war.

A plausible case can be made for the birth of Hezekiah around 732 BC and thus a pregnancy beginning in 733 BC. According to the synopsis of the kings we have been following (see Appendix 2), Hezekiah's twenty-nine year reign (2 Kgs 18:2) most likely dates from 715 to 686 BC. This dating would allow for the sixteen-year reign of his father King Ahaz (2 Kgs 16:2) from roughly 731 to 715 BC, as well as for the invasion of Sennacherib, 701 BC, to occur in the fourteenth year of Hezekiah (2 Kgs 18:13). Second Kings 18:1 makes reference to the accession of King Hezekiah to the throne in the third year of the northern king, Hosea, that is in 728 BC. This reference makes sense if it marks of the beginning of a coregency of Hezekiah with his father. This coregency is also the frame of reference for the mention of the "fourth year" and "sixth year" of King Hezekiah in 2 Kgs 18:9–10. For this dating to work out, we need only assume that King Ahaz named his son coregent when the son was a four- or five-year-old child, perhaps in deep concern about the succession of his family line, perhaps finally impressed by the fulfillment of Isaiah's Immanuel prophecies.

Certainly the pregnancy of Ahaz's wife, Abi, during the Syro-Ephraimite war (734–732 BC) would be a significant sign of hope. Emmanuel would thus be the same son who appears in Isaiah 9:5–6 as the great "prince of peace...from David's throne," and again in 11:1–9 as the saving "sprout from the stump of Jesse" who will rule with justice. These later texts may well have been prophetic hymns composed at the actual birth of Hezekiah or his installment as coregent. It is difficult to imagine the pregnancy and birth of any other son known by Isaiah as a reassuring sign for Ahaz in this critical time.

In a contemporary prophecy, Micah also speaks of the birth of a Davidic ruler, who would be "peace." Micah also mentions the ruler's mother (Mic 5:1–4).

Later, long after the Davidic line had disappeared, the words of Isaiah and Micah would be read again and again as pointing to a future Davidic king. In its excess of meaning, the shadow of a messianic king is projected onto the future. In this shadow, Matthew sees the person of Jesus. Matthew used this text to identify Jesus as the fulfillment of this prophecy, adding the comment about the name, Immanuel, "This means 'God is with us'" (Matt 1:22–23). The Greek Old Testament text used by Matthew identifies the mother as a *parthenos*, a "virgin," which Matthew then connects with the gospel story of the miraculous conception of Jesus. The Hebrew indication of the mother, *'almah*, means simply "young woman."

7:17–25 *The ominous sign*

The sign rejected by Ahaz then becomes an ominous sign. Verses 17–25 contain an oracle of doom in which the king of Assyria (Isa 7:20), whom Ahaz seeks as a savior, becomes the scourge of Judah.

8:1–10 *Immanuel and the Assyrian flood*

The ominous character of Immanuel appears in the next oracles. The destruction of Damascus and Samaria is again emphasized, this time in connection with the birth of Isaiah's second son, Maher-shalal-chash-baz (8:1–4).

As described in the context of the sign of Immanuel, Isaiah's son becomes another possibility for the identity of this special child. The timing of his birth also more or less fits the prophecy. However, identifying Immanuel with Isaiah's son would mean that the sign of Immanuel was one of disaster from the start. Immanuel would thus have to be distinguished from the saving "child born to us" (9:5) or "sprout from the stock of Jesse" (11:1). It is also difficult to understand how the pregnancy of Isaiah's wife would be a dramatic sign of anything for King Ahaz.

In any case, the birth of Maher-shalal-chash-baz becomes a prediction of destruction of Damascus and Samaria (8:3–4). Judah also will be flooded up to its neck by the mighty waters of the Euphrates—Assyria (8:6–8). If the spreading wings also names Assyria, then the sign of Immanuel is a sign of disaster for the people (8:8), as it is for "the distant lands" (8:10)!

8:16–20 *Writing the prophecy*

Because the word of Isaiah is rejected by the king, the prophet wants his instructions written out and preserved for the future, when their truth will become evident (8:20). The mention of "disciples" (8:16) suggests a group responsible for the writing and growth of the Book of Isaiah. Isaiah himself must now assume the posture of "waiting" and "trusting" (8:17).

As typical of the literary prophets, Isaiah had a far greater effect by his "book" after his death than he did by his preaching during his lifetime. The book survived and was pondered, and Immanuel eventually took on more and more of a "messianic" meaning, designating a promised savior in the future who would be an anointed king.

8:23–9:6 [9:1–7] *The invasion of Assyria and the promised child*

A year passed. Then around 733 BC Tiglath-pileser invaded northern Israel and deported to Assyria many Israelites from the territory of Zebulun and Naphtali, the region of Galilee (see 8:23 and 2 Kgs 15:29). This region was then transformed into the Assyrian province of Megiddo.

In a sudden shift, the text describes an extraordinarily joyous event, including the birth of a child, the Davidic "prince of peace." The shift is typical of the editors who juxtaposed prophecies of doom with those of salvation. The shift could also demonstrate the intense hope of Isaiah in God's ultimate intention of salvation.

This hymn of salvation addressed to God begins with the descriptions of a radical reversal of situations (9:1) and the rejoicing that follows (9:2). There follows then three reasons "for" (*ki*) the rejoicing: a) the end of oppression (9:3), b) the end of military wares (9:4), and c) the birth of a Davidic crown prince (9:5–6). The names given to the prince, like "mighty God" or "everlasting father," fit very well with the court hyperbole common at the time (9:5). His dominion, however, is different from other rulers. It is by "fair judgment (*mishpat*) and justice (*tz^edaqah*)" (9:6) not by military might (9:4).

Very significant is the literary form of this text, a hymn of praise addressed to God rather than an oracle in the name of

God addressed to the people. Isaiah is praising or thanking God for something that happened which appears as a saving divine act. The subject matter of the praise therefore appears to be present although Isaiah also draws attention to great future consequences. The birth of the Davidic crown prince is being fêted apparently at some major court celebration, with Isaiah having the honor of composing the official poem, much like the "poet laureates" at our presidential inaugurations. The synoptic time lines of the kings that we are following would point clearly to the birth of Hezekiah or perhaps his installment as an infant coregent sometime after the wars of 733 BC.

In the New Testament, Matthew saw this sudden reversal from darkness to light fulfilled in the ministry of Jesus, who began in Galilee, the land devastated by Tiglath-pileser (Matt 4:15–16). The great hope of Isaiah, never realized in his lifetime or in the centuries that followed, cast a huge shadow onto the future. Matthew saw in Jesus the promised "Immanuel" and Davidic "prince of peace."

11:1–9 *The Davidic ruler*

For a third time Isaiah celebrates a savior figure, this time "a sprout" (*choter*) or "shoot" (*netser*) arising from "the stock" (*geza'*) or "root" (*shoresh*) of Jesse. Unlike the earlier celebration of the birth of a new Davidic ruler (9:1–6), these lines are not necessarily addressed to God. The verbs here point to the future. The text, therefore, seems less like a hymn praising God for a great saving act and more like a prediction of something to come. However, the general parallel of this "sprout" here with the "child" mentioned in 9:5 strongly suggests the identity of the two savior figures as well as an identification with the "Immanuel" of 7:14.

The mention of David's father also parallels Micah's reference to Bethlehem in a similar prophecy (Mic 5:1). The arboreal imagery here in Isaiah suggests new life out of an old stock, but not necessarily out of disaster.

The description of this new Davidic leader, named first as an insignificant "shoot" or "bud" perhaps to indicate a child, focuses on three things:

- First, his tools of office: the new leader will be filled with the spirit of God, with wisdom and understanding like Solomon, counsel and strength like David, knowledge and fear of Yahweh like Abraham (Isa 11:2).
- Second, the exercise of his office: he will recognize and establish the rights of the good and punish the wicked. The principal exercise of his office will be that of an arbiter, especially for the weak (11:3–5).
- Third, the results from his rule: there will be a peace on earth that constitutes in effect a return to paradise (11:6–8). The central benefit, however, is universal "knowledge of Yahweh," which means adherence to God's will (11:9).

11:10 *The root of Jesse*

Added by a later disciple, verse 10 shifts the imagery to the "root of Jesse" as the source of blessings that are to be extended to all nations.

E. Isaiah 28—33 / Isaiah's Prophecies during the Reign of Hezekiah

Isaiah 28—33 is dominated by the prophecies that took place during the reign of Hezekiah, and in particular during the revolt against Assyria sometime around 703 BC. Elements of these prophecies appear from this time also in the earlier parts in First Isaiah and of course in the historical appendix in chapters 36-39, which is for the most part a copy of 2 Kings 18—20.

Isaiah's opposition to Hezekiah's collusion with Egypt and Babylonia appears in the angry texts of Isaiah 28—33, especially as Isaiah rails against the "covenant with death" (28:15) and against the delegations who seek Pharaoh's protection (30:2). The account of the Babylonian Merodach-Baladan's search for allies to help him revolt against Assyria appears in Isaiah 39 (see also 2 Kgs 20:12–19). Despite the urgings of Isaiah, Hezekiah becomes embroiled in the coalition against Assyria.

The result was the siege of Jerusalem in 701 BC. In Judah, all that remained was the city of Jerusalem, "like a hut in a vineyard, like a shed in a melon patch, like a besieged city" (Isa 1:8). Late in 701 BC only Jerusalem stood (see Map 3C.) The accounts in 2 Kings 18:17—19:37 (found also in Isa 36—37) give us a popular rendition of the ensuing events, celebrating God's protection of Jerusalem. The annals of Sennacherib give a different account of his war against "Hezekiah, the Jew" (see Appendix 3c), an account that sounds much more like the description in 2 Kings 18:13–16, which details the tribute paid to Assyria. This more somber account is not found in Isaiah 36—37. Historians are not certain what exactly happened. Two things, however, seem clear: Hezekiah paid a heavy tribute to Assyria, and Sennacherib's armies suffered some setback and were forced to retire to Assyria, thus abandoning the siege.

The survival of Jerusalem was thus interpreted as an eleventh-hour rescue of Jerusalem (Zion) by God. In this section of Isaiah, we will see several passages with this motif, which can be found also in the earlier parts of the book.

28:7–18 *Indictment against Jerusalem*

Isaiah speaks against the ruling classes in Jerusalem. Priests and prophets (28:7–13) have failed. These leaders mock Isaiah's sermons (28:10), but the same words come back as threats (28:13).

This snippet of Isaiah's preaching follows a chiastic structure:

A The drunkenness of leaders (28:7–8)
   B Sarcastic mimicry of Isaiah's preaching (28:9–11)
      C The offer of repose (28:12)
   B' Sarcastic mimicry of Isaiah's preaching (28:13a)
A' The drunkenness of the leaders (28:13b)

Isaiah begins and ends (A–A') with a description of drunken leaders. Isaiah pictures them vomiting from drunkenness, perhaps a disgusting scene he witnessed in the Temple after a sacrificial meal.

Embedded between these lines (B–B') are words best understood as in the mouth of these disappointing rulers. They are speaking about Isaiah ("he") as they first refuse to accept his message and then seem to ridicule his words by mimicking them. The Hebrew has nonsense syllables (*tzav latzav*, *qav laqav*) in the text of 28:9 and 13. These lines are perhaps best translated as "Blah, blah, blah, blah."

In the center of passage (C) is a rendering of Isaiah's message of tranquility. The idea here is much like that in 7:9 or 30:15. True faith in Yahweh means remaining calm. As in the parallel texts, the message is rejected.

Another chiasm follows (28:14–18):

A The covenant with death (28:14–15)
    B God setting of the cornerstone and foundation
       (28:16:17a)
A' The covenant with death (28:17b–18)

In A–A' the arrogant rulers have failed (28:14–15, 17b–18), especially in some alliance that will lead to disaster, the "covenant with death." This covenant probably refers to an anti-Assyrian alliance with Egypt (31:1–3).

In B the tone suddenly changes to hope (28:16–17a). God intervenes as the architect of a new construction, laying "a precious cornerstone as a sure foundation" in Zion. God's construction tools, however, are "fair judgment" (*mishpat*) and "justice" (*tzᵉdaqah*). Once again Isaiah calls for faith so as not to be shaken.

The Isaian text describing the cornerstone (v. 16–17a) was a favorite of the early Christians. Discoursing on the meaning and importance of faith, Paul in Romans 9:33 cites Isaiah 28:16, adding the image of people stumbling on the cornerstone, perhaps a reference to Isaiah 8:14. Describing the church, 1 Peter 2:6 also cites Isaiah 28:16–17a in a more complete form and then adds a citation of Psalm 118:22 with its description of the rejected cornerstone. First Peter then attaches the image of stumbling on the stone as a separate citation. Apparently the combination of Isaiah 28:16–17a; 8:14; and Psalm 118:22 was part of a *testimonia* or written collection of favorite scripture texts for early Christian preachers. The construction metaphor appears frequently in the New Testament as a way of describing God's new people. Paul describes himself as a "master builder" constructing on the foundation laid by Jesus (1 Cor 3:10–16). Ephesians uses the image to describe the apostles as the foundation and Jesus as the "capstone" of the church (Eph 2:20).

29:1–8 *The attack on Ariel and its eleventh-hour rescue*

Ariel is another name for Jerusalem. In popular etymology, the word means "lion (*'arî*) of God (*'el*)." This oracle of woe describes the coming siege of Sennacherib. The enemy—with the support of God (28:3)—appears ready to destroy the city. At the eleventh hour (28:5c) the tide changes and the rest of the oracle describes a dramatic rescue (28:6–8).

This poetic narrative of Jerusalem under attack and rescued by God at the last minute occurs with enough frequency in the sermons of Isaiah (see also 10:27–34; 17:12–14; and 31:4–5) that we can identify a "Zion schema" in Isaiah's sermons. The historical appendix of Isaiah 36—37 follows this schema in his prose narrative. The traditional schema appears also in some of the psalms about Jerusalem, the "Songs of Zion" (see Pss 46; 48; 76). The theme constant in all these texts is God's protection of his holy city. This protection comes during a terrifying attack on the city. It comes only in the last minute. But it comes.

10:27–34 *Attack from the north*

In the earlier part of the book, which mostly represents Isaiah's preaching under Ahaz, 10:27–34 describes an attack on Jerusalem. Mostly likely we have here another version of the "Zion schema." Many of the cities named—Aiath, Michmash (10:28), Geba, Ramah, Gibeah of Saul (10:29), Anathoth (10:30), and Nob (10:32)—can be

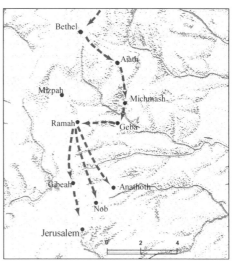

6D—Attack on Jerusalem from the North

located on a path approaching Jerusalem from the north. As far as we know, the actual attack of Sennacherib was from the south. Perhaps the description of this invasion and last-minute rescue describes the Syro-Ephraimite war of 344 BC, which involved an attack from the north (see Map 6D).

30:8–18 *Writing the prophecy*

If written at the time of Hezekiah, this text could be the prophet's last will and testament to his disciples. It is similar to his testament in the time of Ahaz (8:16–18). Here again the written prophetic word is intended to balance the failed preached word. That failure is documented by mention of the constant refusals to accept the prophet's preaching (30:9–11). The written message of Isaiah again describes trust: "By waiting and by calm you shall be saved, in quiet and in trust your strength lies" (30:15). He had the same message for Ahaz (7:9). This confident patience is what Isaiah means by faith.

* * *

Little is known of the fate of Isaiah after the death of Hezekiah in 686 BC. In the years that followed, all the reforms of Hezekiah were reversed by his impious son Manasseh (692–642 BC), who reintroduced the abominations of the Canaanites and persecuted those faithful to the Law (2 Kgs 21:1–9). In the stark words of the authors of Kings, "Manasseh shed very much innocent blood until he had filled Jerusalem from one end to the other" (2 Kgs 21:16). The Book of Chronicles has a kinder evaluation of Manasseh (2 Chron 33:1–20).

III. The Message of Isaiah

A. REVIEW OF IMAGES AND THEMES

Numerous images from the prophet Isaiah have made a lasting impression in the tradition. Among the most prominent are the seraphim and their song of holiness (6:2–7), Daughter Zion (1:8; 10:32; 16:1; 23:12) and the great Temple mountain (2:2),

The Classic Prophets of the Eighth Century

Israel the vine (5:1–7), various images of water, either as gentle and good like the waters of Shiloah (8:6) or those of a destructive flood (8:7–8; 28:2), images of blindness (6:10) like drunkenness and dullness of heart (5:11–12; 6:9–10; 28:1, 7–8, 13), the great light shining in darkness (9:1), the burning or destruction of weapons of war (9:3–4; 4:2), the root of Jesse (11:1; 10), images of some surviving remnant (1:9; 10:20–22)—like the bud (*tzemach*, 4:2), sprout (*choter*, 11:1), or offspring (*zera'*, 6:13)—and the tested cornerstone (28:16–17). Isaiah also uses striking images of the anger (*'af*) of Yahweh (5:25; 10:5; 12:1; 30:27, 30) including his outstretched hand (5:24–25; 9:7–20). Outside the later addition of chapters 24–27, Isaiah says nothing about a divine covenant but uses the image of a covenant with death (24:15, 18).

The major signature themes of Isaiah are the following:

- The importance of faith and calmness (7:9; 28:16–17; 30:15) as contrasted with fear and the foolishness of foreign alliances (8:12–13)
- Immanuel, who is apparently the Davidic newborn son (7:14–16; 8:8, 10; 9:5–6)
- Yahweh as the Holy One of Israel (1:4; 12:6; 30:15) and the danger of his holiness (6:59) or majesty (2:10)
- The last-minute rescue of Zion (10:27–34; 14:24–27; 17:12–14; 29:1–8; 30:27–33; 31:4–5)
- Sin as lack of knowledge (1:2–3) or blindness (6:1) evidenced in the sin of idolatry amidst prosperity (2:7–8)
- Restoration (1:18–31; 9:1–4; 28:5–6; 29:17–21; 30:23–26; 31:7) and "salvation" through a "savior" (*y^eshu'ah*) figure (12:2–3; 33:2)

Other important themes in Isaiah also include the following:

- Judgment and justice (1:27; 5:7, 16; 9:6; 16:5; 28:17; 32:1; 32:16; 33:5) especially in the form of care for the poor (1:16–17, 23; 5:8; 10:1–4; 11:4)
- The low value of cult without morality (1:10–16)

- "That day" (2:11–12, 17; 10:3) a day of terror (3:7, 18; 4:1) or invasion (5:30; 7:18, 20–23) as well as a day of good things (4:2; 10:20, 27; 11:10–11; 12:1, 4; 28:5; 29:18)
- The spirit [of Yahweh] (4:4; 11:2; 28:6; 30:1; 32:15)

B. THE THEOLOGY OF ISAIAH

1. *The Holy One of Israel.* God in Isaiah breaks into earthly life from a heavenly abyss, above "from a high and lofty throne" (6:1), threatening a future abyss of destruction "on that day" when all earthly illusions of power will be leveled (2:11). This God for Isaiah is "the Holy One of Israel." The name becomes Isaiah's trademark, as he peppers his teachings with the title. We see this aspect of God clearly in the vocation scene (chapter 6) where we are reminded of a traditional "theophany"—although the scene is only for Isaiah who can communicate this manifestation of God by the prophetic word.

The dangerous otherworldly character associated with Old Testament "holiness" appears in Isaiah. God burns the lips of Isaiah. He also raises up the Assyrian as the instrument of chastisement—all the while promising an "eleventh-hour" rescue of Jerusalem (29:1–8).

At the same time, this "Holy One of Israel" is not an overpowering volcano. When this holy God offers a "sign," it is not an awesome manifestation of divine power, but rather a simple pregnancy. The holy God remains hidden, mediating his word through the prophet. He commands waiting and calm.

2. *Politics and peace.* Isaiah stands out from the other prophets of his time by the intensity of his political activity. In Isaiah, God directs his messages for the most part to the kings, usually in regard to avoiding some foreign military alliance—with Assyria (chapter 7) or with Egypt (chapters 30–31). Isaiah is a prophet of state, but not a palace ("yes man") prophet. He is not there simply to support the king and provide the consoling messages that the king wishes to hear. Rather, he denounces the king. He threatens God's punishment on the king's refusals. The national government must follow God's justice and judgments.

Such political activity involved a call to international peace. Editors aptly saw this nuance as they developed the first part of the book. All nations are to stream toward Mount Zion, beating their swords into plowshares (see 2:2–4). This call stands in stark tension with the books of Joshua and Judges, where military might is the means to establish security. In Isaiah, peace comes from living under God's "fair judgment" and "justice" and reflecting this justice to others, especially the poor. With God as architect, Zion is to be built with the tools of "fair judgment" and "justice" (28:16–17).

Such an ideal of peace might be unrealistic. Such a desire might involve suffering from the hands of wicked people. The world may be incapable of hearing this word or "walking in the light of Yahweh" (2:5), preferring to secure "salvation" by its own power. In fact, the portrayal of the "eleventh-hour" rescue of Zion (29:1–8) warns us of the suffering that precedes God's rescue.

In a New Testament perspective, we are directed to see this prophecy in the light of eschatology. We understand this prophecy also through the example of Jesus. The Christian church is addressed by Isaiah to prolong the prophecy and exemplify a perfection of peace even if that posture means crucifixion and resurrection.

3. *Failure and hope*. As speaking through Isaiah, God is largely unheeded—not surprisingly, since Isaiah was sent to dull understandings and close eyes from seeing (6:9–10). Like Amos, Isaiah meets refusal. At first the refusal appears in the form of a polite demur (7:12). Later in the book it appears as hostile ridicule (30:11). He was called to fail, but in this experience of present dullness of heart, Isaiah becomes the prophet of "trusting" and "waiting." "I will trust in Yahweh who is hiding his face from the house of Jacob; yes, I will wait for him" (8:17).

In Isaiah we find extraordinary messages of hope. Life arises out of disaster. The fallen stump is holy seed. This hope lies in the vitality of beginnings—the root of Jesse. Isaiah does not simply call people back to beginnings. He affirms that God will provide a new beginning. Thus the Immanuel prophecies appear in the biblical heritage, first as a support for faith, then as a threat, but finally as a message of hope.

This call to faith embodies the famous exhortation "to stand fast" (7:9). Security in a dangerous future consists in having faith, literally, in declaring God as firm, *he'emin*. This great *'amen* is the foundation of life. It is the opposite of worry. It is the opposite of a panic-stricken search for a human solution. It means trusting in God, because God is firm. It must be a way of life for a people constituted by the promises of God. Psychologically, it means inner clarity and peace. "In returning and rest you will be saved; in quietness and trust will be your strength" (30:16).

4. *Immanuel*. In Christian circles, Isaiah is perhaps best appreciated for his "Immanuel prophecies." Matthew's appropriation of these prophecies should not distract us from the historical meaning and the intention of Isaiah. However, from the gospel overlay, we look again at Isaiah with new sensitivities and questions. We are thus drawn to the pattern of divine salvation centered on the birth of a child.

True to Isaian intention, salvation in this form is not from military might or clever political alliance. We are not promised a conquering hero or mighty king. We are promised a spirit-filled child born of a young woman. He strikes not with weapons of destruction but with the rod of his mouth and the breath of his lips. In "the child born to us," we have the embodiment of political justice. This is the ruler who "judges not by appearance or hearsay" but "judges the poor with justice" (11:3–4). This is the ruler who governs by a higher standard—the justice and faithfulness of God (11:5).

Through this child, the Davidic dynasty remains central in God's offer of salvation. The child is from the root of Jesse, who by begetting a son represents and makes present the divine offer of grace. For all the evil and weaknesses of the Davidic kings, the line as a whole remains a sacrament of grace. A great shadow is now sketched onto the future to guide hope through the midst of darkness and gloom. A child *will* be born to us.

7
Micah

I. Overview—Read 2 Kings 15:32—20:21; 2 Chronicles 27—32

A. THE PROPHET

In the opening lines of the Book of Micah, the editor tells us that Micah preached during the reigns of Jotham, Ahaz, and Hezekiah (1:1)—sometime between 750 and 686 BC, contemporary with Hosea in the north and Isaiah in the south, although neither prophet is mentioned in this book. The name "Micah" is an abbreviated form of the name and expression of divine praise, *mi-ka-Yah* (2 Kgs 22:12), and means, "Who is like Yah[weh]?" (See *mi-ka-El*, Dan 10:13.) In addition we are told that Micah came

from Moresheth, a little town southwest of Jerusalem in the western foothill region, called the Shephelah not far from the Philistine city of Gath (see Map 7A). Nothing is said of his family. Since he is known as "the guy from Moresheth," he is certainly not preaching there. Most likely, his mission took place in Jerusalem, whose leaders he constantly ad-

7A—Cities in Micah

dresses. Unlike Isaiah, however, Micah was from the countryside, not a member of the city elite.

Micah speaks of himself only twice in his book. He says of himself, "But as for me, I am filled with power, with the spirit of Yahweh, and with authority and with might—to declare to Jacob his crimes and to Israel his sins" (3:8). Later he states, "But as for me, I will look to Yahweh, I will put my trust in God my savior, my God will hear me!" (7:7). Both texts describe a confident prophet, ready and willing to speak whatever needs to be said. Filled with God's power as God's bulldozer, he has no hesitation to preach demolition.

Another biographical notice comes almost one hundred years later. In one of the very few references one prophetic book makes to another, we are told in Jeremiah that Micah's threat against Jerusalem and the Temple (see Mic 3:12) was instrumental in bringing about the reform of Hezekiah somewhere between 715 and 701 (Jer 26:18–20; see 2 Kgs 18:3–6; 2 Chr 29:8–11). In Jeremiah, the prophet's name appears originally as Micayah (later modified in the text to Micah). The silence in Micah and Jeremiah about Isaiah as influencing Hezekiah and the silence in 2 Kings 18—20 about Micah remain enigmas.

Micah was for Judah what Amos had been for Israel—a prophet who saw the oppression of the poor by the rich as a crime crying out to heaven (Mic 2—3; 6:9–11). Micah, however, goes further than Amos by looking beyond the day of punishment to a future day when a saving figure would come and rule not only Judah but all the nations of the world (Mic 4—5). Micah shares many themes and images with Isaiah his contemporary. Like Isaiah, he addresses the leaders in Jerusalem—although he lacks Isaiah's interest in politics and foreign affairs. Like Isaiah, Micah describes Jerusalem as "daughter Zion" (4:8, 10, 13; see Isa 1:8; 10:32) and portrays divine salvation with the detail of a woman giving birth (5:2).

B. THE BOOK

The Book of Micah seems to include a significant amount of material added long after the prophet's death. For instance, the reference in 5:6–8 to the regathering of the people as a crippled remnant makes sense toward the end of the Babylonian Exile. Similarly, editors apparently appended two psalms from post-exilic times: 7:8–10, a psalm of confidence with close ties to the poetry of Deutero-Isaiah, and 7:11–20, another psalm of confidence in the midst of distress. Such additions mean that the words of the prophet were preserved for generations by a group of followers who read and reread the prophet's words outside their original contexts. Such rereadings have the effect of giving the text a more universal and general application, as the disciples of the prophets search for the "broad" and "typical" in the narrow and specific aim of the prophet—a search continued in our effort to articulate the theology of these texts for our day.

In its present form the book is divided into three main parts:

Micah 1—3: Judgment of Israel and Judah
Micah 4—5: Promises of salvation to Zion
Micah 6—7: More accusations and prayers

(See Appendix 4d for a more detailed outline of Micah.)

C. Torah Traditions in Micah

Apart from the appended psalms at the end of the book, Micah contains one clear reference to the very early (J and E) Exodus traditions with mention of Moses, Aaron, and Miriam by name (6:4), as well as an allusion to the story of Balak, Balaam, and the sin at Shittim (6:5), now found in Numbers 22—25. What appears to be a series of allusions to a story about Jacob, now found in Genesis 35:16–22, suggests Micah was familiar with the patriarch traditions (4:8; 5:1–2; see commentary below). The theophany described in Micah 1:2–3 might be an echo of the Sinai tradition (see Exod 19; especially as celebrated in the ancient hymn of Judges 5:4–5). However, Micah like Isaiah does not seem to know of any book of the Law. The term torah in Micah refers rather to specific divine instructions (see Mic 4:1).

II. Significant Passages in Micah

A. MICAH 1—3 / JUDGMENT OF ISRAEL AND JUDAH

1:1–7 *Divine judgment*

After the opening verse identifying Micah and his times, the book explodes with a summons directed to all peoples of the earth (1:2) and a theophany (1:3–4). This elaborate portrayal of the appearance of God in awesome majesty appears to be modeled on Exodus 19, where God appears on Mount Sinai like a volcano (see also Ps 68:2–9; Judg 5:4–5). As both accusing witness and judge, God comes specifically against Samaria and Jerusalem, the capitals of the northern and southern kingdoms respectively (1:5). God himself will deal with their crime (*pesha'*) and sin (*chatta't*), which appear to be the same as their very existence. Like Hosea, Micah likens the sins of Samaria to those of a prostitute. She is therefore threatened with demolition (1:6–7). At the end of this part of the book, we read of the same demolition planned for Jerusalem (3:12; see Map 7A).

1:8–16 *Lament*

There follows a lament, much like the community laments in the Book of Psalms (see Pss 44; 60; 74; and so on). Twelve cities are mentioned as devastated, as the destroying force reaches into Judah and up to Jerusalem. We can locate seven of those cities: Gath, Beth-leaphrah (1:10), Lachish (1:13), Moresheth-gath, Beth-achzib (1:14), Mareshah, and Adullam (1:15). They all lie to the southwest of Jeru-salem, all on the inva-sion route of Sen-nacherib during his campaign of 701, when he likewise besieged Jerusalem (see 2 Kgs 18:13–20; 19; Isa 36—37; see Map 7B).

The lament is placed in the mouth of

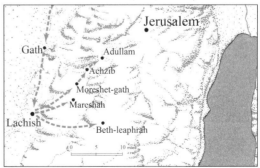

7B—Attack from the South

Micah: "Therefore I lament and I cry…" (1:8). The prophet is drawn personally into the suffering. His life and emotions are part of the prophetic message.

2:1–11 *The crimes against the poor*

The sins for which Judah will be punished are listed in 2:1–2. Like those denounced by Amos (Amos 2:6–8; 5:11–12; 8:4–8), these are crimes against the poor. Introduced by the word, *therefore* (*laken*), indicating a judgment of guilt and the need for punishment, the consequence of this crime is the loss of the perpetrator's own land (2:3–5). Like Amos in the north, Micah is appalled at these social sins. Like Israel, Judah had moved away from a tribal distribution of resources and land to an economy supported by the royal court where society was divided between the increasingly wealthy and the very poor (2:1–2). When a family lost its "inheritance" (*nach^{a}lah*) in Israel, it lost its rights and status in society. It lost its "honor" (*hador*; 2:9).

Micah 2:6 describes the people's refusal to hear his prophecy. Verse 11 then depicts a form of prophecy likened to drunkenness that the people want. Between this double allusion to prophecy, Micah lists more social crimes. The opponents of the prophet are clearly the rich oppressors who defraud the poor (2:8–9). They are also religious people who have God figured out and are convinced that he would never do such bad things to his own people (2:7). In God's eyes, however, these powerful of Judah are as wicked as an invading enemy (2:8–9).

The next two verses (2:12–13) look like a postexilic addition.

3:1–12 *Accusation against the leaders*

Micah points the finger at those responsible for the coming destruction of Jerusalem. The culprits include leaders of the people. He likens these rulers to cannibals (3:1–4). These are the people who should have known what is "fair judgment" (*mishpat*; 3:1), the norms for protecting the innocent in disputes over property and even life. Instead, these leaders abhor it (3:9).

Next listed are the prophets, described as corrupt and venal, for whom money talks—not God (3:5–7). Micah contrasts himself to these prophets by the power of God's spirit that fills him and enables him to declare evil where he sees it (3:8).

Micah then returns to indict the leaders of Jacob (3:9–11), deluded by a form of religious presumption that may have developed from Isaiah's "Zion schema:" "Is not Yahweh in our midst? No evil can come upon us" (3:11; see Isa 12:6; Ps 46:6). In direct contrast, Micah concludes this indictment with a prediction of Jerusalem's demolition (3:12). Although probably impressed by the big city of Jerusalem, the country boy from Moresheth announces its destruction. According to the Book of Jeremiah (26:17–18), these words were uttered during the reign of King Hezekiah and were instrumental in bringing about a reform.

B. Micah 4—5 / Promises of Salvation

4:1–5 *Promises*

It was probably an editor who balanced Micah's accusations and threats here with prophecies of hope. This section, which still contains isolated threats (see 4:9–10; 4:14), opens with verses almost identical to Isaiah 2:2–4 concerning the future importance of Jerusalem, the city that Micah just described as utterly destroyed (3:12). We have no indication that either Micah or Isaiah depended on the other. More likely both used a common source. The tone and teaching of these verses are also similar to Isaiah 60.

The prophecy describes Jerusalem as a religious center for "many nations." Jerusalem is the source of Yahweh's *torah*. The word means "instruction." It is later used to refer to the first five books of the Bible and then is translated as "the Law." Here it is synonymous with "the word of Yahweh," as seen from the inverted parallelism or chiasm in verse 2c: Zion–instruction–word of Yahweh–Jerusalem. Yahweh settles the disputes of nations by his just judgments. The result is international peace, not from conquest and subjection, but as nations voluntarily convert their weapons of death into instruments of farming (see also 5:9). To the material common with Isaiah, Micah adds a note about an individual living undisturbed "under his own fig tree" (4:4; see 1 Kgs 4:25).

4:6–8 *The kingdom of the remnant*

From the description of world peace under Yahweh's instruction, the Book of Micah now gives us a glimpse into the kingship of God on earth. The section is introduced with the oracle or messenger formula, "Yahweh says this" (4:6). God is giving us his own hopes and dreams. The kingdom then promised is not that of the mighty and comely, but one of the lame and the outcasts, described as a gathered "remnant" (*sh^e'erit*; 4:7; 5:6–7). Although they are the despised of the world, they are the ones for whom Yahweh will be king forever. This is not the way an ambitious ruler would normally want to build up his realm. A later prophet will quote God insisting, "My ways are not your ways" (Isa 55:8). Hannah—and later Mary in the New Testament—praised God who "raises the needy from the dust…and seats them with nobles" (1 Sam 2:8; see Luke 1:52–53).

Restored to her former realm, and described as a woman ("daughter Zion"), Jerusalem represents this remnant (4:8). Other names for the city like "Migdal-eder" ("tower of the flock") or "Ophel" ("knoll"?) recall ancient traditions about Jerusalem (see Gen 35:21; 2 Chron 27:3).

The text here aptly expresses the hope of the people after the Babylonian Exile and most probably is postexilic.

5:1–4a [5:2–5a] *A future ruler*

An address emphatically directed to Bethlehem (*we-'attah*; 5:1) parallels a similar address to Jerusalem in 4:8. This address to Bethlehem is a promise of salvation, the promise of a ruler (*môshel*), through whom God will act. As shepherding (5:3), this individual assumes the typical description of a king (see Ezek 34; Jer 23:3–4), although the title "king" (*melek*) seems to be avoided. An origin in Bethlehem suggests the house of David. Ephrathah was apparently an old name for Bethlehem (Josh 15:59); David's father, Jesse, was explicitly called "an Ephrathite from Bethlehem" (1 Sam 17:12). Such a "messianic" text is centered on the Davidic dynasty. In the New Testament, Matthew applies this text to Jesus (Matt 2:6).

The prophet mentions the mother of this ruler, "she who is to give birth." No details are given, but the author may well be thinking of the queen mother (*gᵉbirah*), who held a powerful place in the Davidic palace, in which case we may have some linkage to the Isaian prophecy of Immanuel born of the *'almah* (Isa 7:14). This woman in Micah appears in a discussion of timing: "until the time when…." The issue seems to be a painful delay of God's action.

The language in this section has a strange resemblance to the story Jacob's family in Genesis 35:16–22, with its mention of a woman, Rachel, giving birth (35:16), Ephrath, which is Bethlehem (35:16.19; see Map 7A), and Migdal-eder (35:21; see Micah 4:8). This is the story of Rachel's death after giving birth to Benjamin, the youngest of the patriarchs. Perhaps the connection is meant to emphasize the origins of Israel, the way death does not stop the protection and salvation of God, and the important place in God's plan of the youngest and least impressive—like the story of the selection of David (1 Sam 16).

The effects of this future ruler are extraordinary. He will incarnate "peace" (*shalom*) itself. "His greatness will reach to the ends of the earth" (5:4). In Micah's time, such a prophecy would be an expression of great hope in the Davidic dynasty. As the Davidic line died out and these lines were read over and over again, this promise would have directed readers to look forward to a future ruler. In the New Testament, Matthew applies this text to Jesus (Matt 2:5–6).

C. MICAH 6—7 / ACCUSATIONS AND PRAYERS

6:1–8 *Accusations*

The prophetic *rîb* or trial against Israel now proceeds. This section is in three parts, according to three different speakers, all perhaps part of a Temple liturgy. God speaks first (6:1–5), calling on the mountains as his witnesses. Divine distress and suffering appear in 6:3 as God recalls the origins of Israel: "O my people, what have I done to you…?" Christians use this line for the Good Friday liturgy.

The people respond (6:6–7) offering to perform elaborate acts of religion, even to the point of returning to the abomination of infant sacrifice (see 2 Kgs 16:3; 21:6).

As the third voice, the prophet concludes the section with the familiar theme: a moral life is far more important than acts of religion. The words of Micah define true religion:

> You have been told, O man, what is good, and what Yahweh requires of you: only to make fair judgments (*ᵃsot mishpat*), love goodness (*'ahᵃvat chesed*) and to walk humbly (*hatzne'a leket*) with your God. (6:8)

III. The Message of Micah

A. Review of Images and Themes

We can group the characteristic images in Micah as either threatening or consoling. Among the threatening images: Yahweh destroying mountains and valleys (1:3–4), the drunkenness of the people (2:11), and the divine lawsuit against Israel (6:1–8). Among the consoling: Jerusalem as the exalted city, open to the Gentiles, source of peace and justice (4:1–3), Daughter Zion, a women in labor pains (4:9–10), and the woman giving birth to a ruler in Israel (5:1–2).

We can group the more developed themes in Micah similarly. Among the negative themes:

- The readiness of God to destroy Samaria and Jerusalem (1:6–7; 3:12)
- The evil of oppressing the poor in the quest for wealth (2:1–2)
- Resistance to the prophetic word (2:6), particularly on the part of the leaders (3:1–12)
- The strength of the prophet through the spirit of God to denounce sin (3:8).

Among the positive themes are the following:

- The restoration of Jerusalem (4:4–8)
- The remnant (4:6–7; 5:6–7)
- The call to ethical conduct as more important than cultic sacrifices (6:6–8)

B. The Theology of Micah

The Book of Micah begins with God crashing into the world: "Yahweh comes forth from his place…the mountains melt like wax" (1:3–4). This theophany is the announcement of the utter destruction of human accomplishment, the very cities of Samaria and Jerusalem (1:6; 3:12). Like Amos and Isaiah, Micah announces God's doom against those who dispossess people of their inheritance, those who dishonor the poor. God will deal with this sin by death and destruction. The denunciation of evil is intense.

The visions of future blessings are also intense. In its final form, the Book of Micah carries us from the rubble of a totally demolished Jerusalem (3:12) to the heights of the same city exalted above the mountains (4:1). The prophet denounces the corrupt leaders of that city (3:1–3) and then speaks of a ruler from Bethlehem who will shepherd his flock by the strength of the Lord (5:1–4).

If the prophet does not hesitate to portray God as furious at the sins of his people, he also depicts God as hoping and dreaming of better things. These are the oscillations of a loving parent whose family is hell-bent on destructive activity. The parent knows there is no way to avoid terrible suffering, yet he or she must envision a future of redemption and peace, a family gathered again, although now limping and bearing the wounds of its affliction. Daughter Zion, like a woman writhing in birth pains, eventually will be rescued. Death and destruction cannot be the last word.

In the middle of the eighth century BC, Micah predicted the demolition of Jerusalem. The burning of the city did not occur for some 150 years, and even to this day it was never the plowed field or forest ridge that Micah predicted. It becomes clear then that the preaching of a prophet does not give people control over the future by passing on cryptic information about it. The aim of the prophet is always the present and the moral reform needed at that time. As for the future, God's loving and mysterious freedom warns us never to presume control over his plans. Yahweh is a transcendent God who descends from his holy place in the heights. This God cannot be controlled by any city or organization that presumes to understand his prophetic utterances regarding the future.

What God makes clear through the mouth of Micah and his predecessors is the importance of ethics. "Make fair judgments, love goodness, walk humbly…" (6:8). This is more important than "thousands" of religious sacrifices in the Temple. God desires living temples that reflect his justice and goodness. Religion concerns not what we do for God in church, but how we live in general and treat each other. God desires a worship that turns human beings back to one another with attitudes of love and care.

Perhaps what best distinguishes Micah is his insistence on the strength he has from the spirit of God. Faced with opposition (2:10–11), he shows no hesitation in proclaiming God's harsh words. He has placed his trust in God, his savior. He has nothing to fear. This image of a prophet will contrast with the prophets of the next century, especially that of Jeremiah.

PART II

The Prophets of the Seventh Century and of the Period of the Exile

8
Historical Background

Read 2 Kings 21—25; 2 Chronicles 33—36.

I. In Mesopotamia

The latter part of the seventh century BC in the Middle East was a time of war and turmoil. After reaching its zenith of power under King Assurbanipal (668–626 BC), Assyria started a precipitous slide. During his own reign, Assurbanipal faced revolts throughout his empire. In alliance with the kingdom of the Medes, Nabopolassar of Babylon (626–605) launched a series of attacks against Assyria. The former Assyrian capital of Assur fell to the Babylonians in 614. Two years later, the new capital of Nineveh was destroyed. Babylonia, often called "Chaldea" in the Bible, replaced Assyria as the major superpower of the Middle East.

Nabopolassar continued his expansion west. In a striking shift of alliances, Egypt went to the rescue of Assyria, its former enemy. Pharaoh Neco II (610–595) marched a massive army north from Egypt through Palestine to encounter the Babylonian army at Haran in the Gozan region of northern Syria (see Map 8A). After easily defeating a much smaller Judean army led by King Josiah (640–609) near the old Israelite city of Megiddo, Neco battled the Babylonian army. The Egyptians at first succeeded in stalling the Babylonian advance, but when the Babylonian army finally crossed the Euphrates at the city of Carchemish, the Egyptians were unable to counter. The battle of Carchemish (605) ended in a rout of the Egyptian army. The world belonged to Babylonia.

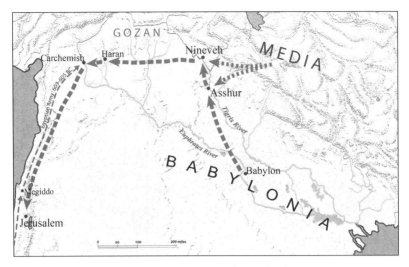

8A—The Advance of Babylonia

Nabopolassar died shortly after this battle and was succeeded by his son Nebuchadnezzar (605–562), known throughout Ezekiel and in parts of Jeremiah, as "Nebuchadrezzar," apparently following the Babylonian form, and "Nebouchodonosor" in the Greek texts of the Old Testament. After some time needed to consolidate power and heal the recent wounds of battle, Nebuchadnezzar continued the military expansion west, quickly taking possession of the small kingdoms left in the ruins of the Egyptian empire. Judah was one such kingdom.

In 598, Nebuchadnezzar entered Jerusalem, deposed the pro-Egyptian king, Jehoiachin, replacing him by his presumably pro-Babylonian uncle, Zedekiah. At this time, Nebuchadnezzar deported to Babylonia the upper class of Judea along with Jehoiachin.

About ten years later, hearing word that Zedekiah was in league with the Egyptians and had refused to pay tribute, Nebuchadnezzar again marched west, quickly repelling an Egyptian army sent to help Zedekiah and then destroying the rebellious cities of Judea, including Jerusalem. In 587, his armies burnt to the ground the city of Jerusalem and its Temple to Yahweh. The ensuing deportation to Babylonia this time included most of the population.

II. Meanwhile in Judah

Manasseh, the worst of Judah's kings according to 2 Kings, ruled until 641, when he was succeeded by his son, Amon, who continued the idolatrous policies of his father (2 Kgs 21). Two years later, Amon was assassinated and was succeeded by his eight-year-old son Josiah (2 Kgs 22). Josiah reigned until his death in battle in 609.

In 628, the now twenty-year-old king Josiah instituted a series of religious reforms, purging Judah and Jerusalem of the idols and idolatrous practices that had taken root in the reigns of Manasseh and Amon. According to 2 Kings, the covenant with Yahweh was solemnly renewed and Passover celebrated with memorable pomp and ceremony (see 2 Kgs 22—23; 2 Chr 34—35). On the part of the people, however, the reform remained only skin-deep, as is apparent from the events under Josiah's successor.

According to 2 Kings 22:8, the reform was aided by the finding in the Temple sometime around 622 of "the book of the Law [*sefer ha-torah*]." Only the biblical Book of Deuteronomy refers to itself with that expression (Deut 29:20; 31:26). Other descriptions in the story of 2 Kings connected with the discovery of the Law also echo teachings characteristic of Deuteronomy (see 2 Kgs 23:3, 15, 19, 24). These details suggest that the discovery might have been a part of this biblical book. Apart from editorial editions in the accounts of 1 and 2 Kings, this description of the discovery of "the book of the Law" is the earliest description in the Old Testament of what we know today as "a biblical book" described as "the Law," to be consulted to discover God's covenantal will. Up to this time, the word of the prophet was the source for divine guidance. After the Exile, the "book of the Law of Moses" becomes the center for religious life in Judaism, not just for the king but for all the people (see Neh 8:1–12).

Three years after the fall of Nineveh, on the plains of Jezreel (Esdralon) in northern Israel, Josiah died in a futile attempt to prevent Pharaoh Neco from helping the beleaguered Assyrian armies against the Babylonians at Haran in Syria. The battle of Megiddo (609) was a shock to the Judeans. Good King Josiah was killed by the "evil" forces of the Egyptians. According to the theologians and historians of the day, military and political success was linked to fidelity to God. Something went wrong at the battle of Megiddo. Somehow this battle between the forces of good and evil needs to be fought again at some future Har-Megiddon.

Josiah left behind three sons: Jehoahaz, Jehoiakim, and Zedekiah, all of whom along with a grandson, Jehoiachin, eventually succeeded him as king. According to 2 Kings, the confusing succession of the house of Josiah (made worse by the change of names) appears in the following family tree (Diagram 8B), which also indicates the order of the reigns:

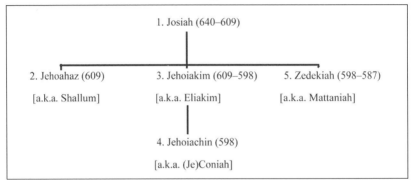

1. Josiah (640–609)

2. Jehoahaz (609) 3. Jehoiakim (609–598) 5. Zedekiah (598–587)

[a.k.a. Shallum] [a.k.a. Eliakim] [a.k.a. Mattaniah]

4. Jehoiachin (598)

[a.k.a. (Je)Coniah]

8B—The Family of Josiah

Jehoahaz succeeded his father for three months. In the late summer of 609, Pharaoh Neco returned from his war against the Babylonians at Haran, deposed Jehoahaz, and established Jehoiakim his brother as king of Judah (2 Kgs 23:29–37; 2 Chr 36:1–4).

For eleven years (609–598), Jehoiakim reigned as a cynical, godless butcher in the tradition of Manasseh and Amon. He murdered prophets, oppressed the faithful, and reestablished the Ba'alist cults abolished by Josiah (2 Kgs 24:1–6; 2 Chr 36:5–8; Jer 26:20; 36:15–26).

When Nebuchadnezzar absorbed Judah after defeating the Egyptians again at Carchemish in 605, Jehoiakim was forced to submit to a new master. Sometime during his ten-year reign he sided with the pro-Egyptian party and rebelled against his Babylonian overlord. He died in 598 just before Nebuchadnezzar's siege of

Jerusalem opened (Jer 22:18–19), leaving his son Jehoiachin to succeed him on the throne.

When this Babylonian siege of Jerusalem ended in 598 BC, Nebuchadnezzar deposed the young King Jehoiachin, known in Jeremiah as Coniah or Jeconiah. The Babylonian king then had Jehoiachin carried off as a hostage to Babylon replacing him with his uncle, Zedekiah, the last and weakest of Josiah's sons. Jehoiachin remained a captive until 562 when a new Babylonian king, Evil-Merodach, restored him to royal honors but did not permit him to return to Judah (2 Kgs 24:10–17; 25:27; 2 Chr 36:1–10). Some eight generations of royal descendants of Jehoiachin are listed in a genealogy of that family in 1 Chronicles 3:17–24.

Back in Judah, Zedekiah, a weak and vacillating puppet, eventually sided with the pro-Egyptian faction at court and joined a coalition of nations in revolt against Babylon. This time the Babylonian juggernaut rolled on Judah for the last time. After disposing of an Egyptian army sent to help Judah and after an eighteen-month siege, Nebuchadnezzar's generals breached the walls of Jerusalem in the summer of 587. Zedekiah was captured. His sons were executed before his eyes. He himself was blinded and carried captive to Babylon (2 Kgs 24:18—25:7) where he died (see Ezek 12:12–13).

In the months following, the city was utterly destroyed. Houses and Temple were burnt to the ground. The walls were demolished, and the cream of the population carried off to Babylon (see Map 8C). To all appearances this should have been the end of Judah (2 Kgs 25:8–21; 2 Chr 36:11–21; Jer 52).

Jeremiah and Ezekiel had pleaded with the leaders of Jerusalem not to place false hopes in the Temple and learn to submit to God. Despite these prophets' efforts, Judah followed her northern sister into exile. The exile, however, was not in Assyria but in Babylon. It is in Babylonia that Deutero-Isaiah will address the dejected exiles.

The chronology of the last hundred or so years of Judah can be sketched as follows:

695–641   The reigns of Manasseh and Amon, Judah's worst kings

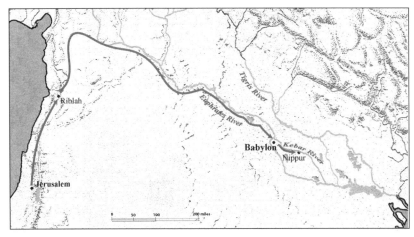

8C—The Babylonian Exile

640–609   The reign of Josiah, who in 628 introduces religious reforms

640–630   The preaching of Zephaniah

626–580   The preaching of Jeremiah

622   The finding of the "book of the Law" in the Temple

612   The fall of Nineveh to the combined armies of the Babylonians and Medes; the preaching of Nahum

609   The crushing of the last Assyrian armies at Haran in Syria by Nabopolassar

609   The three-month reign of Jehoahaz, who is deposed by Pharaoh Neco

609–598   The reign of Jehoiakim, the mortal enemy of Jeremiah

605   The battle of Carchemish; the preaching of Habakkuk

605–562   The reign of Nebuchadnezzar, king of Babylon, following his victory over Pharaoh Neco at Carchemish in 605

598   Jehoiachin's three-month reign, deposed by Nebuchadnezzar; the first invasion of Nebuchadnezzar and the first deportation

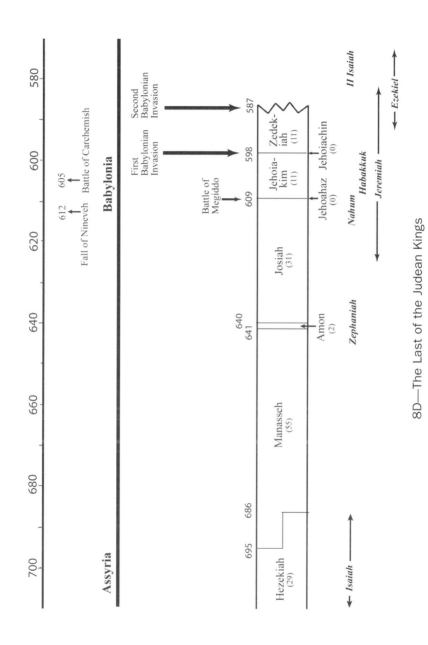

8D—The Last of the Judean Kings

598–587   The reign of Zedekiah, appointed by
          Nebuchadnezzar
587   The second invasion, destruction of Jerusalem
          and the Temple, second deportation
587–537   The Babylonian captivity lasting almost fifty
          years, ending when Cyrus the Great, king of
          Persia, conquers Babylon and allows the Jews to
          return to Jerusalem

9
Three Pre-exilic Judean Prophets of the Seventh Century

In the last years of the southern kingdom, more prophetic voices cry out. Zephaniah warns of God's ultimate option, the annihilation of the universe. When Nineveh capitulates in 612 BC, Nahum sings a song of triumph to express the savage delight of the oppressed satellite nations at the downfall of the hated tyrant. When Babylon under Nebuchadnezzar replaces Assyria and like Assyria oppresses the subject nations, the prophet Habakkuk searches his soul and questions the apparent injustice of God allowing Babylon to take over the reins of the empire.

I. Zephaniah

A. Overview

Zephaniah preached in the reign of Josiah (Zeph 1:1), who reigned from 640 to 609 BC. Given the negative tone of the prophet, his preaching probably occurred in the early period of Josiah's reign, perhaps before 628, when the king was too young to act for himself and before the call of Jeremiah. The reformation of religion and morals that did occur under Josiah (2 Kgs 22:3—23:25) indicates perhaps that Zephaniah's preaching had a powerful effect, at least in the short term.

The prophet is described in the opening inscription as the son of Cushi ("the Cushite"?) and as the great-great-grandson of a person named Hezekiah (1:1). This could be King Hezekiah. We have no other example of a book tracing the ancestry of a prophet back four generations.

The book can be divided into three parts:

Zephaniah 1:2—2:3:   The approaching "day of Yahweh"
Zephaniah 2:4—3:8:   Oracles against the nations and
                     Jerusalem
Zephaniah 3:9–20:   Promises of salvation for a remnant

(See Appendix 4e for a more detailed outline of Zephaniah.)
Except for the brief reference to Sodom and Gomorrah (2:9), Zephaniah shows no clear connection with patriarchal or Exodus traditions.

B. Significant Passages in Zephaniah

1:1–13 *Divine annihilation*
After the introductory superscription (1:1), the book starts with a sweeping condemnation of all creation. God is speaking in a prophetic oracle. He declares that he will "sweep away" and "cut off" everything, including humanity, from the face of the earth. Never before was the destructive presence of God so radically portrayed. The imagery is obviously exaggerated. After all, who is going to do the pillaging mentioned (1:13)?

Yet the divine threat clearly portrays the ephemeral and illusory character of the great earthly pillars of security, the "Ba'als" and "Milcoms" (1:4–5), the "princes" and "kings" (1:8), the "merchants" and "wealth" (1:12), the "houses" and "vineyards" (1:13)—as "the face of the earth" (1:2) is destroyed. With his broom sweeping away all things of human importance, only God remains speaking from the great abyss. There God appears for who he is.

1:14–18 *The day of wrath*
This text inspired Thomas of Celano's famous Christian chant, *Dies irae dies illa*. The theme of "the day of Yahweh" was introduced into the literature by Amos as a day of destruction for Samaria (Amos 5:18–20). Isaiah expanded the theme to include other nations in the punishing destruction (Isa 2:9–17; 13:6). In Zephaniah it receives a clear "eschatological" sense, as we would say. (The Greek word *eschatos* means "last," in effect, the final word.) The scene is universal in scope, embracing "all who live on the earth" (1:18).

With his portrayal of "the day of Yahweh," Zephaniah appears at the fountainhead of a new tradition, that of apocalyptic. He identifies "the day of Yahweh" as one of destruction for the entire earth—as we would say, "the end of the world." The theme will be picked up sporadically by other prophets like Joel. Some four hundred years later it will give birth to a whole literary tradition speculating on the nature and timing of this end. In the New Testament, the Book of Revelation is a clear heir to this tradition.

2:3 *The humble*
The section ends with an appeal by the prophet directed to the humble and poor (*'anawim*) of the earth. They are to "seek Yahweh." This injunction is placed in parallel with "seek justice [*tzedeq*], seek humility [*'anawah*]." The "humble of the earth" are also described as those "who observe his fair judgments [*mishpato*]."

To those who seek God comes an offer of shelter. More exactly, the prophet offers the possibility of shelter: "Perhaps (*'ulay*) you may be sheltered." An appeal for God's help is approached in hope, not smug certitude. God cannot be manipulated even by a moral life.

3:9–13 *The hope of salvation*
After oracles against surrounding nations (2:4–15) and against unnamed Jerusalem (3:1–8), Zephaniah shifts suddenly to speak about salvation, with no attempt to be consistent with the preceding terrible predictions. The prophet simply points out two aspects of God's action, one destructive, the other saving, making no attempt to reconcile the two.

In the form of a divine oracle, the promise again first speaks about the "nations" (*'ammim*). God will purify their lips that they may "call on the name of Yahweh and serve him with one accord (literally, with one shoulder)" (3:9). The vision is expansive, from the far north to the land "beyond the rivers of Cush (Ethiopia)" (3:10). People from these areas will all bring offerings to Yahweh. The prophecy is striking in its universalism and eventually will join Trito-Isaiah in an effort to expand the faith of Israel to all nations.

The oracle then promises salvation to Jerusalem. Like Micah (see Mic 5:6), Zephaniah focuses attention on "a remnant of

Israel" (she'erit Yisra'el), described as "humble and lowly" ('anaw wᵉdal; Zeph 3:12–13). The text of 3:19 appears to have been added later to the book. The promises in that verse to "the lame" and "the outcasts" reflect Micah even closer (see Mic 4:6).

3:14–17 *"Daughter Zion"*

Again as in Micah and Isaiah, the prophet addresses Jerusalem as a woman, "Daughter Zion," "Daughter Jerusalem" (3:14). She is promised that she will have nothing to fear. Her hope rests in God alone: "Yahweh, your God is in your midst" (3:17).

Echoing Hosea, Zephaniah affirms Yahweh's love for his people (3:17). For Zephaniah this is a joyful love. Yahweh "will rejoice in his joy." "He will exult in his gladness." This is a rare picture of happy divine emotions.

In the New Testament, Luke focuses on the humble and lowly as the primary recipients of Jesus' attention (Luke 4:18–19). His opening two chapters select humble and lowly characters to portray Israel as it moves into the time of Jesus. He may have had Zephaniah's text in mind when he quotes the words of the angel Gabriel to Mary, "Hail, favored one! The Lord is with you" (Luke 1:28; see Zeph 3:14–15).

C. THE MESSAGE OF ZEPHANIAH

1. Review of Images and Themes

Zephaniah develops his theology around the images of the day of wrath (1:15), the merchants weighing their silver (1:11), the humble and poor of the earth (2:3), and Daughter Zion/Jerusalem (3:14).

The principal themes that appear in Zephaniah are the following:

- The day of Yahweh as the end of the world (1:2–18)
- The importance of seeking justice (2:3)
- Promises for the Gentile nations (3:9–10)
- Salvation for the "remnant of Israel" (3:12–13)
- Yahweh, the mighty savior in your midst (3:15–17)

2. The Theology of Zephaniah

The message of Zephaniah is harsh. He proclaims a "day of Yahweh" as a devastation of the whole earth. This is the first time in scripture that we have such a picture of the ultimate abyss for created reality. In effect this is a summons to seek God in the abyss—beyond the earthly illusions of security and happiness. To seek God means to reach beyond the earthly idols of security, even as total devastation becomes the mark of God's presence. To seek God means to reach into the abyss.

From this abyss we hear also the summons to seek the fundamental values of ethical life, "fair judgment" and "humility." This is not an abyss of absurdity and despair—although definitely beyond human comprehension. With religious life in Israel gangrened almost to death by its false gods (1:4–5) and by its dismissal of any significance of Yahweh in the business world (1:11–13), perhaps no other message would be adequate. This is an abyss that declares its love for Daughter Zion (3:17).

Later apocalyptic literature would complete the picture of annihilation by a promise of a "new creation." Zephaniah does not yet have that picture; however, his promises of salvation to "the remnant of Israel" (3:13), the "people humble and lowly" (3:12), hint at a divine economy that can bring hope out of the worst disaster.

II. Nahum

A. OVERVIEW

Writing probably around 612 BC, the year Nineveh fell to the Babylonian and Median armies, Nahum of Elkosh sees in these events God's moral government of the world and his punishment of Assyria for misusing its great power. Nahum's whole book is an oracle against one nation, Assyria. Nahum's voice is raised to describe God's anger against nations abusing power, destroying peoples, heaping up injustice.

We know of no city in Israel by the name of Elkosh. Near the ruins of ancient Nineveh, the village of Al-Qush today claims to be the city of Nahum (see Map 9A). Perhaps this book—the prophecy of Nahum identifies itself as a "book" (*sefer*, 1:1)—was written from Assyria among the deportees of 722 BC.

The book has three parts:

Nahum 1:2–8:   A partial alphabetic (or acrostic) poem of twelve Hebrew letters describing God's vengeance and anger

Nahum 1:9—2:3:   Promises of "good news" to Judah in the form of a dialogue addressed alternately to Judah and Nineveh

Nahum 2:4—3:19: The fall of Nineveh

(See Appendix 4f for a more detailed outline of Nahum.)

This short and specialized oracle against Nineveh shows one brief connection with an Exodus tradition. The words of God identifying himself to Moses, "slow to anger...but not declaring the guilty innocent" (Exod 34:6–7), are found verbatim in Nahum 1:3.

B. SIGNIFICANT PASSAGE IN NAHUM

3:1–7 *The fall of Nineveh*

The description from within the city flashes with scenes of war (3:2–3). The poetry here engages both hearing and sight. The

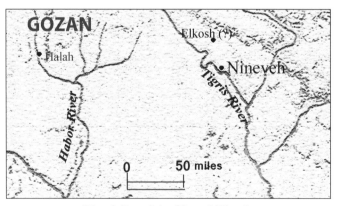

9A—A Possible Site of Elkosh

repeated accusation frames the description: Nineveh has been unrestrained in its plundering (3:1) and she plays the role of whore and witch (3:4). History testifies to the savagery of the Assyrian armies and the deceitfulness of its diplomacy. The Assyrian rape of the Egyptian city of Thebes (*No-amon*) in 633 BC was particularly brutal (see *ANET*, 277, 294–95), the memory of which might be reflected in Nahum 3:8.

Punishment is decreed for Nineveh, portrayed as a fallen woman, stripped naked, covered with filth, shamed (3:5–7). In his effort to describe an object of hatred and scorn, Nahum compares the city to a prostitute and witch (3:4), an image that would speak to a patriarchal society.

C. The Message of Nahum

1. Review of Images and Theme

Nahum builds his theology on the images of God as jealous and avenging (1:2), Nineveh as whore and witch (3:4), the disgrace of a prostitute (3:5–7), and urban warfare (3:2–3).

The Book of Nahum revolves around the one theme of the destruction of the evil city by an angry and avenging God (2:2—3:19).

2. The Theology of Nahum

Other nations also stand before the abyss of God's justice. What Nineveh did was wrong. God will redress this injustice. He must destroy the city. In a way, Nahum picks up the eschatological message of Zephaniah and focuses it on one city, one far beyond the borders of Israel.

Like the oracles against the nations in the larger collections of other prophets, this "oracle" with its vindictiveness against Nineveh presents a major challenge to the believer committed to the exhortation, "Love your enemies" (contrast Matt 5:38–48). Here we must focus on the substrate, an intense sense of justice. This is the cry of a powerless, oppressed people.

Another huge hermeneutic challenge arises from the picture of God the warrior abusing and humiliating Nineveh, portrayed as a disgraced prostitute. Nahum could speak this way only from within the perspective and framework of a violent patriarchal society. This perspective appears here as the controlling presupposition of Nahum, but today appears to us for all its own brutality (contrast John 8:1–11).

Here and in other "difficult passages" of the Old Testament we find sinful elements in the framework and presuppositions of the message, lust for revenge, violence against women. The sinfulness of these elements appears in a proper use of "canonical criticism," the attempt to understand a passage in the light of the whole Bible—including the gospels. This is not the posture of standing over the Bible and cutting out the parts we do not like. We are using the Bible as a whole to recognize when God's word comes in fact smeared with human sinfulness.

If we can at first understand and then pull away from this framework and perspective, then Nahum appears as a proclamation of God's law and justice, applicable to all peoples and nations. Yahweh is the God of all peoples—even those who do not believe in him. This reach of divine justice of course can only be seen in faith. Evil powers seem to operate with impunity. Yet however invisible, the power of God's justice remains in force and eventually manifests itself.

III. Habakkuk

A. OVERVIEW

As Nebuchadnezzar rose to power after his defeat of the Egyptian army at Carchemish in 605 BC, the prophet Habakkuk wondered just how God's justice could be served by a nation as wicked as Babylon. His "vision" deals with the perennial problem of evil.

The reference to the Chaldeans (1:6), another name for the Babylonians, without any allusion to the capture of Jerusalem in 598, places the historical setting of these prophecies between 605 and 598. Judah had become subject to Babylon around 601. The invasion of the Babylonian armies began when Judah revolted three years later (2 Kgs 24:1–2). Once the Babylonian invasions began, it was evident that Judah would be punished by the foreigners from the Euphrates.

Apart from his name and his link to the time of the Babylonians, we get no specific information about this prophet from the text. The style of pouring his anguish out to God, however, suggests a major change from the confident strong positions of earlier prophets like Amos, Micah, and Isaiah. The prophet feels the emotions of fear and dread (see especially 3:16) and expresses those emotions to God. This style will appear again in Jeremiah, a contemporary of Habakkuk.

The Hebrew text of Habakkuk poses some problems. Several key words in the text appear to be corrupted in the transmission, requiring some level of guesswork. Hence the variety of translations.

The book falls into three parts:

Habakkuk 1:2—2:4a: Dialogues between the prophet and
                            God on the mystery of evil
Habakkuk 2:4b–20:   Five woes
Habakkuk 3:1–19:   The canticle of Habakkuk

(See Appendix 4g for a more detailed outline of Habakkuk.)

An Exodus tradition appears perhaps in the description of God coming with theophanic splendor from the south or southeast (3:3–6). The one reference to "law" (*torah*), however, is in parallel with "fair judgment" (*mishpat*; 1:4) and most likely refers to specific legal instructions, not the Mosaic Law.

B. Significant Passages in Habakkuk

1:2–11 *The first dialogue*

Contemplating the paradoxical situation, Habakkuk prays to God in the form of a lament pointing out injustices surrounding the prophet. The wicked overpower the just. This is not a prophetic denunciation or judgment directed to evildoers. This is a complaint to God: "Don't you see this?" "Do I need to point these evils out to you?" In the Old Testament, such arguments with God are never considered sins. A large part of our Book of Psalms is made up of such laments.

In this first dialogue, the descriptions of wickedness appear like those typically denounced by other prophets. Habakkuk challenges God on the extent of social injustice within Israel, where justice is perverted by political corruption (1:4, 13; 2:6). This is the period of the reign of Jehoiakim (see 2 Kgs 23:34–24:5), placed in power by Pharaoh Neco and the pro-Egyptian faction in Jerusalem against the advice of the pro-Babylonian factions. Habakkuk's complaints about "strife and discord" (1:3) may well reflect his disgust at the destructive political wrangling. Judah is being punished by destruction and violence. Like many depressed psalmists (see Pss 4:3; 13:1–2), Habakkuk asks, "How long ('ad 'anah)?" How long will sinfulness go unpunished (1:2–4)? Wickedness cannot be the final word.

God answers by describing worse things to come (1:5–11). God is raising up the Chaldeans, described with vivid imagery of power, speed, and confidence. The focus now is on international affairs. In effect, God is saying, "You ain't seen nothin' yet!" The domestic evils that Habakkuk complained about are to be punished by far more severe suffering.

1:12—2:4 *The second dialogue*

In a second round of the conversation, the prophet again challenges God: "Why?" (*lamah*). This is the fundamental question also characteristic of laments (see Ps 22:2). Why does God use such events as war, which involves indiscriminate suffering at the hands of people who seem to scoff at God (1:12–13). In effect, Habakkuk challenges God, "Are you really the God I worship?" "Are you not the holy and eternal one?" (1:12). "Are you not the God who abhors suffering and misery?" (1:13). There must be a larger picture in which such destruction can make sense. Why is this happening?

In his complaint, Habakkuk describes some destroyer, probably the Babylonian emperor, as a "fisher of men," an image of wicked destruction (1:14–16). Jesus will use this image with the opposite meaning (see Mark 1:17). The prophet then likens himself to a sentinel waiting at his post, an image that Ezekiel will pick up (Ezek 3:17), watching for a response from God (Hab 2:1).

In the section of this book that forms the heart of Habakkuk's message, God tells the prophet to wait (2:2–4). He also gives a command to preserve the prophetic word in writing for the future, which will not disappoint (2:3). But no vision of the future is given. If there is any answer given to the problem of evil, it lies in the oracle, "The just man, because of his fidelity (*'emunah*), shall live" (2:4). If this fidelity means waiting in calm patience and steadfastness for God to act in his own good time, then Habakkuk's teaching is close to Isaiah's. Only by a faithful commitment, which reflects the faithful commitment of God to his people, will the just person survive these evil times.

3:1–7 *The canticle of Habakkuk—part 1*

Using archaic descriptions and names, a concluding canticle celebrates that vision. The first part of the canticle (3:3–7) describes the awesome theophany of God the warrior (see also Isa 59; 63; Ps 76), advancing from the southeast. Unlike the theophany of the Exodus story, however, God here is connected to Mount Paran, not Mount Sinai or Horeb (see Map 9B). Paran was the name of a wilderness north of the wilderness of Sinai where the Israelites camped after they left Mount Sinai and sent spies into Canaan (see Num 10:11–12; 13:3). Placed

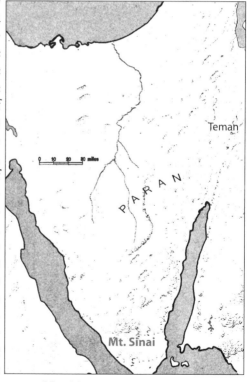

9B—Mount Paran and Teman

here in parallel with Mount Paran, Teman is a territory in Edom. The ancient canticle of Deborah also describes a theophanic coming of Yahweh from Edom (Judg 5:4–5; see Mic 1:3–4).

3:8–19 *The canticle of Habakkuk—part 2*

In the next section of the hymn (3:8–15), images of the waters and the sea fit together to portray God's battle with the powers of chaos. The canticle begins (3:2) and ends (3:16–19) with a statement of trust in God, even in moments of great fear.

C. The Message of Habakkuk

1. Review of Images and Theme

Habakkuk first creates a series of images dramatizing the power of the Chaldeans: with horses swifter than leopards (1:8), flying like eagles (1:8), powerful like a storm wind (1:9), a fisher of men (1:15), with the brandished sword (1:17). The prophet then sees himself as a sentinel (2:1). He portrays the warrior God dominating the rivers and seas (3:8) and ends with himself like a deer bounding up a mountain (3:19).

Habakkuk has one basic theme expressed in different ways:

- The presence of unpunished evil in the world (1:2–4)
- The question of how God can use evil instruments (1:13)
- The challenge of living by faith and trust (2:4; 3:16–19)

2. The Theology of Habakkuk

Habakkuk stands out from the preceding prophets by his anguished concern for "the problem of evil." This "problem" in fact has remained the hallmark of any critical discussion of evil down through the centuries. How can there be a God when the world is such a mess? How could a God who allows this be good?

In effect, Habakkuk is not satisfied with the traditional theology of suffering, focused on God punishing his people for their sins at the hands of enemy nations. Habakkuk's dissatisfaction lies in his theology. The prophet portrays God as directing all nations. This is the God from all eternity, who is above the vicissitudes of history. This is the God who is "holy" and "pure." How then does he personally stir up forces of evil on earth with their power to wreak untold destruction?

Habakkuk does not solve the "problem." No light is shown on this "problem." In fact, the prophet places the issue more as a mystery to be reverenced than as a problem to be solved. The just person is simply called to maintain "fidelity" (*'emunah*, 2:4). This is the attitude Isaiah urged for Ahaz, the attitude of relying on God as firm (*'aman*). The challenge here is not to give up on God's fidelity, even if that fidelity appears in an abyss of darkness and suffering. Faith and waiting are attitudes of attention, with nothing specifically present to be attentive to. Faith and waiting mean looking beyond the things that happen in front of you to a great void, empty of things, where God's fidelity rules.

In the New Testament Paul twice quoted Habakkuk 2:4, "The just man, because of his faith, shall live," using this text to describe the crucial attitude of openness to God's saving power , an attitude that allows the gift of salvation to be gift (Rom 1:17; Gal 3:11). The author of Hebrews gives a more complete citation as motivation for Christians to endure painful circumstances (Heb 10:36–38). Such calls to faith are not answers as to why God allows evil. They are calls to wait, calls to a faithful commitment to a coming kingdom—despite the surrounding injustice and evils.

Habakkuk simply affirms a larger, if hidden, vision of God, who in his own way eventually brings salvation. According to Habakkuk, the "answer" lies in the future. "The vision . . . will surely come" (2:3). But the future does not *solve* present problems. The future is precisely the dimension of reality that lies outside our control. The future calls for reverence and confidence. The incorporation of "the canticle of Habakkuk" (chapter 3) into this collection of prophecies suggests that this "future" is God himself, who comes in his cosmic role, dominating the forces of chaos. Later apocalyptic writings will appeal to the cosmic transcendence of God and the coming of his kingdom as the only serious response to the "problem of evil."

Ultimately, only eschatology can resolve the issue. God's plan of salvation must extend beyond what we see and experience here on earth—rightly called a "vale of tears." God's plan must extend beyond the here and now. In the New Testament stories of Jesus, only the resurrection makes sense of the crucifixion. St. Paul exhorts his readers to look at "the sufferings of the present time as nothing compared to the glory to be revealed for us" (Rom 8:18).

Unlike Micah, who stood with the strength of God before opposition, Habakkuk shows anguish and internal turmoil: "Why, O Lord?" With this prophet we see again the pain that prophets must experience if they are to stand between God and the people. The pain eventually must be seen to be the very pain God experiences when dealing with the sins of his people. God deals with sin, not from a position of serene power but by entering into the turmoil and dealing with sin on its own level. The prophet will be part of this turmoil. We will see this participation even more in Jeremiah. In the New Testament, Mark will portray Jesus in the same prophetic role (Mark 14:34–36).

10
Jeremiah

I. Overview—Read 2 Kings 22—25; 2 Chronicles 34—36

A. THE PROPHET

Of priestly descent, Jeremiah, son of Hilkiah, was born during the reign of Manasseh at Anathoth (1:1), a village about three miles north of Jerusalem (see Map 10A). Called in 626 BC, the thirteenth year of Josiah's reign (1:2; 25:3), Jeremiah prophesied until about 580 (see chapters 40–44), although the introduction to the book describes the end of his career in 587 (1:3). For the most part his work took place in Jerusalem. At the end of his life, he was taken into Egypt where he disappears (43:5—44:30).

Jeremiah's mission extended through the last five kings of Judah. To some degree the material in the book is ordered accord-

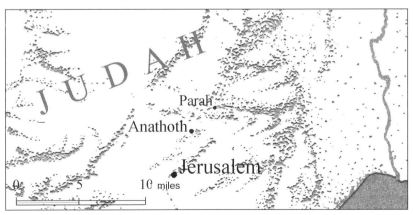

10A—Cities and Places in Jeremiah

129

ing to reigns of those kings—who are known by different names often given by the conquering suzerains.

Jeremiah is the suffering mystic in the marketplace. He faced the bitter opposition of his fellow townsmen, his family, and compatriots from the time of Josiah's death in 609 down to his own death, which according to Jewish legend was by stoning. Quiet and peace loving, he was sent by God to rebuke royalty. He thundered warnings in the ears of the populace and in consequence drew upon himself the scorn, contempt, and even homicidal hatred of others—including his own relatives.

To begin with, he did not want to be a prophet (1:4–8). Once a prophet, no one would listen to him, neither people nor kings (5:10–13; 6:10; 7:21–27). His own relatives and fellow townsmen tried to assassinate him (11:18–19; 12:5–6; 18:18). He was beaten and imprisoned (20:1–2; 32:1–3; 37:11–16; 38:1–12). Contradicted on every side, he began to wonder if even God had deserted him (15:10–18). Disheartened, he accused God of having seduced him into accepting the prophetic office (20:7–10).

B. THE BOOK

The Book of Jeremiah stands out among the literary prophets by its amount of narrative material. Chronological confusion arises, however, when we read of Jeremiah's Temple speech in chapter 7 and read about it again in chapter 26 or when we read of the siege of Jerusalem (588–587), mentioned during the reign of Zedekiah in chapter 21, and then in chapter 26 we read of events in the beginning of the reign of Zedekiah's predecessor, Jehoiakim. Apparently, the book as we have it contains several independent collections of the prophet's sermons, and the separate collections were for the most part placed end to end instead of being edited into one chronologically ordered whole.

The following division of the book best indicates the different individual collections arranged by a postexilic editor:

Jeremiah 1—25:
   Many sermons against Judah with little narrative. This
   section can be further divided into three parts:

a. Chapters 1–6 from the time of Josiah
b. Chapters 7–20 from the time of Jehoiakim
c. Chapters 21–25 mostly from the time of Zedekiah. Jeremiah 25:1–13a, the original ending of the book, is an epilogue with more from the time of Jehoiakim.

Jeremiah 26—35:
Another account of Jeremiah's preaching but mainly narrative, probably written by Baruch

Jeremiah 36—45:
A biographical narrative in the third person almost entirely taken up with the sufferings of Jeremiah, especially his last years after the fall of Jerusalem

Jeremiah 46—51:
A collection of Jeremiah's oracles against the nations. The collection actually starts in 25:15–38 but is broken off in the Hebrew text until chapter 46. The Greek Bible places these oracles immediately after chapter 25, although the individual oracles are in a different order.

Jeremiah 52:
A historical appendix taken from 2 Kings 24–25.

(See Appendix 4h for a detailed outline of the book of Jeremiah.)

C. TORAH TRADITIONS IN JEREMIAH

As we now have it, the Book of Jeremiah exhibits several of the ancient traditions of Israel. He alludes to the Exodus traditions by having God identified as "Yahweh who brought us up from the land of Egypt, who led us through the desert" (2:6; 7:22, 25; 11:4; 16:14; 31:32). By paraphrasing several of "the Ten Commandments" (7:9; see Exod 20:13–16) or by using repeatedly the covenant formula, "You shall be my people and I will be your God" (11:3; 24:7; 31:33; 32:38; see Exod 6:7), Jeremiah shows familiarity with the covenant traditions. The short section in Jeremiah that stresses observance of the Sabbath (17:19–27), however, appears to be a later editorial addition to the book.

Furthermore, in Jeremiah the Exodus tradition is linked to the covenant tradition. The two are together as they are in our Pentateuch: "Cursed be the man who does not observe the terms of this covenant, which I enjoined upon your fathers the day I brought them up out of the land of Egypt" (11:3–4; see also 7:22–23; 31:32). However, the most elaborate narration of the Exodus tradition in Jeremiah follows the pattern of the ancient hymns describing the rescue from Egypt, the wandering in the desert, and the entrance into the promised land, with no mention of Sinai (Horeb) or any making of a covenant during this trek (2:6–7; see Deut 6:21–23; 26:5–9; Josh 24:2–13).

Like Amos, Jeremiah rejects the link of sacrificial cult to the Exodus tradition, "On the day I brought them out of the land of Egypt, I gave them no command concerning holocaust or sacrifice" (Jer 7:22; see Amos 5:25)—again probably an indication that the Pentateuch as we know it did not exist at the time of Jeremiah, which otherwise could easily have been used by Jeremiah's adversaries to refute the prophet.

For the first time in the prophets, however, we see in Jeremiah references to the Law (*ha-torah*) of God in the sense of a basic way of life given by God to his people, a covenant law (2:8; 6:19; 8:8; 9:12; 16:11; 26:4; 32:23; 44:10, 23). These references are mostly in the first collection (see above), where Jeremiah decries the nonobservance of this Law. In the later collections, Jeremiah predicts a Law written in the heart (31:33), which implies a superior existence of a Law of God already known to Jeremiah's audience, the transgressions of which Jeremiah laments.

Although much is said about the book (*sefer*) the prophet himself wrote, Jeremiah never refers to "the book of the Law" or the discovery of that book that figured so prominently in 2 Kings 22:8—23:3, where curiously Jeremiah is not mentioned either. The absence in Jeremiah of any mention of this "book of the Law" is intriguing.

As described in 2 Kings, this discovered book of the Law has many connections to our Book of Deuteronomy. Likewise, Jeremiah, for his part, has many teachings and images typical of Deuteronomy, like "the circumcision of heart" (4:4; see Deut 10:16; 30:6), the sign of a true prophet (28:9; see Deut 28:21–22), the general stress on the interior of a person (31:33; see Deut 6:5) as well as the insistence on divine "curses" on those who break the covenant (11:3; see Deut 28:15–19). So why no mention of the "discovery" of this book? Why no mention of Jeremiah in Kings? What is the connection between Jeremiah and the deuteronomistic reform?

Jeremiah mentions Moses by name in 15:1 (see also Mic 6:4), where he refers to Moses' prayer of intercession, apparently an allusion to the story now found in Exodus 32:30–34. Jeremiah also describes a leader who approaches God even though it involves a deadly risk (30:21). The description suggests the story of Moses—now found in Exodus 19:20, 34:29–35, or Numbers 12:7–8—who could consult with God "face to face" even at the risk of death (see Exod 33:20). Jeremiah's own call narrative also suggests familiarity with the image of Moses as the archetypal prophet ("like me") in Deuteronomy 18:15–18 (or Deuteronomy shows familiarity with Jeremiah), where the key to authentic prophecy lies in the action of God putting "my words into the mouth of the prophet" (see Jer 1:9).

Jeremiah also shows familiarity with some patriarchal traditions. Abraham, Isaac, and Jacob are mentioned by name as giving rise to the descendants of Israel (33:26). In a more generic way, these patriarchs are alluded to as "your ancestors" to whom God promised a land flowing with milk and honey (11:5). Jeremiah also mentions the destruction of Sodom and Gomorrah (49:18; 50:40), apparently a favorite story among the literary prophets (see Amos 4:11; Zeph 2:9).

Jeremiah is also familiar with creation traditions. One text in particular (4:23–26) shows some vocabulary connections with both the "priestly" (P) and the "Yahwist" (J) accounts in Genesis 1 and 2. Other references to divine creation, stressing God's wisdom and power (10:12–13; 27:5; 32:17), show closer affinities to wisdom traditions (see Prov 8:22–31; Job 28:3–11).

II. Significant Passages in Jeremiah

Our study of Jeremiah will try to follow a chronological order by regrouping the sermons and narrations drawn from the different collections and looking at them according to the order in which they appear to have taken place. At the same time, we will try to keep track of the major sections of the present Book of Jeremiah where these texts are found by **bold references** to the sections embedded in the commentary.

A. Significant Texts from the Reign of Josiah

Chapters 1–6, the first part of **the first major section,** appear to be a collection of sermons uttered during the reign of Josiah (see 3:6).

1:4–19 *The call of Jeremiah*

After the introductory superscript (1:1–3), the book describes the call of the prophet. The two parts of this description both begin with "The word of Yahweh came to me" (1:4, 11; see also 1:13). Jeremiah is constituted a prophet by this word, which he is then to proclaim in his role as a messenger (see 2:1–2). For the most part, Yahweh does not appear in this text; we only hear his voice.

Like Moses, Jeremiah is extremely hesitant to accept the burdens of the prophetic office (see Exod 4:10–15). This is not a task he sought after. He thinks he is too young and too unskilled at rhetoric to function as a prophet, not just to his own people, but also to Gentile nations and kingdoms. Furthermore, it is a task "to root up and to tear down…to build and to plant" (1:10), negative and positive images from farming and construction. The formula is repeated several times later (18:7–9; 24:6; 31:28). Yahweh reassures Jeremiah with the promise made to Moses, "I am with you" (1:8; see Exod 3:12).

Similar to the vocation scene of Isaiah, Jeremiah experiences a purification of his mouth as God touches it and sets his words in it (1:9). In this gesture we again see the fundamental role of a prophet (see Deut 18:18).

At the time of this experience, the call of God is a fait accompli. It already happened perhaps some eighteen years earlier—depending on our guess of how old the "youth" (*na'ar*), Jeremiah, is here. Only now is God letting Jeremiah know about it. "Before you were born…I dedicated you, a prophet to the nations" (1:5). In a series of verbs describing what God has already done for Jeremiah, we see God's love for the prophet: "I formed you…I knew you…I dedicated you…I appointed you" (1:5). The intense connection between Jeremiah and God is the key to understanding this prophet's mission. In the New Testament, Paul uses similar words to describe his own congenital calling (Gal 1:15–16; see also Luke 1:13–25).

The second part of the call narrative involves two visions and a reprise of the divine commissioning. The first vision of the "watching/almond tree" plays on the Hebrew word for almond tree (*shaqed*) representing God watching (*shoqed*) over his word to bring it to realization (1:11–12). The certitude of God's word here is given as the basis of Jeremiah's vocation. In the second vision, the boiling cauldron from the north represents the Babylonian armies, which one day will come down from the north to besiege and destroy Jerusalem (1:13–16). This vision may have occurred at a much later date when the Babylonians did indeed invade. In that case, an editor would have placed the account here with the account of Jeremiah's call. In any case, the vision is not just an insight into international war but on a deeper level represents God pronouncing his "judgments" against the cities of Judah (1:16).

God repeats the commission (1:17–19), stressing Jeremiah's adversarial role and reiterating the promise, "I am with you" (1:19). Just as the call of Isaiah was developed along the double stress of God's transcendent holiness and Isaiah's mission to aggravate the blindness and sin of his audience (Isa 6), so the call of Jeremiah grows around the lines of the opposition the weak prophet was to face (1:17,19) and the promise of God to strengthen and protect him (1:18).

2:1–3 *Israel's original love of God*

Opening the subsection (chapters 2–6) that appears to be connected with the reign of Josiah (see 3:6), the words Jeremiah repeats from Yahweh sound very much like those of Hosea 2:16–18. The desert experience is compared to the honeymoon period of God's marriage with Israel. The prophet's later call to conversion (see 3:12, 14; 4:1) is thus a call to return to beginnings, to "the devotion (*chesed*) of your youth, how you as a bride loved (*'ahavat*) me, following me in the desert." At the beginning of this oracle, God addresses Israel in the second-person feminine Hebrew form. As in Hosea, Israel is God's beloved wife. The basic duty of Israel is to love God.

The focus is on God's memory. The stress is on God's reluctance to punish Israel.

2:4–37 *Accusations of sinfulness*

At this point, the prophet begins by addressing "the house of Jacob…the house of Israel" calling on them to listen to the word of the Lord (2:4). A very similar address occurs at 4:3, this time "to the men of Judah and of Jerusalem." The two verses may be organizing titles, where the material from 2:4 to 4:2 is addressed to the Jews of the former northern kingdom and the material from 4:3 to 6:30 is addressed to the existing kingdom of Judah. The whole subsection presents God's legal indictment (*rîb*; see 2:4) of both houses.

The dominant sin addressed by the prophet in the days of Josiah's reign was Ba'alist idolatry. For the material addressed to Judah, Jeremiah could be speaking in the period before the religious reform begun by the king in 628 BC, a period still filled with the pagan practices pushed by kings Manasseh and Amon (see also Zeph 1:4–6). For the material addressed to Israel, Jeremiah may be exhorting the reform of the north before or during the time when Josiah apparently pushed his reform against Ba'alism around the cities of Bethel and Samaria (see 2 Kgs 23:15–19).

References to the "harlotry" practiced "on every high hill" allude to the fertility cults of Ba'al (2:20). The "piece of wood" and the "stone" refer respectively to the wooden posts (*'asheroth*) symbolizing a Canaanite mother goddess and the upright boulders (*masseboth*) symbolizing the penis of a Canaanite god (2:27). Jeremiah sarcastically points out how the leaders of Israel (kings, princes, priests, and prophets) have it all screwed up referring to the wrong objects as mother or father.

God protests, "Does a virgin forget her jewelry, a bride her sash? Yet my people have forgotten me" (2:32). God remembers

Israel's past love (2:2), but Israel has forgotten God. The issue of unswerving love is above all an issue of memory. Without memory, sexual love becomes fickle lust, like that of a frenzied camel in heat running through the desert after every passing sniff (2:23). For Israel at this time, God is known above all from past actions. To forget the past is to abandon God.

4:1–2 *Appeals to conversion*

"Return (*shûb*) to me" (4:1) is the basic prophetic call to conversion. Literally it means turning around and going back. In this text Jeremiah describes religion with three traditional terms. It is religion "in truth" (*'emet*), "in fair judgment" (*mishpat*), and "in justice" (*tz^edaqah*; Jer 4:2).

4:3–4 *Circumcision of the heart*

Leading off the material arranged as directed to the kingdom of Judah, Jeremiah in effect calls again for a conversion but one that involves an interior change much more than a change of outward behavior: "For the sake of Yahweh, be circumcised, remove the foreskins of your hearts" (4:4). The wording is almost identical to the words of Deuteronomy (Deut 10:16; 30:6; see also 6:9–10; 11:8). The relationship between Jeremiah and Deuteronomy is difficult to determine. We know for sure only that the two shared intense interest in the interior and the need for a religion of the heart.

Paul used Jeremiah's image of circumcision of the heart to describe what constitutes a real Jew, what constitutes the new people of God, whether from an ethnic point of view they be Jew or Gentile (Rom 2:25–29).

4:13–26 *Suffering from sin*

A collection of prophetic sayings from Jeremiah begins with a threat that describes God as an attacking enemy (Jer 4:13). The appeal, "Cleanse your heart of evil" (4:14), continues the stress typical of Jeremiah on interior reform.

The description of suffering and anguish (4:19) is clearly a description of the prophet, but here it is attached to a "saying of Yahweh" (*n^e'um Yahweh*; 4:17) and flows smoothly into the following lines in the mouth of God (4:22). The anguish of the prophet ultimately reveals the anguish and suffering of God at the sins of his people (see also 8:18–23).

The fundamental sin is named, "They do not know me" (4:22; see Isa 1:3). The consequence of sin is the chaos (*tohu wabohu*) that results, with its loss of lights of the heavens, the birds of the air, and the man (*ha-'adam*)—the undoing of the orderly creation of Genesis 1 (4:23–26).

5:26–29 *Social injustice*
In this section we find also the traditional accusation against oppression of the poor. Those in charge of the legal process pervert justice: "They do not defend the cause [*dyn*] of the fatherless or judge the poor with fair judgment [*mishpat*]" (5:28). Instead the rich grow richer, as they fill their houses with gains from "treachery" (5:27).

6:20–21 *False religion*
Jeremiah picks up also the traditional criticism of formalistic religion: "Of what use to me is incense that comes from Sheba.... Your holocausts find no favor with me, and your sacrifices please me not" (6:20; see Amos 5:21–25; Hos 6:6: Isa 1:10–15; Mic 6:6–8).

6:22–26 *Invasion from the north*
The prophecy flows into another where Jeremiah proclaims a not-so-veiled threat of foreign invasion, a "people from the north" (6:22). The Babylonian army was camped near Haran, northern Syria, as they made their way along the Fertile Crescent, eventually coming into Israel from the north. "The north" thus became the traditional direction from which any enemy of Israel comes.

The woman in birth pains appears as a symbol of the people (6:24; see also 4:31), but the image here is completely negative, unlike the hopeful use of this image in later apocalyptic literature (see Isa 26:16–19).

B. Significant Texts from the Reign of Jehoiakim

7:1–34 *The Temple speech*

In the Temple precincts Jeremiah delivered an oral excoriation of Judah, calling the Temple "a den of thieves" (7:11), a phrase later used by Jesus (Matt 21:13). We have this "Temple speech" at least twice in the Book of Jeremiah, duplicated by the juxtaposition of the earlier collections (see also 26:1–24). Here in **the first major section** of the book, Jeremiah warns against religious complacency: "Put not your trust in the deceitful words: 'This is the Temple of Yahweh! The Temple of Yahweh! The Temple of Yahweh!'" (7:3). The magnificent building constructed by Solomon three centuries earlier symbolized Israel's special blessings (see Pss 46; 48). It was saved from Sennacherib's destruction by an apparent miracle (Isa 36—37), leading to the theology of "the Zion schema" (see Isa 31:4–5; Ps 48). Some twenty years later it would be a heap of burning rubble. Jeremiah uses the image of Shiloh to destroy the theology of Jerusalem's indefectibility (7:14). Shiloh, the first central shrine of Israel (Josh 18:1), was apparently destroyed during the Philistine wars described in 1 Samuel 4—6.

For the Temple to mean anything, the people must "reform your ways and deeds" (7:3). By this, Jeremiah means the practice of care of the poor and vulnerable in society, not shedding innocent blood in the Temple and not worshiping "other gods" (7:9; see also 22:3). Then in a third repetition of the same message, Jeremiah lists several of the "Ten Commandments," mostly related to neighbor along with not shedding innocent blood and worshiping "other gods" (7:9; see Exod 20:13–16; Deut 5:6–21). Without such ethical life and a firm commitment to Yahweh, any exercise of religious cult is a charade (7:22), a charade that God would demolish (7:14–15).

Jeremiah emphasizes the secondary character of religion by disjoining any duty to offer holocaust or sacrifice from the Exodus experience (7:21–23). This disjunction was already proclaimed by Amos 5:25, an indication that the merging of the extensive religious law found in the present Torah with the Exodus tradition is probably a later simplification. In any case, both Amos and Jeremiah downplay religious cult as a striking way to emphasize the importance of ethical conduct.

Along with other foreign religious practices, Jeremiah bitterly laments the evil of killing and burning infant sons and daughters in the valley of Ben-hinnom (7:31; see 2 Kgs 16:10; 23:10; Lev 30:3; Ezek 23:29). The "valley of Hinnom," (in Hebrew, *ge' hinnom*) will later become the symbol of ultimate perdition (see Matt 5:22; Mark 9:43–47, and parallels). The place was also called "Topheth."

The Temple sermon was an exercise in futility. The problem lay not just in impious and unjust conduct but more in the evil hearts from which this conduct arises. As Jeremiah describes, Israel and Judah are a people of "hard hearts" and "stiff necks" (7:24, 26). The expressions describe the radical impossibility of listening to the voice of God (see Exod 10:27) and hence the history of Israel's rejection of the prophets (7:25–26; see 25:4; 26:5). Even though one function of a prophet is to intercede before God on behalf of the people, God tells Jeremiah, "Do not intercede for this people; raise not a pleading prayer in their behalf!" (Jer 7:16).

26:1–24 *The Temple speech again*

In **the second major section** of this book, Baruch, Jeremiah's scribe, gives us another version of the Temple address, specifically dating it to the beginning of Jehoiakim's reign in 609 BC (26:1–6). This account stresses the real possibility of avoiding disaster. "Perhaps ['*ulay*]" the mission of Jeremiah will succeed and God will "relent [*nacham*]" of his punishment. The account here echoes the theology of the conditional covenant found in the Book of Deuteronomy, blessings for good behavior, disaster for bad (see Deut 11:26–32). Along with the importance of listening to the words of the prophets (26:5; see 7:25), the speech also mentions "living according to the law" given by God (26:4).

Baruch describes how Jeremiah is persecuted and threatened with death. Various powerful groups take different positions regarding Jeremiah:

a. The "priests and prophets," along with "all the people," call for his death because he threatened the Temple and the city (26:7–11).

b. "The princes" allow Jeremiah to defend himself in some legal court, where he insists that he is just the messenger of Yahweh and that killing him will bring innocent blood on the people (26:10–15). "The princes" support Jeremiah (see also 36:11–19) and are now joined by "all the people" (26:16).

c. "The elders of the land" join in the defense of Jeremiah by recalling the prophecies of Micah, who threatened total destruction of Jerusalem and was listened to by King Hezekiah (26:16–19; see Mic 3:12).

The execution of the prophet Uriah warns us of what probably would have happened to Jeremiah if the princes had not interceded for him (26:20–24). This story contrasts Uriah with Micah. More important, it contrasts King Jehoiakim with King Hezekiah. In the end, "the people" are still trying to kill Jeremiah, who is protected by one of the princes, Ahikam ben Shaphan (26:24; see 2 Kgs 22:14).

The similarities of the scene of Jeremiah's speech and arrest with Matthew's account of the arrest and trial of Jesus (Matt 26–27) are unmistakable.

36:1–32 *The scroll of Jeremiah*

In **the third major section** of this book, Baruch gives us the story of Jeremiah's sufferings, a story extending from the time of Jehoiakim to Jeremiah's forced exile in Egypt (36:1—45:5). This major section also begins with the story of a prophetic proclamation in the Temple.

In this story Baruch will read the written prophecy of Jeremiah, a speech Jeremiah dictated to Baruch, who writes it on a scroll (*m^egilat sefer*; 36:1–4). Like the Temple speech some four years earlier, this scroll is a threat against the nation. Several months after the writing of it, at some important fast proclaimed by the king, Baruch proclaims the scroll in the Temple with the help of some sympathetic leaders (36:9–10). The details of the account of Baruch's reading give us perhaps the general procedure prophets followed in delivering oracles of God in the Temple. The scroll was a call to conversion and an offer of forgiveness (36:3). The scroll was in effect the written word of God that placed the king and the nation at the point of judgment.

The reading of God's words had no more effect than the Temple speech. King Jehoiakim not only refuses the summons but determines to destroy the scroll, in stark contrast to the story in Kings of Josiah, who accepted the "book of the Law" when it was discovered and who listened to the prophetess, Huldah (2 Kgs 22:8–20). As though fearing the power of the word of the prophet, Jehoiakim personally burns Jeremiah's scroll piece by piece in his fireplace (36:20–23).

Cynically rejected, this scroll is replaced by another one more threatening (36:27–32), including the prediction of the desecration of Jehoiakim's corpse (see also 22:19; but contrary to 2 Kgs 24:6) and the end of the kingly line of David through Jehoiakim (Jer 36:30; but see 2 Kgs 24:8). It would seem that this second scroll formed the core for the written prophecies of Jeremiah that we now have in this biblical book.

This scroll, it seems, is the origin of the concept of the written word of God. Isaiah had written on small tablets (Isa 8:16–20; 30:8). Isaiah's writings were the prophet's own instructions to be preserved for the future as a witness to the prophet's word unheeded in his own lifetime (8:20; 30:8). Jeremiah's lengthy scroll, however, appears as a revelation to the king. Somewhere down the road, this concept of "the written word of God" will be applied to all the important documents and teachings of Israel.

8:18–23 [8:18—9:1] *The prophet's grief*

Back in **the first major section** of the book, we see another description of Jeremiah's personal involvement and suffering in the impending disaster of his people (see 4:9; 14:17). The prophet appears weak and vulnerable, unlike Micah, the bulldozer (Mic 3:8), and the other "strong" prophets of the eighth century.

Like the description in Jeremiah 4:9, this cry of pain is connected with the preceding oracle of Yahweh (n^e'um-Yahweh; 8:17) and is followed by the same (9:1–2). Thus the opening words, "my grief…my heart," appear to be that from God, describing his pain and involvement with the impending disaster. This initial ambiguity again suggests the way in which the prophet is called to manifest in his life not only the words of God but also the emotions of God (see also 12:7–13).

13:1–11 *God's underwear*

A number of stories in **this first section** describe prophetic actions and symbols. They follow a pattern. Along with the gestures, we see verbal interpretations woven into the story to give meaning to the actions.

The story of the "linen loincloth" describes a special piece of "intimate apparel" that turns rotten after being left at the "Parath." Parath is the Hebrew name for the Euphrates River. If this meaning is the one indicated in the text, then the story is a parable. Jeremiah could hardly walk twice to the Euphrates River, some seven hundred miles from Jerusalem. On the other hand, if "the Parath" is a spring at the village of Parah (Josh 8:23), modern Kirbet 'Ain Farah, some five miles northeast of Jerusalem near Anathoth (see Map 10A), then the story describes a "prophetic gesture," where the message from God is embodied in the action of the prophet.

In this action dealing with the rotten underwear, the main point is indicated by the explicit interpretations (13:8–11). Despite Israel's and Judah's intimacy with God, the people are becoming rotten and destined to be discarded like a filthy rag. If the intention is to allude also to the Euphrates River, then the story is a hint about the coming Babylonian captivity where Judah and Jerusalem will be buried for some fifty years.

16:1–4 *Jeremiah's celibacy*

Another prophetic gesture involves the prophet's entire life. He is not to marry or have children. Thus Jeremiah joins a list of prophets from Hosea to Ezekiel whose marital life was part of their mission. If understood in the historical context of Jeremiah, this command is extremely harsh on Jeremiah. A life without children was considered a curse, whereby one's name could not survive into the next generation. His enemies would apparently succeed in blotting out his name (12:19).

The action, or nonaction, is then explained by verbal interpretation as a threat against the nation (16:3–4). Disease, sword, and famine will destroy the sons and daughters of the land. In effect, Jeremiah's celibacy is a testimony to the end of the world as he knew it. He was not to become part of this world by having a family. Rather, by his solitude, he was to testify that this world was rapidly coming to an end. By this solitude, he also testifies to the suffering of God who is losing his people, his family.

18:1–12 *The divine potter*

Later, Jeremiah is commanded to watch a potter at work, noting how the artist reworks the clay back to a ball and tries something else rather than have it turn out poorly. The interpretive words (18:5–10) turn the work of the potter into a parable-allegory. The clay worker represents God with absolute control over human beings and nations, represented by the clay. Israel is totally in God's power. Like a potter, he can smash down his work and redo it—until it comes out the way he wants it. In this imagery, the smashing down is not done as an end in itself but is part of a larger picture. The intended pot cannot be made unless the defective clay form is again crushed.

As long as the clay is wet, hope exists. The teaching about "repenting (*shûb*) from evil" and the promise of God "relenting" (*nacham*) from the threatened evil as part of the divine explanation (18:8) underlines the element of hope in this potter's scene. God's plan remains open.

The imagery will appear later in Jewish writings (Isa 64:7; Sir 38:29–30) and in St. Paul (Rom 9:20–23). The imagery centers on the idea of God's freedom. Any potter, however, would see in the imagery also a sense of pain and disappointment on the part of the potter who must destroy the work of her hands.

19:1–13 *The potter's flask*

A bit further in **the first section**, the prophetic gesture of smashing the potter's flask takes the divine threat of destruction further. Jeremiah enters a Ba'alist shrine in the valley of Ben-hinnom along the southwest side of Jerusalem, mentioned earlier as a place of infant sacrifice (7:31). Jeremiah excoriates the Jews assembled there, shattering before their eyes a clay pot, then explaining the meaning of the gesture: "Thus says Yahweh of hosts: Thus will I smash this people and this city, as one smashes a clay pot so that it cannot be repaired" (19:10).

The imagery here suggests finality. Once it is fired and hardened, the broken flask cannot be repaired. Another version of this story might be found in 13:12–14.

The consequences for Jeremiah are a scourging and imprisonment at the hands of the religious authorities, as described in 20:1–6.

* * *

An editor of the book placed the last of Jeremiah's expressions of discouragement (20:7–18) as a conclusion to the collection of sermons under Jehoiakim. This is the fifth of a series of very personal expressions of suffering directed as prayers to God for help. They are known in scholarship as Jeremiah's "confessions." Starting with 11:18, we can identify four earlier ones:

11:18—12:6 *The first confession*
The composition here follows an a–b–a'–b' structure, alternating between Jeremiah's lament and God's response:

a. 11:18–20: Jeremiah describes adversaries who try to kill him. Jeremiah describes himself as a "trusting lamb led to the slaughter" whose enemies are trying to "cut him off from the land of the living" (11:19). He pleads for help from God "as just Judge" (11:20).
b. 11:21–23: God answers indicating that the adversaries are Jeremiah's own countrymen of Anathoth (11:21). God promises to punish them (11:22–23).
a'. 12:1–4: Jeremiah complains like Habakkuk about the prosperity of the wicked (12:1–4). Like Habakkuk, Jeremiah is appalled at the situation given the nature of God, who is always in the right (12:1) and knows Jeremiah's heart (12:3). Like Habakkuk, Jeremiah cries out "why?" (12:1) and "how long" (12:4).
b'. 12:5–6: God's answer is not reassuring or consoling. It appears as a rebuke by God. Things are going to get much worse (12:5).

Jeremiah's description of himself as a "lamb led to the slaughter" under the threat of being "cut off from the land of the living" echoes some fifty years later in "Second Isaiah" where a prophet in exile describes the redemptive suffering of a "servant of Yahweh" described like a "sheep led to the slaughter…cut off from the land of the living" (Isa 53:7–8). Jeremiah's innocent suffering may very well have begun a reflection on the way suffering may actually be a divine means of redemption. In this way, Jeremiah begins a line that climaxes with Jesus rejected and crucified.

15:10–21 *The second confession*
In the second confession, Jeremiah's bitterness and God's answer appear again in a double dialogue:

a. 15:10–14: Jeremiah starts by a traditional way of complaining bitterly, wishing he had not been born (see also Job 3:3–10).

b. 15:11–14: God's answer is hard to see as responding to Jeremiah's complaint, except as saying, "Look at the terrible things I have to do." (Serious textual problems with these verses lead some to think of a mistaken repetition of 17:3–4).

a'. 15:15–18: Jeremiah complains to God that his sufferings have resulted because "I devoured your words" and "bore your name" (15:16). The prophet does not hesitate to accuse God of being undependable, "like waters that cannot be relied on" (15:18).

b'. 15:19–20: In response, God suggests that Jeremiah repent and reminds the prophet, "I am with you," and that his enemies will not prevail. The promises remind us of those at the call of Jeremiah (1:18–19), promises that do not seem to have been fulfilled.

17:14–18 *The third confession*
In the third confession, Jeremiah prays desperately for help. He mentions specifically the ridicule received because of the non-fulfillment of his prophecies. The attack on God here appears in the line, "Do not be my ruin!" (17:17). This is directed to the God who is supposed to be the prophet's refuge.

God does not respond to any more of these prayers.

18:18–23 *The fourth confession*

The fourth confession begins with the words of the adversaries to destroy Jeremiah. Getting rid of him will not upset any of the powers of the status quo, the priests, the sages, or the prophets.

Jeremiah prays for their punishment following the traditional formulas of vengeance often found in similar lamentations (see Pss 3:8; 7:16–17; 20:9–11).

20:7–18 *The fifth confession*

In the fifth confession, Jeremiah opens his heart to God. The bold lament reproaching God has three parts: Jeremiah's anger at God (20:7–10), his expression of confidence (20:11–13), and his wish that he had never been born (20:14–18). The shift from anger to confidence to anger again perplexes a modern reader but follows the pattern of the psalms of an individual's lament (see Pss 6; 22; 28). The curse of one's birthday may be a stereotype of grief (see also 15:10; Job 3:3–12).

Jeremiah accuses God of "seducing" him into his service (20:7). The image is that of a victim who *mistakenly* trusted someone (see Judg 14:15). This is a real attack on God's goodness and reliability. Yet stories exist of God deliberately deceiving prophets (see 2 Kgs 22:10; Ezek 14:9). The fact that the lament is still addressed to God, however, bespeaks the prophet's deep-rooted faith.

Still there is no answer for Jeremiah. Things do get much worse—no miraculous rescue from the pit, no raven to bring him food. He is left to feel abandoned by God. This is the mystery of suffering at its worst, to be reenacted again when Jesus cries out in the words that share the same sense of abandonment, "My God, my God, why have you abandoned me?" (Matt 24:46 and parallels; John 12:27).

C. SIGNIFICANT TEXTS FROM THE REIGN OF ZEDEKIAH AND FOLLOWING

In 598 and again in 587 BC, the Babylonian emperor, Nebuchadnezzar, invaded Israel and deported the population to exile. The military and political dramas of these attacks form the background for the remaining part of Jeremiah's career. It is at this hour of darkness that we hear promises for the future. As part of **the first major section** of the Book of Jeremiah we find a collection of sermons proclaimed under Zedekiah (see 21:1):

23:1–8 *Promises*

Jeremiah predicts an ideal reign and introduces a ray of hope. The oracle is in three parts, vv. 1–3; 5–6, and 7–8, each introduced with a verse that contains the oracle formula, "a saying of Yahweh" ($n^e um$ *Yahweh*).

The first (23:1–4) starts as an oracle of woe to the ruling kings ("shepherds"). However, the promise that follows is double. Like a shepherd, God himself will gather at least a "remnant" (*sh^e'erit*) of his flock (23:3), and he will appoint good shepherds for them (23:4). It is not clear which exile the prophet has in mind when he speaks of the gathering. However, the result is prosperity and peace. The flock will "be fruitful and multiply," the exact words of God's blessing in the creation account (Gen 1:28).

In the second part (23:5–6), we see a promise of a "righteous bud" to David (23:5). The description of the new ruler as "Bud" (*tzemach*) is similar to Isaiah's prophecy of "Sprout" (*choter*) coming from the stump of Jesse (Isa 11:1). "Bud," however, will rule as "king" (*melek*), with the royal name, "Yahweh is our Justice."

That name in Hebrew, *Yahweh Tzidkenu*, reminds us of King Zedekiah. As concerning this king, the oracle would fit in the collection that started in 22:10 and followed with the mention of kings from Jehoahaz to Jeconiah (Jehoiachin). The next king in line would be Zedekiah. The oracle may have been part of some enthronement ceremony expressing extreme religious hope in the new king, involving both the northern kingdom of Israel, destroyed since 722 BC, and the southern kingdom of Judah, which will suffer two deportations during the lifetime of Jeremiah (23:6).

Very quickly, however, it became clear. Jeremiah could hardly count on the existing Davidic dynasty to accomplish anything. The new Davidic "Bud," who would rule wisely and with "fair judgment" (*mishpat*) and "justice" (*$tz^e daqah$*; 23:5), then becomes a ray of hope for the future.

The third part (23:7–8) is a doublet of 16:14–15. It predicts a return from Exile which would outclass the Exodus from Egypt. This message is a theme found also in Deutero-Isaiah (see Isa 43:18–19). If these lines come from Jeremiah, he would most likely be referring of the exiles of 598 BC.

24:1–10 *The two baskets of figs*

In this vision account of two baskets of figs, brought to the Temple as offerings to God, Jeremiah dramatically foretells the future of his people. The good figs represent Jeconiah (Jehoiachin) and the exiles in Babylon. Echoing Amos's vision of the basket of overripe fruit (Amos 8:1–3), Jeremiah sees the bad figs as representing Zedekiah and the Jews remaining in Judah. The bad figs will be wiped out (24:10). The good figs will become the remnant out of which a new Israel will be born. This will be a time for "building" and "planting" (24:6). Forget the "tearing down" and "rooting up" part of Jeremiah's mission (1:10).

Here Jeremiah also introduces the image of God providing a new heart (24:7; see also 32:39). This is the gift by which the people can "know" Yahweh. With this gift they can return to God "with their whole heart." Ezekiel will also stress the imagery of the "new heart" (Ezek 11:19; 36:24). After centuries of the people exhibiting a "hard heart," one incapable of receiving the word of God, the prophets of this period make it clear a more radical gift is needed and will be provided.

* * *

In **the second major section** of the Book of Jeremiah (chapters 26–35), we have warnings mostly under the reign of Zedekiah along with some of the most important promises of salvation in the whole Old Testament. Unlike the first major section of the book, these fragments of preaching are imbedded in extensive narrations about Jeremiah. The narrative elaborations might be the work of Baruch, Jeremiah's scribe, or part of the elaboration on the oracles of Jeremiah by the spiritual leaders who in exile reflected on the accuracy of Jeremiah's prophecies and worked to keep the covenant faith alive for the people.

Chapters 27–29 form a unit detailing Jeremiah's efforts around 593 BC (see 28:1) by sermon and by letter to avert the suicidal policy of resistance to Babylon. Jeremiah describes such resistance as contrary to God's directives. The Babylonian domination is a divine punishment that Judah must accept with patience and humility.

27:1–22 *Serve Babylon*

Wearing a yoke as a symbol of Babylonian domination, Jeremiah stands before several groups of leaders to urge them to accept Babylonian domination. The text fits well the time around 594 BC (verse 1 with its reference to Jehoiakim is apparently misplaced here).

a. Jeremiah appeals first to a group of ambassadors of the satellite kings gathered in council at Jerusalem apparently to discuss with Zedekiah their revolt against Babylon (27:3–11). These representatives of non-Jewish kingdoms are the first to be addressed by the prophetic word. It is perhaps in this scene that Jeremiah fulfills his mission as "a prophet to the nations" (1:5). To these foreign ambassadors, Jeremiah stresses the need "to serve" Babylon. Yahweh has decreed this, and he is the God not just of Israel, but of all nations including Babylonia, whose king, Nebuchadnezzar, God refers to as "my servant" (27:6; see also 25:9; 43:10). Jeremiah adds a warning against prophets who preach otherwise.

b. Then Jeremiah addresses basically the same message to the king, Zedekiah (27:12–15).

c. Finally, Jeremiah addresses the priests and the people (27:16–22), again urging them to submit to Nebuchadnezzar. To the priests and the people, Jeremiah adds the warning about the destruction of Jerusalem and the sacking of the Temple.

Along with the need to submit to Nebuchadnezzar, the warning against deceptive prophets is a major theme in this story. They prophesy lies (27:10). They are not sent by Yahweh (27:15). The word of Yahweh is not with them (27:18). The words reflect the lengthy invective against prophets of lies in **the first section** of the book (23:9–40) as well as the next story about Hananiah, the false prophet (28:1–17).

28:1–17 *Jeremiah versus Hananiah*

The theme of the conflict between Jeremiah and the "prophets of lies" comes to the forefront in the next story, dated also to around 594 BC (28:1). Here Jeremiah engages in a public debate with the prophet, Hananiah, who prophesies peace and happiness. In fact, there does not seem to be anything wrong with the message itself, as we will see Yahweh promise almost the identical thing in Jeremiah 30:8–11. However, Jeremiah warns, "The prophet who prophesies peace is recognized as truly sent by Yahweh only when his prophetic prediction is fulfilled" (28:9; see Deut 28:21–22). Such a criterion is not much help to the audience listening to the conflicting voices.

The story insists that Jeremiah is not speaking on his own. Personally, he would much prefer the message of Hananiah (28:6). In fact, he must wait "some time" for a message from God before he can counter Hananiah (28:12). However, the message does come. Hananiah is wrong. The punishment for a prophet of lies is death (28:16–17).

29:1–23 *The letter to the exiles*

The confusion caused by the conflicting prophetic messages continues to surface in the story of Jeremiah's letter to the exiles of 598. In this unusual form of written prophecy, Jeremiah encourages the exiles to settle into the new land, to be good subjects of Nebuchadnezzar, even to pray to God for the welfare of Babylon—a rare teaching in the Old Testament about praying for your enemy (29:4–7). Jeremiah turns his regard also to the future (29:10–14). He promises an end to the Exile after "seventy years." God intends "peace [*shalom*]" not harm for the people (29:11). This peace will involve the great gathering of Israel from all the nations and a return back home to "this place" (29:14).

By contrast, Jeremiah warns about the disaster in store for the Jews in Judea, who avoided the Exile, including the king. We see here an allusion to the "two baskets of figs" described **in the first major section** (chapter 24). Jeremiah warns also against prophets among the exiles in Babylon who preach otherwise, naming names (29:8–9, 20–23). The following story about the exiled prophet, Shemaiah, illustrates the problem (29:24–32).

Ezekiel was in fact among these exiled prophets but is not mentioned by Jeremiah.

The mention of "seventy years" of exile is found also in the conclusion of **the first major section** of the book (25:11–12). Apparently the number signifies a "long time," perhaps a lifetime (Ps 90:10). Seventy is often a symbolic term for "many" (Judg 1:7; 8:14; 1 Sam 6:19; 2 Sam 24:14). Four centuries later in another time of crisis, the author of Daniel will refer to Jeremiah's prediction of seventy years and reinterpret it to mean 490 years ("seventy times seven") to bring the promises of Jeremiah roughly into his own time of troubles, roughly 167 BC (Dan 9:1–27; see also 2 Chr 36:21).

* * *

Chapters 30–31 also form a unit in **this second major section** of the book, perhaps all part of the book (*sefer*) mentioned in 30:2. Here we find images of hope. Jeremiah proclaims divine promises, perhaps the most important promises made by Jeremiah or any prophet of the Old Testament. These are promises that occur in the darkest moments of Israel's history—sometime before or after the destruction of 587 BC. The first and larger part (30:4—31:22) appears to be addressed mostly to the exiles, with a mention of both Judah as well as the defunct northern kingdom of Israel (see 31:9–20). Judah and Jerusalem become the explicit concern in the second section (31:23–40). As in the story of the good figs (24:6), gone are the threats and the descriptions of God's determination to root up and tear down. Now Jeremiah speaks only of God's building and planting.

30:1–3 *Promises in the book*
The next section begins with an elaborate introduction, stressing the divine origin of the message. The words are to be written in "a book [*sefer*]" (30:2), indicating that the message is for the future: "Behold, the days will come" (30:3). This writing is totally different from the threats that composed "the scroll" of 605 BC (see chapter 36). This writing promises a restoration, literally, "a change of the captivity" (*shuv et-shvut*), a return to the land given to the fathers (30:3).

30:8–11 *Breaking the yoke*

Yahweh promises to break the yoke of oppression from the neck of the Jewish people. The similarity of words with those of the false prophet Hananiah is striking (see 28:2–4). The words here, however, are from Yahweh. That makes all the difference.

God promises "David, their king" will be raised up for the people. The promise joins that of the future "righteous shoot to David" (23:5; see 33:14–18) and insists on the central role of the Davidic dynasty in the faith of the people.

The promise, "I am with you, says Yahweh, to deliver you," also reminds us of God's promise to Jeremiah (1:8) and suggests the way the prophet represents the people.

30:18–22 *Renewing the covenant*

The promise of restoration continues with mention of the dwellings, the city, the palace, and the rulers of Jacob.

The new leader will be from the people, as were the kings of old. He will be able to approach God because he will be summoned by God (30:21). The image here is of Moses, who could consult with God "face to face" (Num 12:7–8; Exod 19:20; 34:34). Moses, the greatest of the prophets, combined the prophetic with the governing role. The new leader will do the same. A hint of the dangerous holiness of God appears as closeness to God is described as a "deadly risk" (Jer 30:21).

This will be a time of joy and happiness (30:19). The "day of Yahweh" is ultimately a day of salvation. Jeremiah sums up all these blessings in terms of the covenant promise: "You shall be my people, and I will be your God" (30:22).

31:1–9 *Yahweh brings back the remnant*

The promises for the future are based on the unfailing love of God. For the first time in Jeremiah and indeed since Hosea (see Hos 3:1; 11:1), a prophet proclaims God's love for his people: "With an age-old love (*'ah*ᵃ*vah*) I have loved you (*'*ᵃ*havtik*); therefore I have maintained my mercy (*chesed*) toward you" (Jer 31:3). Although rare in the pre-exilic strata of the Old Testament, the identification of God as "father" is explicit in this text of Jeremiah, "I am a father to Israel, Ephraim is my firstborn" (31:9;

see Hos 11:1; Exod 4:22). The focus at this point is the northern kingdom. The extension to Judah will occur at 31:23. The deliverance of this "remnant of Israel" (31:7) appears to be an end of suffering, a dramatic contrast and change of status.

31:15–17 *The emotions of Rachel*

The picture is developed by a text well known to the readers of the Gospel of Matthew: "In Ramah is heard the sound of moaning of bitter weeping! Rachel mourns her children, she refuses to be consoled because her children are no more" (31:15; see Matt 2:18). In the Gospel, this matriarch of the northern tribes appears to epitomize suffering. In Jeremiah, the text functions to describe the end of suffering: "Cease your cries of mourning, wipe the tears from your eyes" (31:16).

The important element of this picture is the portrayal of the parent who suffers the pain of her children and can then rejoice in their recovery. The destruction of Israel is not just some historical or political piece of information illustrating the vicissitudes of history. Israel is a family. It is God's family (31:9). A family lives most intensely as family around a mother. Thus, the figure of Rachel. The upheavals of Israel are the heartrending disasters that befall the beloved children of this family.

31:23–34 *The New Covenant*

As the promises of restoration shift explicitly to Judah and her cities (31:23), the prophecies begin to describe a more radical action of God, one that brings about a change within the heart of human beings. The inevitability of disaster appeared always in terms of Israel's inevitable failure to hear the word of God. This impossibility to listen to and understand God was rooted in Israel's "heart" (see 3:17; 5:21.23; 7:24; 9:26; and so on). In promising "a new covenant" (31:31), God therefore promises a transformation of the human heart. Although it is described in explicit contrast to the old, the new covenant will not involve so much a new set of laws but a way in which the law of God will exist in the hearts of human beings: "I will place my law within them and write it upon their hearts; I will be their God and they shall be my people" (31:33; see Lev 26:12).

The consoling words of Jeremiah have reverberated through scripture into the New Testament. Ezekiel will develop the idea by adding the theme of the spirit as gift (Ezek 36:26). When the Deuteronomic reform focused on loving God with all one's heart (Deut 6:5; see Matt 22:37 and parallels), it was building—intentionally or not—on the promise of Jeremiah that God would make this possible by writing his law in the human heart. In the New Testament writings, Jesus will insist on the interior observance of the Law (Matt 5:17–30; Mark 7:17–22). In the account of the Last Supper of Jesus according to Luke and Paul, Jesus will refer to the cup of wine as "the new covenant in my blood" (Luke 22:20; 1 Cor 11:25). The author of the Letter to the Hebrews cites this text of Jeremiah at length to show how the new covenant has replaced the old (Heb 8:7–13). Paul alludes to this text as he defends his apostolate. His credentials consist in a letter written in the hearts of the readers, which makes Paul a minister of a new covenant (1 Cor 3:1–6).

32:1–15 *The purchase of land*

In 588 BC, a year before the final destruction of Jerusalem, Jeremiah's message of hope and consolation takes the form of prophetic action that is worth special attention. As the account describes, Jeremiah is visited in prison by his cousin Hanamel, who has come to ask Jeremiah to buy his property in Anathoth, a couple of miles outside of Jerusalem (see Map 10A), a city about to be besieged. Given the military events unfolding, the farmland was not what we would call "prime." But God sends the message for Jeremiah to purchase the land. It was a prophetic gesture explained by the words of verse 15: "For thus says Yahweh of hosts, the God of Israel: Houses and fields and vineyards shall again be bought in this land." The risky investment is an act of trust and hope in the future, an act of faith in the words of Yahweh.

Although different in a number of details, another account of this transaction appears in Jeremiah 37:11–16.

* * *

Forming most of **the third major section** of the book (chapters 36–45), Baruch's narrative describes the arrest of Jeremiah by King Zedekiah, who reigned over the city as it was captured and destroyed by the Babylonians (chapters 37–39). The tragedy of Jerusalem continued. Jewish factions refused to listen to Jeremiah, assassinated Gedaliah, the appointed governor; and forced the Jewish remnant including Jeremiah into Egypt, where we hear the last of him (chapters 40–44).

45:1–5 *Divine pathos*

This section comes to a close with a summary prophecy, dated to 605 BC, the year of Jeremiah's writing of the threatening scroll at the time of Jehoiakim. (A similar retroshift occurs at the end of section one, 25:1). We hear of a book (*sefer*) written by Baruch at the dictation of Jeremiah (45:1). We have references to many "books" in this Book of Jeremiah (25:13; 30:2; 51:63). However, the material here as well as the date given corresponds to that described in the writing of the "scroll" (*m^egilat sefer*) in 36:1–19, at the beginning of **this third major section** of the book of Jeremiah. Most likely, editors returned to this "scroll" or "book" at the end of **this third major section** to create something of a framework for the section and to bring an insight into the meaning of the work of Jeremiah.

The words that conclude the section deal with suffering and grief. Baruch complains of his pain, which he sees as coming from God himself. The surprising answer to this suffering is a description of divine tragedy. Jeremiah explains to him that God must undo his work: "What I have built, I am tearing down; what I have planted, I am uprooting, even the whole land" (45:4). This is the tragedy of sin that draws God into the turmoil.

Nothing is said of divine emotion. However, a stark contrast is drawn, the contrast between the personal involvement of God in building and planting and the personal involvement of God in destruction. All this suggests a God who is himself torn by grief, like the loving parent of a rebellious child (see Hos 11:8). In the context here the pathos of God becomes the explanation of the suffering of Baruch. Baruch in effect manifests the very suffering of God. Baruch and Jeremiah's suffering are part of a tragedy of cosmic—even divine—proportions. This is the role of the prophet.

III. The Message of Jeremiah

A. REVIEW OF IMAGES AND THEMES

The selected passages above give us a wealth of poetic images, starting with the mission of Jeremiah as rooting up and tearing down, building and planting (1:10; 18:7–9; 24:6; 31:28). We see also the vivid images of circumcision of the heart (4:4), God's loincloth (13:1–11), the clay and the potter (18:1–10), the broken flask (19:1–13), the shoot or bud of David (23:5–6), the two baskets of figs (24:1–10), and the seventy years (29:10; see also 25:11–12).

In addition, we find in Jeremiah a special class of poetic images which are prophetic actions: Temple sermon (7:1–34; 26:1–6), the writing of the scroll (36:1–32), Jeremiah's celibacy (16:1–4), his personal suffering (15:10, 15–18; 20:7–10, 14–18), carrying a yoke (27:2; 8:10), the letter to the exiles (29:1–23), and the purchase of the field (32:6–15; see also 37:11–12).

The religious themes in Jeremiah are also numerous. We can group them into two categories.

1. Traditional prophetic themes:

- Israel as bride of God (2:2)
- Israel's forgetfulness of God (2:32) or lack of knowledge of God (4:22)
- The call to conversion (4:1)
- The need for "fair judgment" and "justice" (4:2)
- God as the attacking enemy (4:13)
- The sin of social injustice (5:27–28)
- The low value of religion without justice (6:20–25; 7:3–15)
- A future Davidic king who brings salvation and security (23:5–6; 30:9; also 33:15)

2. Themes characteristic of Jeremiah, although not all unique to him:

- Zion as a woman suffering in painful labor (4:31)
- God suffering from the sins of his people (4:19–22; 45:4)
- God as shepherd of the remnant of Israel (23:3)
- The divine gift of a new heart to understand God (24:7; 32:39)
- The harm done by "prophets of lies" (27:10, 14, 16; 29:21)
- God's love as "father" of Israel (31:3, 9)
- The new covenant written in the heart (31:31–34; see also 32:40)

B. THE THEOLOGY OF JEREMIAH

1. *The destruction of a theology.* When Jeremiah came on the scene in 626 BC, hardly an Israelite alive would have admitted that the city of Jerusalem could be taken and the Temple destroyed. Life was full of illusory meaning, based on the earthly city with its Temple. In the popular mind, God was bound to Jerusalem and to the Davidic kings. Jerusalem, the city of God's choice, was inviolable because he had chosen it. The retreat of Sennacherib in the time of Isaiah had only confirmed this theology. That theology alone explains the senseless revolts against Babylon.

Jeremiah's task was to destroy this theology, "to root up and tear down" (1:10). He reminded the people in his Temple address that God was not bound to the Temple, that he could and would destroy it as he had destroyed Shiloh in times past (7:1–34). He insisted that Jerusalem and the nation were but pieces of clay in the hands of the divine potter (18:1–12). For this task, Jeremiah was derided, beaten, and imprisoned. His enemies carried the day. God had promised to be with Jeremiah, but that divine presence was not very apparent.

The day of Yahweh came for Jerusalem, and the great abyss yawned for the nation. For those who remembered Jeremiah, the parables of the loincloth, the potter, and the broken flask were now seen in a new light. In exile the people remembered that Jeremiah had spoken of the "good figs" who would someday return to Judah. They remembered his buying of the seemingly worthless property. They remembered the sermons of consolation (chapters 30–31) and especially the promise of a new covenant.

2. *A theology of suffering.* As the suffering mystic in the marketplace, Jeremiah stared into this terrifying abyss of chaos (*tohu wa-bohu*, 4:23). In his own life, however, for Jeremiah this abyss was not so much that of a destroyed universe as preached by Zephaniah, but rather an interior abyss, that of a holy life apparently abandoned by God. It is through the abyss of this suffering that Jeremiah stood in the council of God and heard God's word.

As the editors assembled the preaching and writings of Jeremiah and Baruch, something struck them about the prophet's sufferings. If he preached destruction, he was himself like Hosea deeply and personally involved in that destruction. Understanding this involvement may have led the editors to include so much narrative material precisely about Jeremiah.

To no other prophet did God express such closeness. "Before I formed you in the womb, I knew you…I dedicated you…I appointed you…I am with you" (1:5, 8). Yet from no other prophet do we hear of such sense of injury precisely from God. "You seduced me, Yahweh. . . . You were too strong for me" (20:7). His suffering was rooted in his closeness to God. "My heart within me is broken…because of Yahweh, because of his holy words" (23:9).

The closeness binding God and prophet makes it difficult sometimes to know who is talking and who is suffering. Is it God or the prophet who cries out, "My suffering! My suffering! How I am pained!" (4:19)? This sounds like Jeremiah, yet the lines following are clearly from the mouth of God: "Fools my people are, they know me not" (4:22). In Jeremiah God is repeatedly portrayed as having to smash down his work like clay (18:4), to tear down what he has built, and uproot what he has planted (45:4). It is as if the life of the prophet is a manifestation of God's own distress.

How can we picture God suffering? Jeremiah insists on the love of God for his people (31:3), and love means becoming vulnerable. In love we bind ourselves to others. The problems of the beloved become our problems. The death of the beloved becomes our death. Can God really suffer and die for his people?

The objection arises that God is not God if he suffers. This objection is based on the understanding of God's "impassibility," the unchanging quality of God because he is infinite and exists in eternity, not time. This understanding must be respected, but we also must recognize that we do not know what "unchanging" means when applied to the infinite. Similarly we do not know what "love" and "suffering" mean when applied to the infinite. All these concepts are images taken from our human experience that we can use to target our judgments *toward* the infinite. *In some way* our understanding of God as loving and suffering applies, just as our understanding of God as unchanging *in some way* applies—although Christians firmly believe that this *unchanging* God *became* "flesh." We do not know how these concepts apply. We know only that denying these understandings of God moves us further from the truth.

When we attribute seemingly contradictory traits to God, we are placing our faith in the conviction that the traits do converge in the infinite prolongation of our understanding, a prolongation that escapes our comprehension or conceptualization. We then must speak the language of paradox. In fact, the New Testament provides a vision of an incarnation of God that allows us to affirm realistically this paradox of divine love and suffering. In Jesus God suffered and died. Jeremiah seems to be a shadowy anticipation of this incarnation of divine suffering.

3. *A new covenant.* Jeremiah lived at a turning point in Israel's history and bridged the gap between the old and the new. The events of 587 BC had a profound influence on the development of Israel's theology. They forced Israel's thinkers to look deeper into their covenant theology and reassess their expectations. The results are in fact the Pentateuch and Deuteronomist history, which achieved substantially their present arrangement during or shortly after the Exile. Faith continued to live, through the dreadful days of siege and destruction and through the years of

exile. Faith was the link that joined the Israel of old to the Judaism that arose from the grave of exile to become a nation again. It was Jeremiah's message that helped forge the link.

Jeremiah preached the funeral oration on the defunct kingdom of Judah and at the same time predicted the institution of a new covenant. He declared the Davidic kings rejected but heralded the coming of a new David. Sin he says is "engraved upon the tablets of their hearts" (17:1), but then Jeremiah promises a remedy for sin as a new law written "on their hearts" (31:33) or even an act of God creating for human beings "a new heart" (24:7; 32:39). A "new covenant" between God and Israel will replace the broken Sinai covenant (30:18–24; 31:31–34). The painful destruction of Jerusalem and the burning of the Temple were the acts of a divine potter preparing the lump of clay to be a better vessel (18:1–12).

Israel's resurrection from national death in Babylon is one of the great works of God. But God works through human beings, like Jeremiah. Jeremiah was not the failure he had seemed to be during the long years of his tortured life. In the end, his message took root and bore abundant fruit. In the double abyss of personal and national destruction, Jeremiah fulfilled his call "to build and to plant" (1:10).

11
Ezekiel

I. Overview

A. The Prophet and His Style

One of the priests deported from Jerusalem to Babylon in 598 BC was called to be a prophet among the exiles (see Map 11A). His name was Ezekiel, son of Buzi. His call was in 592 (1:2); his last dated sermon, 570 (29:17). If the miraculous trip described in 8:3 is a literary device to show Ezekiel's strong identification with the people in Jerusalem, then all of his preaching, it would appear, was done in exile. He was married but lost his wife the year Jerusalem fell to the Babylonian army (24:15–19).

Ezekiel is one of the most colorful personalities in the Bible, labeled by his own people as "the one who is forever spinning parables" (21:5) and recognized as an irrepressible mime and actor. In his inaugural vision, he sees the strangest of theophanies (1:4–28). When commissioned a prophet, he is given a written scroll to eat and digest (2:1–9).

Like Jeremiah, he foretells the siege and fall of Jerusalem but in his own unique way. He acts out the message in pantomime (chapters 4–5) and mimics the escape of the fugitives by digging through the wall of his house and fleeing into the night (chapter 12). When the time comes for Nebuchadnezzar's armies to march upon Jerusalem, Ezekiel pantomimes the march with a sword, setting up guideposts for the sword as it leaves Babylon on its way to Jerusalem (21:14–19). He clenches his fists, stamps his feet, cries "ach!" and groans until the bystanders call for an explanation out of curiosity (21:11–12).

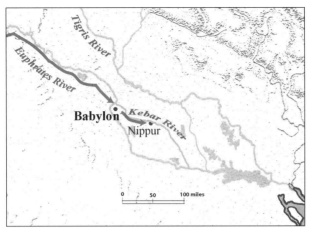

11A—Ezekiel in Exile

Whatever we think of his style, Ezekiel made a vivid impression on the minds of the doubting and discouraged exiles. What he did was not easily forgotten. He succeeded in interesting the crowd by his unusual behavior, and before long his words and actions were being discussed from house to house and in the streets (33:30–33). When Jerusalem fell in 587 BC, the significance of Ezekiel's behavior became obvious, and his reputation as a prophet was established. From that time on, we see little pantomime, much serious preaching, and elaborate planning for Israel's return and restoration.

B. THE BOOK

Unlike the books of Isaiah and Jeremiah, that of Ezekiel is well ordered both topically and chronologically—despite changes and additions by later editors. While strong and lofty on occasions, the style is heavy with symbols and allegories and much too repetitious for modern tastes.

The book falls clearly into four major parts:

Ezekiel 1—24: Before 587 BC, threats against Jerusalem and predictions of her certain destruction
Ezekiel 25—32: Oracles against the nations

Ezekiel 33—39: After 587 BC, encouraging prophecies of
national and religious restoration

Ezekiel 40—48: The Torah of Ezekiel

(See Appendix 4i for a detailed outline of the Book of Ezekiel.)

C. TORAH TRADITIONS IN EZEKIEL

The opening line in the Book of Ezekiel includes an unexplained reference to "the thirtieth year" as the beginning of Ezekiel's mission, which can be dated around 593 BC (1:1–2). If this "thirtieth year" refers back to the discovery in 622 BC of "the book of the Law" described in 2 Kings 22:8–17, then we have a confirmation of an important step in the development of the Torah, a step that the editors of Ezekiel would have known about.

Valuable for knowing what oral traditions or texts existed at the time of Ezekiel himself, a number of allusions or echoes of details now found in our Pentateuch appear in this book. Some of these are now found in our Book of Genesis, like the "garden of Eden" (36:35; see Gen 2:8; 3:24), the role of the spirit in giving life (37:1–14; see Gen 2:7; 6:3, 17; 7:15), Noah (14:14; see Gen 6—9), and the names Magog, Meshech, and Tubal (38:2; see Gen 10:2). Several others are found now in the Book of Exodus, like the saving mark that spares divine destruction (9:11; see Exod 12), the mobile "glory" (*kabod*) of God (2:12; 10:4; see Exod 24:15), and the "cherubic" throne of God (10:1–22; see Exod 25:18–20; also Ps 80:2). The story in Ezekiel of God's pardon based on divine self-interest as the motive (36:20–38) has a strong resemblance to Numbers 14:13–19.

Ezekiel appears very conversant with the legal traditions that fill our Pentateuch. As an extended text, the "holiness code" in the Book of Leviticus, chapters 17–26, with its detailed prescriptions for cult, shows the most parallels with Ezekiel, especially chapters 20, 22, 33, and 44. The examples of wrongdoing that he uses in his discussion of personal responsibility seem to draw on the material we have now in Exodus 22:25–27 as well as Leviticus 15:19–24. In the first major part of his book, Ezekiel also rails against Israel for its repeated violations of the Sabbath (20:13–24; 22:8, 26; 23:38).

The special section of Ezekiel 40—48, the so-called "Torah of Ezekiel" poses intriguing questions. Why are these chapters so similar in form to the cultic and architectural prescriptions of Exodus, Numbers, and Leviticus, yet substantially different in the content of the prescriptions? Clearly Ezekiel 40–48 is an attempt to reestablish the identity of Israel on the basis of cult and law—an effort that would culminate later in the work of Ezra. On the other hand, the distinctiveness of Ezekiel's prescriptions argues that he did not know the Torah as we have it. It would thus appear that Ezekiel's efforts here are an early sketch of many efforts that would eventually produce our Pentateuch—probably some two hundred years later.

II. Significant Passages in Ezekiel

A. Ezekiel 1—24 / Before 587 BC

1:1–28 *Vision of the glory of God*

The first part of Ezekiel's inaugural vision is that of the glory of God. The year is 593 BC, as explained in the editorial addition of 1:2. This is "the thirtieth year" (1:1)—probably from the discovery of the book of the Law by Josiah, the only event around 623 BC that seems worthy of establishing a calendar. Ezekiel is living in one of the colonies of Jewish exiles in Babylonia, "the land of the Chaldeans by the river Kebar" (1:3), probably southeast of the city of Babylon (see Map 11A).

He describes his overpowering contact with God by means of two images, "the hand of God" and "the spirit." The first part of his vision is attributed to God's hand (1:3), an image of a compelling power coming from outside human experience ("in God's grip"), perhaps also an allusion to God's way of helping Elijah (2 Kgs 18:46).

The storm and the fire seen by Ezekiel make us think of the classic theophanies (see Exod 19:16-25; Ps 18:11–15). The vision of the "living creatures," with their four faces, their wings, and the wheels, is without biblical precedent. The four faces suggest the similar combinations of human heads and animal parts common to some Babylonian divinities, somewhat like the ancient sphinxes and griffins, except these creatures stood upright like human beings in human form. The wings, which touched each other, suggest the *kerubim* in the Holy of Holies of the Jerusalem Temple (1 Kgs 6:27). The wheels suggest a war chariot. The whole scene is dominated by the theme of motion, which in turn is depicted as ruled by "the spirit" (Ezek 1:12, 20).

More awesome yet is what appears above "the firmament," the dividing barrier between the created and the divine (Ps 14:2; 33:13; 80:15; 102:20). There Ezekiel sees what looks like a human being, surrounded with fire and brightness, along with the gentle colors of the rainbow, a symbol of God's "everlasting covenant" with humanity as a whole (Gen 9:12–16; see Ezek 16:60). This vision is identified as "a likeness of the glory (*kabod*) of Yahweh" (1:26–28). Ezekiel is depicting God as far more glorious and dominant than any local divinity, who is incapable of exercising dominion outside its own territory and is subject to conquest by other divinities. Ezekiel's God is the God of the whole universe, of all nations and peoples. This picture of the transcendent God may be the key to the whole Book of Ezekiel. It leads the prophet to fall on his face.

2:1—3:11 *The commission of Ezekiel*

The second part of Ezekiel's inaugural vision starts with a command, "Stand up!" (2:1). The spirit enters Ezekiel, apparently the same spirit that moved the heavenly creatures and chariots. The prophet is commissioned or "sent" to speak the message of "our Lord Yahweh" to the Israelites, a people "stiff of heart" (2:4; 3:7). The commission is doomed to failure, reflecting God's failure: "The house of Israel will refuse to listen to you, since they will not listen to me" (3:7).

Ezekiel is strengthened for the conflict. "I will make your face as hard as theirs…like diamond, harder than flint" (3:8–9). This is a promise that goes far beyond God's promise to Jeremiah (Jer 1:8), who seems to have suffered far more from his mission than did Ezekiel. Unlike Jeremiah, Ezekiel never protests the orders of God. This promise of hardness, however, ties into the portrayal of Ezekiel as rather cold and impassionate, even at the death of his wife (see Ezek 24:15–18). But then, the God of Ezekiel seems a bit cold and impassionate.

The words that the prophet is to deliver are written on a scroll that Ezekiel must eat, an image picked up later by apocalyptic literature (see Rev 10:9–11). The message is clearly not the prophet's message but is given to the prophet to deliver, as an ambassador delivers the message from his or her government. Although the words on the scroll are ominous, "lamentation, wailing, and woe!" (2:10), the scroll tastes "sweet as honey," as did the words of God for Jeremiah (Jer 15:16).

This message thus enters into the very life of the prophet: "Take into your heart all my words that I speak to you" (3:10). Like bread from heaven, this word of God nourishes and strengthens the prophet. The biblical text here is clear: God and the prophet now walk together. The otherworldly word of God is assimilated and thus incarnated in this earthly "son of man."

3:12–15 *The sound of God*
The third part of the prophetic call is attributed to "the spirit" who lifts Ezekiel up. The experience begins with hearing the "loud rumbling" sound of the divine glory. In Exodus the divine "glory" (*kabod*) appeared as a great cloud that hovered on top of Mount Sinai (Exod 24:16) and then filled the inner sanctum of the meeting tent (40:34–38). It represents the presence of God.

Again we are alerted that Ezekiel is among the exiles near Babylon, "at Tel-abib, by the river Kebar" (Ezek 3:15).

3:16–21 *The watchman*
This third part of the prophetic commission continues with a description of Ezekiel's responsibility as "a watchman" or sentry (see also Hos 9:8; Hab 2:1; Isa 21:6). We are introduced to the theme of personal responsibility in terms of the prophet's role. That theme will appear in wider development later (chapter 18). Here Ezekiel has the responsibility of a sentry who must warn Israel of God's word as if God himself were the enemy. The scene

will be repeated at 33:7–9, when the second phase of Ezekiel's mission begins.

3:22–27 *Ezekiel's dumbness*

The fourth part of Ezekiel's inaugural vision, attributed again to "the hand of God" (3:22) but also to "the spirit" (3:24), is another vision of the glory of God. It takes place "in the plain" but is meant to recall the first vision by the river Kebar.

Ezekiel is supposed to shut himself up in his house and be bound up by rope (3:24–25), a rather awkward situation for a public speaker. To make things harder, the prophet is struck dumb, at least for normal everyday speech. At this point we can note that he has not said a word during the entire three-chapter account of his call. He will talk (see chapters 5–7), but his speech, as mentioned here, will be totally at the service of God. During this first part of his ministry, much of Ezekiel's teaching will be by speechless pantomime, mostly symbolizing the coming siege and destruction of Jerusalem (chapters 4–7).

4:1–8 *Prophetic pantomime*

The next two chapters describe a series of wordless actions of the prophet, whose gestures carry the prophetic message (chapters 4–5; see also chapter 12). The first pantomime here involves Ezekiel and a toy model of the city of Jerusalem with models of war machines. By silent drama he prophesies the siege of the city. The text we read here gives us the words to interpret the gestures, but the people watching Ezekiel apparently hear nothing.

In the second part of the account, the prophet lies on the ground, first on his left side to symbolize the exile of Israel and then on his right to symbolize that of Judah. In those positions, he must "bear the sin (*ᵃwon*) of the house of Israel" and "the sin of the house of Judah" on him (4:4, 6), as if he thus vicariously bears the sins of the people. The vocabulary reminds us of the scapegoat that is made "to bear the sin" of the Israelites (Lev 16:22). Also like Moses who was willing to bear the penalty of the Hebrew's sins (Exod 32:32), the prophet is drawn into the sinfulness of the people, representing them in their misery. Ezekiel also anticipates the description of "the suffering servant" of Deutero-Isaiah, "on whom Yahweh laid the sin of us all" (Isa 53:6; see below).

8:1–4 *Ezekiel transported to Jerusalem*

Chapters 8–11 may in fact be messed up by clumsy editorial additions. Scattered through this section, however, are details central to Ezekiel's message, details that depend on each other for a basic portrayal of God's mobility. The point of the prophecy is the independence of God from his Temple in Jerusalem.

The first details appear in the beginning of chapter 8, in which through literary fiction or a miraculous transport, the prophet gets to Jerusalem where the visual elements of the prophecy can be located. The scene starts in Babylonia and is dated to the fourteenth month after the inaugural vision, which is visually recalled by the return of the fiery humanlike figure and the glory of God (see 1:26–28). This fiery figure along with "the spirit" together then transport Ezekiel to Jerusalem—by his hair!

9:1–11 *The punishment and the protecting mark*

After giving Ezekiel a tour of the Temple with the "abominable evils" of the worship of false gods (8:5–18), the fiery figure introduces a scene of divine judgment and destruction, beginning with the Temple sanctuary (9:6). The prophet attempts a prayer of intercession—apparently in vain (9:8–10).

The scene also includes a picture of God starting his move. "The glory of God" lifts from the *kerubim* figures and pauses at the threshold (*miphtan*) of the Temple. God has his bags packed (9:3).

The story, however, describes also how a part of the population of Jerusalem is spared because of a saving mark given to them. "A man dressed in linen" writes the letter *tau*, the last letter of the Hebrew alphabet, as the saving mark on the foreheads of select people. (In the ancient Hebrew alphabet used at the time of Ezekiel, the letter *tau* looked like a cross.) The heavenly figure charged with this task appears as an angelic figure dressed in the high priest's robe equipped with the instruments of a scribe. Although the whole scene echoes the Passover events of Exodus 12, the selection of those receiving the saving tau is based not simply on being a Hebrew but on one's personal attitude toward the sins of the city (9:4). Ezekiel is preparing the way for the concept of personal responsibility that he will develop in chapter 18 (see also 33:10–20).

10:1–22 *God moves out of the Temple*
Still in Jerusalem, Ezekiel again sees a vision of the heavenly throne (see 1:26) and the man dressed in linen introduced in the previous chapter. In the previous chapter his action as a scribe was that of saving and sparing, now his action of scattering burning coals on the city is that of punishment (10:2). Other elements of the inaugural vision seem to interrupt the drama: the throne, the wheels, the four-faced living creatures—now described as *kerubim* (10:9–17, 20–21).

The vision of the glory of God rising from the Temple, however, begins the important scene that dramatizes God's independence from his Temple. Repeating the first move of God to the threshold (*miphtan*; 10:4), the text then describes God moving to the east gate of the Temple (10:18–19; see Diagram 6B). In the final rather awkward form of this chapter, the stationary throne of God (see Exod 25:18–20; Ps 80:2; 1 Kgs 8:6–11) becomes mobile, as the *kerubim* or "the living creatures [*chayyot*]" get wheels along with their wings (10:9–13).

11:14–21 *Promise of a new heart and spirit*
Unexpectedly embedded in these oracles of threats is one of consolation. It starts as a declaration of God countering the false hopes and grasping attitudes of the remaining inhabitants of Jerusalem (11:15). It is directed to the exiles and promises a future "gathering" and restoration to the land. Most important, however, is the promise of "a new heart and a new spirit" to replace Israel's "hard heart." These promises are repeated in the second part of Ezekiel's prophecies to Israel (36:24–28).

The inability of Israel to hear and follow the word of God lay in their "hard heart." The promise of life required a change nothing less than this cardiac transplant and the gift of the divine spirit described here. Paul writing to the Corinthians will combine the imagery of Ezekiel with that of Jeremiah to describe "the new covenant" of the spirit (2 Cor 3:2–6).

11:22–23 *God moves out of the city*

Completing the vision of God's mobility are two verses in the following chapter describing the glory of God leaving Jerusalem. The movement is to the east. God's glory pauses on the mountain east of Jerusalem, the mountain named in Zechariah 14:4 as the Mount of Olives. In the New Testament, Luke portrays Jesus pausing on the Mount of Olives before ascending to heaven (Acts 1:12).

This mobility of God is a way of expressing his transcendence. He is not bound to any place, even to his Temple. The Jerusalem theologians had argued that God would not let the city be destroyed for the sake of his glory (Isa 29:5–8; 31:4–5; Ps 46). Along the lines of Jeremiah, Ezekiel counters that the glory of God is not bound to Jerusalem.

15:1–8 *Parables, allegories, and instructions*

Chapter 15 begins a series of parables and allegories, along with other instructions that continue through the end of chapter 17. The literary form of these stories is interesting. Some of the stories are taken from everyday life but given a twist that causes the listener to be attentive to a deeper meaning. The stories develop one main point, where the details simply contribute to the story line. We call such stories "parables." Other stories use details that have their own symbolic meaning that needs to be deciphered. These we call "allegories." Along with the two-liner "proverb," the parable and the allegory—and mixtures of both—were developed by the wisdom teachers who were deeply interested in moral education. They gave the name *mashal* to all of these forms without distinction.

Here Ezekiel combines his wisdom background with his prophetic calling to develop a series of *mashalim*, all emphasizing the threat of God's punishment of Jerusalem. The first is the parable of the vine, the image of Israel canonized by earlier prophets (see Hos 10:1; Isa 5:1–7; Jer 2:21; see also Ps 80:9–15) and later used by the New Testament (see John 15:1–10). Focusing on the branches rather than on the fruit, Ezekiel describes scraggly wood suitable only for burning. In this condemnation of the inhabitants of Jerusalem (15:6), the prophet seems to be taking an image that evoked God's care (see Ps 80:9–15) and turning it on its head.

16:1–43 *The faithless spouse*

The allegory of the faithless spouse develops the daring imagery, introduced by Hosea (Hos 1—3) and picked up by Jeremiah (Jer 2:2–13; 3:8), of Israel as the wife of Yahweh. Most of the chapter is a description of the erotic love of Yahweh for Israel. The eroticism of Ezekiel is even more graphic in chapter 23, the description of Israel and Judah as two prostitute sisters.

The story, unusually long in prophetic literature, begins with the heartwarming motif of a foundling, which usually develops into a story of happiness (see Exod 2:1–10). In fact, the story starts in that direction, where the guardian of the child falls in love with the maturing woman, marries her, and provides lavishly for her. Ezekiel, however, again turns the story on its head and describes Israel's faithlessness, with references to Ba'alist prostitution (16:15–16) and infant immolation (16:20–21; see Jer 7:31). The description of God's passionate love thus serves to underline the senselessness of Israel's sin—although the gruesome details of the punishment for adultery (16:37–41) may produce in the modern reader a sense of revulsion for the story itself (see our comments on the Message of Nahum above). Both in this story and in chapter 23, Ezekiel points out the root of Israel's wickedness as stemming from its origins. There is no ideal period to return to (see Hos 2:16–17). There is no mention of promises to patriarchs and former kings. The relationship with God is over and never should have started.

The image of Jerusalem as the wife of God appears again in Trito-Isaiah in a positive light (Isa 62:4–5). In the New Testament, Ephesians will develop the image of the wife to describe the church as the faithful wife of Christ (Eph 5:22–33). This was an image apparently already used by Jesus (Mark 2:18–20) and Paul (2 Cor 11:2).

16:59–63 *The everlasting covenant*

After the allegory of the wicked daughter (16:44–58) comes a brief oracle of salvation. God promises "an everlasting covenant" based on the covenant he already made with Israel, which he will *remember* (16:60). Israel's memory is short (16:43), but God does not forget. The action is described as an act of generosity. God is not bound by that covenant, which Israel broke. Nevertheless, he will *reestablish* it (16:61–62). The stress here is on continuity with the old through an act of grace. Ezekiel will later speak of a future "covenant of peace" (34:25; 37:26).

The oracle of salvation is connected to the preceding by references to the sisters of the wicked daughter (16:61; see 16:55). God's grace and salvation given to these "sisters" will bring shame and repentance to Israel. In the New Testament, Paul will see God's gift of grace to the Gentiles not as a rejection of Israel but as a way to make Israel "jealous" and thus be saved (Rom 11:13–15). In these stories, God brings about conversion in the end by the abundance of his grace and love.

17:1–24 *The great tree*
The third story is an allegory-parable (*mashal*) about a great cedar and vine, symbolizing Israel, attacked by eagles, who symbolize foreign powers (17:3, 7). The story contains a reference to "the crest of the cedar" ripped off from the tree, representing King Jehoiachin exiled by King Nebuchadnezzar, and a secondary planting that becomes a low-lying vine, representing King Zedekiah, that sends out in a futile attempt roots and shoots to the second eagle, probably Pharaoh Psammetichus II, son of Neco (595–589 BC).

The symbols of the allegory are then interpreted (17:11–21) and expanded by a prophetic oracle with a very different orientation (17:22–24). The oracle basically promises salvation. The stress is on God's action on behalf of a new Davidic king ruling in Jerusalem, the "high and lofty mountain" (see 40:2; Isa 2:2; Mic 4:1). Illustrating the contrast between beginnings and endings, the "tender twig" from the cedar becomes a majestic tree and "birds of every kind shall dwell beneath it" (Ezek 17:22–23). The result is some form of international recognition ("all the trees of the field") of God's ways.

This story as found in Ezekiel seems to have influenced later religious storytellers (see Dan 4:7–9) including Jesus, who speaks about the mustard seed that grows into a great tree and the "birds of the air come and dwell in its branches" (Matt 13:31–32 and parallels).

18:1–32 *Personal responsibility*

The idea of personal responsibility becomes a major theme in Ezekiel. Faced with inevitable rejection, the prophet's own mission was made understandable earlier in terms of personal responsibility (Ezek 3:17–21; 33:7–9). Here in chapter 18 Ezekiel expands the theme to the whole nation, earning for him the title, "prophet of individual responsibility."

The development here illustrates Ezekiel's redundant and nitpicking style. This is the style of the priest explaining sacred law (see Exod 22). Ezekiel first deals with the issue of responsibility within a family, running through the various possibilities. The overall point is clear. One is not held responsible for the sins of one's parent or child, nor can one count on the virtues of one's parent or child (18:1–20). Ezekiel speaks then about an individual life. One will not be punished for the past sins of which one repents. Likewise, one will not be saved by the past virtuous deeds from which one strays. There will be no averaging out of one's life. The decisions of the present moment determine life or death (18:21–32).

This doctrine of individual responsibility becomes clear at a time when the structures of Israel's solidarity had been destroyed. No monarchy held the people together. Even the common Temple liturgy had no place in the life of the exiles. Ezekiel tells the exiles to take charge of their own lives: "Make for yourselves a new heart and a new spirit" (18:31).

The idea of individual responsibility is not totally new. It is briefly presupposed in some ancient stories (see Gen 18:25; 1 Sam 26:23). It also appears as a command of God in Deuteronomy 24:16 and as an isolated literary displacement in Jeremiah 31:29–30. However Ezekiel seems to give a deathblow to the dominant idea of rigid collective responsibility (see Exod 20:5). By overemphasizing collective responsibility, the exiles could have been attributing their misfortunes to the sins of their ancestors (Ezek 18:2), thus evading the call to repentance.

Understood in the context of Ezekiel's preaching, the point of this teaching is one of hope. God's focus is on the present not the past, whether that be a national past or individual past. The nation and the individual can be freed from the guilt of the past by a determined turning to God to which they are *now* called. Forget the past sins; it is in the present moment that God offers life. Ezekiel also challenges the persons who appear righteous in their own eyes. The journey is not over. Every present moment is a moment of decision.

24:15–24 *The death of Ezekiel's wife*

Another glimpse of the prophet's personal involvement in his message occurs at the end of the first major part of the book, in the story about the death of his wife, "the delight of your eye" (24:16). Ezekiel is in the place of Israel, which must view the death of Jerusalem, "the delight of your eyes, the desire of your soul" (24:21). The opening of Ezekiel's career was marked by his "bearing the sins" of Israel and Judah (4:4–6). Now Ezekiel's grief is one with the grief of his people. The prophet is not drawn up and away from the misery of the people but immersed in it. The "prophet of individual responsibility" appears here in remarkable solidarity with the people.

Gestures of mourning are forbidden. By defying the customary rituals of grief, Ezekiel turns his domestic tragedy into a prophetic gesture. He becomes "a sign" for them (24:24). Ezekiel tells the people they must concentrate on their sins rather than mourn the loss of their beloved (24:23). At the same time, God promises Ezekiel that he will be relieved of his temporary dumbness on the day Jerusalem falls (24:25, 27) or, more precisely, on the day a messenger arrives with the news of the fall (24:26). He will again speak, this time in words of consolation and hope.

It is difficult to make sense of Ezekiel's prophetic gesture here—not at all helped by additions and rearrangements in the text. The main point again insists on God's control of the events, whether they be Ezekiel's loss or the people's loss. These moments of devastation are part of God's plan, which ultimately must be a plan of salvation. Not to mourn for the dead is not natural. Neither, however, is God's plan to raise the dead to life. Ezekiel and the people are called to a complete surrender to God.

B. EZEKIEL 33—39 / AFTER 587 BC

In the first period of his preaching (chapters 1–24), Ezekiel prepared the people to understand the impending destruction of Jerusalem as a punishment for Israel's sins. In the later part of his preaching (chapters 33–48), Ezekiel turns from sermons of threat and doom to sermons of hope and consolation. His mouth is opened and freed. The people are listening in a new way, no longer scoffing but listening humbly and penitently. The temptation after 587 BC was to despair. To all appearances, Israel was dead. Ezekiel addresses such a temptation with sermons of restoration and the reestablishment of the covenant.

33:1–22 *Ezekiel recommissioned*

In this new phase of Ezekiel's preaching, we are given another account of his calling, the part that describes him again as "a watchman," emphasizing again his personal responsibility as a prophet (33:1–9; see 3:17–21). The doctrine of general individual responsibility is also repeated here (33:10–20; see 18:1–32), this time as a remedy for discouragement. The sins of one's past count for nothing the day one repents and does what is right and just.

The news of the destruction of Jerusalem comes with a "refugee" from Jerusalem, as the story here continues from 24:25–27. As promised, the power of speech returns to the prophet (33:21–22). The "hand of Yahweh" comes upon Ezekiel as it had at the beginning of his career (1:3). A new phase of his career begins.

34:1–31 *The shepherds and the sheep*

A threat and a promise occur in the sermon about the shepherds, a common image of kings in the ancient Middle East. Ezekiel issues a woe to the past shepherds of Israel (34:1–10). They failed their mission of strengthening the weak, healing the sick, binding up the injured, bringing back the strayed, seeking out the lost (34:4). The people are like sheep without a shepherd (see Matt 9:36). God insists twice that the people are "my sheep"

(34:5–6). "Therefore" (*laken*) God will intervene against the shepherds (Ezek 34:7–10).

The promise part of this sermon comes in three messages. The first message describes God himself coming as the shepherd of Israel (34:11–16). God himself will "seek out those driven away, bring back the strayed, bandage the injured, and strengthen the sick" (34:16). God's promise is clear: "I will rescue them from every place where they were scattered....In good pastures I will feed them....I myself will give them rest" (34:12, 14, 15). These are images of the divine power to heal and to gather. The people will return from exile to their land.

The image of God the good shepherd rings throughout scripture (Jer 23:3; Ps 23:1–4). It is the image of God's direct care of his people. In the New Testament, Jesus uses the image of a shepherd searching for a lost sheep as an image of the Father's love for individuals (Matt 18:12–14 and parallels). John's Gospel also adapts Ezekiel's parable to describe Jesus in conflict with false shepherds, or "hirelings" as he calls them (John 9:40—10:21).

In the second message, God pledges to judge "between one sheep and another, between rams and goats" (Ezek 34:17–22), protecting the weak who have been oppressed by the strong. The fact of direct divine care of the people does not reduce the importance of responsible human leadership. The failure is not just on the part of the rulers, but extends into the people themselves, as the propertied class apparently dispossessed the poor. The prophet is describing the capacity of the members of the flock to harm one another. We have here a clear echo of Amos's and Micah's concern for social justice. The text stands as a source for the story of the final judgment described by Matthew, in which Jesus as king comes to judge between the sheep and the goats (Matt 25:31–46).

In the third part, God then also pledges to appoint "my servant David" as the shepherd of Israel (Ezek 34:23–24). He is not called "king" but "prince" (*nasi'*). This prophecy joins the series from Isaiah 11:1 to Jeremiah 23:4, predicting a future Davidic leader who as God's "servant" (*'ebed*) will bring peace to his people. Through this future David, God is at work. The imagery is striking, given Ezekiel's condemnation of the Davidic kings. Despite these failures, the dynasty remains sound in its source.

The promise of God appointing "David" as shepherd is a promise to return to beginnings.

All this is part of a "covenant of peace," characterized by the fertility of the land and the security of the people (34:25–31; see Lev 25:18–19; 26:4–6, 13). "Peace" (*shalom*) connotes wholeness, well-being, harmony—in a word, salvation. The basic covenant with God is reaffirmed: "I, Yahweh, am their God and they are my people, the house of Israel" (34:30; see Lev 26:12). Ezekiel emphatically shows God revealing himself by this act of salvation: "Thus they shall know that I am Yahweh" (34:27, 30).

36:16–38 *The promise of a new heart and a new spirit*

The core of Ezekiel's restoration theology occurs in this text. As the prophet searches to understand the reason for God's decision to restore Israel, he discusses God's motivation. Hosea and Jeremiah focused on God's love for his people (Hos 2:16–17; 11:1; Jer 31:3). Ezekiel focuses on what looks like divine self-interest. The theme seems to come from an earlier Elohist story about Moses' intercession with Yahweh on behalf of the people (Num 14:13–19). Moses argued that God's reputation is now connected with Israel, and if he wants to maintain his reputation among the Egyptians he needs to spare Israel. Ezekiel uses a similar reasoning. God will restore Israel, not for anything Israel has done, but to demonstrate "the holiness of my great name…among the nations" (Ezek 36:23). Both texts show a remarkable universal outlook in regard to the role of God and Israel among Gentile nations. God relents and shows mercy because of *his name* among the nations. In effect Ezekiel plugs into the Elohist story of God revealing his name to Moses, which defines God as a power of compassion and love. "Yahweh…Yahweh, God of compassion and gracious love, slow to anger and rich in kindness and fidelity" (Exod 34:5–6; see Num 14:19).

As Ezekiel works up again to the covenant formula in verse 28b, "You shall be my people, and I will be your God," he lists five aspects of the renewal, repeating much of the doublet in 11:17–21. The list forms a chiasm with the focus of the message at the center, C.

A God will assemble his people on their own land (v. 24).
  B By the sprinkling of clean water, he will purify them from sin, especially idolatry (v. 25).
    C He will transform them interiorly, removing their stony hearts and giving them hearts of flesh (v. 26).
  B' He will give them his spirit so that they will obey his Law (v. 27).
A' They will live in the land of their ancestors (v. 28a).

The central element focuses and clarifies the four balanced elements. A–A' describes the return to the land. B–B' describes a moral purification attributed to washing by water and to the gift of God's spirit, a combination of cleansing agents that Paul will echo again in the New Testament (1 Cor 6:11). At the center of the chiasm is the key element. The Law will be observed because the heart of stone, which made observance impossible, has been removed. Previously Ezekiel had told the people to "make for yourselves a new heart and spirit" (18:31). Here the prophet describes the transformation as God's work.

The last section of this prophecy (36:29–38) translates the promises into earthly economic terms. Cities are rebuilt. Crops are abundant. The desolate land is transformed into "a garden of Eden" (36:35). The inward purification of the heart is matched by the outward prosperity of the land.

37:1–14 *The field of dry bones*

Attributed to "the hand of God" and also "the spirit" (37:1), the vision of the dry bones continues the theme of God's work. The vision is of resurrection from the dead, not of individuals but of the people as a whole. Only centuries later will the image of resurrection shift to individuals rising from the dead (see Dan 12:2; 2 Macc 7:22–23). The dead of Ezekiel's vision are very dead! Not only are they dead bodies, they are dead bones—not only dead bones, but dry bones! This is an image of the exiles' national despair.

As instructed, the prophet prophesies the word of God to the bones and then calls on "the spirit" to come and restore life. God is drawing Ezekiel as an instrument into his mighty power to save from death. God gives life through the prophetic word. As an illustration of the saving power of God, this story insists on two things. First, it demonstrates the extent of what is possible for God. Secondly, it points toward the ultimate purpose of God's saving power, to restore life.

The word *spirit* (*ruach*) in Hebrew is the same for breath. We are reminded of the Yahwist story where God gives life by breathing into Adam (Gen 2:7). One's breath became a symbol for one's life (Gen 7:15; Ps 104:29). This breath of life is then linked to God's breath or spirit (see Gen 6:3, 17). Through his breath God can bring to life the dead nation of Israel and have them settle on the land (37:11–14). It is not the survival of Jerusalem or the Temple that should ground the hope of the exiles, but God and his life-giving spirit. Eventually in the New Testament, the Spirit of God is welded to the hope of resurrection also of individuals (see Rom 8:11).

37:15–28 *The reunification of Israel and Judah*

Immediately attached to the vision of the dry bones is a promise of reunification for the people, split since 932 BC between the northern kingdom of Israel (named here Joseph or Ephraim) and the southern kingdom of Judah (37:16–22). In the preceding story of the resurrected bones, the explanation insisted, "These bones are the whole house of Israel" (37:11). In this story, the longing for the reunification of the people is explicit. The imagery of two sticks joined will be picked up later by the Book of Zechariah (Zech 11:10,14).

The unity of the people leads to a promise of "one shepherd" over this people, David himself (Ezek 37:24–25). The promise of David again as one "king" (*melek*) and one "shepherd" (*ro'eh*) recalls the earlier prophecy (34:23) where God promised David as the one shepherd and prince (*nasi'*) for all his people. Without using the expression of Jeremiah 31:31, Ezekiel is in effect promising a new covenant, "a covenant of peace" and "an everlasting covenant" (37:26).

God then promises to place his "sanctuary" (*miqdash*) and his "dwelling" (*mishkan*) in their midst forever. Such a temple would allow the nations of the world to know God (37:26–28). Later Ezekiel will try to visualize what that new sanctuary should look like in stone (chapters 40–43). Much later St. Paul would remind the community of Corinth, "You are the temple of God" (1 Cor 3:16).

* * *

The promises of national restoration flow into three symbolic visions of a holy war, with little connection to history or geography (chapters 38–39). The text looks a bit out of sync with the rest of Ezekiel and interrupts a natural flow from chapter 37 to 40 on the theme of the Temple. The two chapters may have been added by later disciples of the prophet, who could look back on the prophets "in former days" and felt the need to cite them as support (38:17). In each of the three visions, God leads his army against an enemy named "Gog." The story depicts the struggle between good and evil and promises the ultimate resolution of the struggle by God's conquest of "Gog." The names Magog, Meshech, and Tubal appear to be borrowed from Genesis 10:2 where they are all grandsons of Noah, although Ezekiel uses them as place names (38:2). Using the same story, the Book of Revelation in the New Testament transforms Magog into a second evil leader but still focuses on the overwhelming power of God to destroy evil (Rev 20:7–10).

C. EZEKIEL 40—48 / THE TORAH OF EZEKIEL

Concluding the book is a series of visions, attributed to "the hand of Yahweh." This part of the book has been called "the Torah of Ezekiel." Like the instructions given Moses on Sinai, these visions detail the geographical layout of Jerusalem and the Temple (chapters 40–42), the worship connected with the Temple and the major feasts (chapters 43–46), along with the boundaries of Israel and the distribution of the twelve tribes (chapters 47–48). It is basically a promise of Israel's restoration.

The prescriptions do not all agree with those of the later-compiled Pentateuch dealing with the same matters. Ezekiel's prescriptions were never implemented as written. To some degree they were an embarrassment in later Jewish theology, which simply left the matter in God's hands and for the messiah to explain (see Babylonian Talmud, *Shabbat* 13b; *Menachot* 45a).

The visions are dated to 571 BC, fourteen years after the destruction of Solomon's Temple (40:1). Ezekiel begins to look ahead but keeps an eye out on the past. His plans remove the palace of the prince far from the Temple and curtail previous royal privileges (43:7–9; 46:1–18). He sets up an elaborate series of gates and courts to screen out the unworthy and the foreigners (44:5–9). At the same time he describes a flow of special blessings proceeding from the new temple (47:1–12). He also provides for a new division of the land for all twelve tribes around the temple (48:13–35).

43:1–9 *The return of God's glory*

Perhaps the most important description in this elaborate reconstruction is that of the return of the glory of God to the new Temple. The movement described is the direct opposite of the one in 11:22–23, the departure of God's presence from the old Temple. The approach of God is accompanied with such glorious light and roaring sound that Ezekiel must fall on his face. However, the spirit lifts him up and allows him to hear God himself speaking.

With this return, the very meaning of the Temple is restored. Here God dwells among his people. God is not contained in the building. As God says, it is simply the "dwelling" where "my throne shall be" and where "I will set the soles of my feet" (43:7). This is the God of the cosmic thunderstorm, whose throne is above the firmament (chapter 1). However, as the house of God, the Temple in some way assures the nearness of God and a fellowship with God in his holy transcendence. In the old description of the people as "hard-hearted," such nearness to God was deadly. In the new description, with a new heart and a new spirit, this nearness is life-giving and a source of blessing.

44:4–9 *Exclusion from the Temple*

One of the first stipulations Ezekiel insists on is the exclusionary character of the new Temple. The discussion starts with the issue of service in the Temple. Apparently those responsible for the cult had preferred to hire non-Israelite servants rather than perform the jobs themselves (44:8). In a "baby with the bathwater" move, however, the prohibition becomes broader:

"No foreigners, uncircumcised in heart and in flesh, shall ever enter my sanctuary" (44:9 This exclusivism dominates the Book of Ezra (see Ezra 9). It stands in stark contrast to the open attitudes earlier of Isaiah and Micah (Isa 2:2–4; Mic 4:1–3) or later of Trito-Isaiah (see Isa 56:1–8; 66:18–21). At the time of Jesus, an inscription was placed somewhere in the Herodian Temple, prohibiting entrance to Gentiles under pain of death.

47:1–12 *The life-giving stream*

Before he closes, Ezekiel provides an image that will enrich the apocalyptic poetry of both Judaism (see Zech 14:8) and Christianity (Rev 22:1). It is the image of a life-giving stream flowing from the Jerusalem Temple. From this bountiful stream comes both food and healing. It starts at the "threshold" (*miphtan*) of the Temple on the east side, streams toward the desert of Judah and the Dead Sea, flowing as a shallow stream from under the south wall and rapidly increasing in volume until it is a deep river. The growth of the water suggests the pattern of small beginnings and great endings, like story of the mustard seed in the New Testament (Matt 13:31–32). By this water, the land is transformed into a great garden and the sea is changed into fresh water filled with life.

The transformation of this barren world into a garden of paradise is a dramatization of God's saving power. The stream flows because God now dwells in his Temple. Human fellowship with God transforms all creation. The previous stress on exclusion from entry into the temple is balanced here by the life-giving stream that flows outside and away from the Temple. The Fourth Gospel in the New Testament will envision a temple not made of stones, but rather of the body of Jesus (John 2:19–22) from whom also life-giving waters will flow (John 7:38; 19:34).

III. The Message of Ezekiel

A. REVIEW OF IMAGES AND THEMES

It takes a long list to name the prominent images in Ezekiel. We can organize them loosely around four topics:

First, we have images of Yahweh: the glory of Yahweh (1:28; 3:12, 23; 8:4; 9:3; 43:2–5; 44:4), in particular the image of that glory on the move, leaving the Temple of Jerusalem or returning there (10:4, 18–19; 11:22–23; 43:1–9). Connected with these images of God are those of his heavenly entourages, the cosmic creatures and the wheels (1:5–20; 10:9–22).

We also have images of God in his actions toward Israel: as ordering the saving mark on the forehead of some people in Jerusalem (9:3–6), as shepherd of Israel (34:11–16), and as judging between good and bad sheep and goats (34:17–22). Connected with these images are those of divine life-giving powers coming from God: the spirit giving life and transforming people (11:19; 18:31; 36:26–27; 37:5–9) as well as the spirit acting on the prophet (2:2; 3:12, 14, 24; 8:3; 37:1; 43:5), and the life-giving stream from the Temple (47:1–12).

We have images of Israel as a whole in her sinfulness, especially the scraggly vine (15:1–8) and the faithless spouse (16:1–43).

We also have images of Israel that are images of hope: the great tree (17:1–24), the new Davidic shepherd (34:23–24; 37:24–28), and two sticks (37:15–22), the dry bones that come to life (37:1–14).

Finally we have the actions of the prophet that were filled with meaning: eating the scroll (3:1–4), pantomiming and being unable to speak (4—5), lying on the ground bearing the sins of Israel and Judah (4:1–8), and losing his wife (24:15–23).

The characteristic themes of Ezekiel that organize his message seem to be the following:

- The divine covenant (16:8, 59, 61; 17:19; 44:7), called an everlasting covenant (16:60) and a covenant of peace (34:25; 37:26)
- The mobility of God (10:4, 18–19; 11:22–23; 43:1–9)
- Personal moral responsibility (18:1–32; 34:17–22)
- God's gift of a new heart and a new spirit for people (11:19–20; 36:26–27)
- The restoration of the Temple (40–44), with its exclusion of Gentiles (44:5–9)

B. The Theology of Ezekiel

1. *The glory and majesty of God.* As Jeremiah gazed into the abyss of God's presence, so also Ezekiel watched "the huge cloud" and "storm from the north" (1:4). In this dark abyss, Ezekiel saw the flashing glory of God, surrounded by life and motion, enthroned above all things in blazing fire, demanding purification and holiness on the part of anyone who would approach him. This glorious majesty of God becomes for Ezekiel the solid foundation by which he can understand the catastrophic events of history. No longer is the Temple or the city of Jerusalem the unshakable hope of the exiles. That Temple and city are destroyed. But God is above both. It is not therefore religious practice but fidelity to God that constitutes the covenant. This is the prophetic vision of God.

In Ezekiel, God is the God of the universe, clearly enthroned above the firmament. No longer seen as bound to the Temple and the city, he manifests his glory in the "unholy" plains of Babylonia (1:1–28). He is the God of all nations. The overall point and motivation behind God's promise of the "new heart" and "new spirit" is the vindication of his holy name among the nations. By his salvation of Israel, "the nations shall know that I am Yahweh" (36:23; see 39:7). The everlasting "covenant of peace" God promises to the reunited nation of Israel and Judah has repercussions for all the nations (37:26–28).

In the end, the great abyss closes and is replaced by a new Temple on earth and new prescriptions for cult (chapters 40–48). Perhaps such a Temple was the only way Ezekiel could imagine a complete restoration of Israel after the end of the Exile. It is clear that the priestly character of Ezekiel colors this aspect of his prophetic message. He draws importance to a distinct and identifiable place where God "dwells" among his people, albeit with divine mobility. In the final chapters of his book, he highlights the life-giving and healing character of the waters that flow from that Temple (Ezek 47) and links the imagery of life-giving waters to the Temple.

2. *Suffering and destruction.* Ezekiel opens a can of worms when he insists, "Only the one who sins shall die" (18:20). The

prophet may have been insisting on people taking control of their situation and not blaming the past generation for their suffering. However, by forging the link between sin and death in the way he does, Ezekiel rubs salt in the wounds of suffering people who have tried to be good. The Book of Job will protest this link.

Ezekiel himself, however, is aware how he must participate in this punishment. He must bear in his paralyzed body the sins of the people (4:4–8). He must experience the loss of his life's delight, just as the people must experience the loss of the Temple (24:15–24). He does not confess his sinfulness.

The visions of future restoration—the dry bones coming to life, the reconstruction of the Temple—all seem to be part of some attempt to deal with suffering and destruction. Punishment is not God's last word. The larger picture—including some future events—forms a perspective for dealing with present disaster. Ezekiel basically proposes hope.

3. *Ezekiel and Jeremiah.* The comparison of Ezekiel with Jeremiah is a valuable tool to discover Ezekiel's special message. Although both surrender themselves to God, in personalities they are really miles apart. Jeremiah is the emotional and sensitive youth. Ezekiel is the disciplined man of power. Both are thrown into distressing turmoil because of the sins of the people. Jeremiah must face the hostility of the leaders, the same hostility that God faced. Ezekiel, however, does not seem to face much personal opposition. On the other hand, he must go into exile with the punished people. The distress and turmoil of Ezekiel is that of one who does not know sin but must become one with the sinfulness of the people as God draws the prophet into the destructive forces of sin.

Both Jeremiah and Ezekiel are from priestly families, but the priesthood of Ezekiel fully marks his prophetic message. In Jeremiah, God converses with the prophet, responds to his hesitation, touches his lips. In Ezekiel, God simply commands (chapters 2–3). The lowly "son of man" does not challenge the decisions of the enormous and awesome reality that overpowers any human being coming in contact with its majestic glory, blazing in supernatural splendor. God is God. This is the priestly vision of God.

4. *The new covenanted community.* Ezekiel sees this new life starting earlier with a community removed from the land of Israel. The Judean establishment is described as perverse from the beginning of their history (chapter 16). The promises of the past mean nothing now. Instead God reaches outside the land of Israel to find a small, humble group with whom he can set up his "everlasting covenant" (16:59–63). Under a new David, this covenant will be established (34:23–30), and the establishment of this new community will be nothing less than the resurrection of the dead, caused by the gift of God's spirit (37:1–14).

Ezekiel insists that all future salvation will involve a new heart and a new spirit in the breast of the worshiper. God will purify his people by their return to Temple cult but more importantly by the purifying waters of his spirit that he will place within them (36:24–28). St. Paul will insist that the Corinthian community is the temple of God precisely because the Spirit of God dwells in them (1 Cor 3:16).

The historical intention of Ezekiel and all the others who contributed to this book was focused on the exiles in Babylon and on keeping their hope alive until God in his mysterious ways brought them back to Judah. Yet his descriptions of God's salvation contained a sketch of God's ways that would appear in bold lines in the New Testament.

Paul would draw heavily on both Ezekiel and Jeremiah as he struggled to comprehend what God had done in Jesus. The law written in the heart by the ink of the Spirit (2 Cor 3) combines images from both Old Testament prophets. A community based on faith in the resurrection of the dead, a community that begins the resurrected life through the down payment of the Spirit, a community not living in Jerusalem, worshiping a God not welded to the Jerusalem Temple, a community that is to radiate its light to the nations, not by the exercise of imperial power but by the observance of God's law of the heart—these are all themes that Paul saw as constituting the "new covenant." But these are themes already sketched in Ezekiel in his vision of the "everlasting covenant."

12
Deutero-Isaiah (Isa 40—55)

I. Overview

A. AUTHORSHIP OF ISAIAH 40—55

Until a century ago, most believers held that all sixty-six chapters of the Book of Isaiah had been written by hand by the eighth-century Judean prophet, even though chapters 40–66 clearly addressed the Jews in exile some 150 years later. As scholars learned more about the editorial process at work behind the compilation of the book, they discovered solid reasons for thinking that chapters 40–66 were the work of one or more later prophets. Besides the differences in style and theological emphasis between these chapters and the work of the eighth-century Isaiah, the following points became convincing for many scholars:

a. The prophet addresses himself to the exiles in Babylon and shows a knowledge of Babylonian worship of idols and stars.
b. Nothing whatever is said about events in Jerusalem at the time of Hezekiah.
c. The captivity and the destruction of Jerusalem are described as past, not future.
d. The prophet is concerned with the end of the Exile and the return to Jerusalem.
e. Cyrus is described as a contemporary.
f. Neither Jeremiah nor Ezekiel mention or show any familiarity with the prophecies of Isaiah 40—66.

We know that Isaiah had disciples who cared for his writings (see Isa 8:16). It is not improbable, therefore, that a "school of Isaiah," made up of preachers, writers, and editors, developed the message of the prophet, using favorite images of the prophet—like "the Holy One of Israel"—during and sometime after the Exile. They then would have collected all their writings in one volume under Isaiah's name. The prophet (or prophets) behind the writings of chapters 40–55, therefore, appears as a parallel to Ezekiel addressing his fellow exiles in Babylonia.

Isaiah 56—66, with its shift to a postexilic perspective as well as with its different style and mood, appears to be the work of yet another later author. We will look at those chapters when we treat the prophets who arose after the Exile.

B. THE PROPHET

Beyond the few details we can glean from remarks in his work, we know almost nothing about the prophet responsible for Isaiah 40—55, whom we generally call "Deutero" (the Greek word for "second") Isaiah. Internal evidence in these chapters indicates that he preached in Babylon in the last decades of the Exile. The writing of these chapters occurred probably around 539 BC. Cyrus, the Persian king mentioned in this book, defeated the Babylonians in 539 BC. His decree in 538 BC allowing the Jews to return home from exile is not mentioned in this book, suggesting that Deutero-Isaiah ended his preaching before that date.

The brief mention of a command, "Cry out!" along with the hesitating response starting with the words, "What shall I cry out?" seems to be all we have of a "call narrative." Yet these brief lines would suggest that the author saw himself in the pattern of the prophets. We can picture him as a powerful speaker who pursued his mission with determination. His writing moves consistently on lyric heights. When contemplating the great things God has in store for Israel, it turns rhapsodical. When faced with the exiles' stubborn resistance, it becomes tragic.

As it appears, Deutero-Isaiah's purpose is to console, encourage, and inspire the disillusioned and fainthearted exiles, who saw no hope of returning to Jerusalem and were in danger of being won over to the morals and idolatry of Babylon. The Jews in exile could continue some community life, and nothing suggests they suffered any persecution. Nevertheless, it was a terrible time for the exiled believers in Yahweh. Jerusalem and the Temple were destroyed. The Davidic dynasty had ended. The priesthood had stopped functioning. The ruined land was under foreign domination. Judging from appearances, Yahweh had ceased acting for his people.

The prophet addressed these dispirited exiles, who were wavering between putting their trust in God and abandoning hope. To encourage and inspire them, Deutero-Isaiah stressed the very figure of God, highlighting his care and power.

C. THE BOOK

The subdivision of Isaiah 40–55 remains conjectural; however, a shift occurs between chapter 48 and 49 both in mood and themes. Furthermore, chapters 40 and 55 seem to form an inclusion by the repetition of several common motifs, a rhetorical technique used freely by Old Testament and New Testament authors to indicate the beginning and ending of a passage or of a whole book. We therefore group the sermons now collected in Deutero-Isaiah as follows:

Isaiah 40:   Opening introduction
Isaiah 41—48:   The New Exodus of Israel
Isaiah 49—54:   The Word of Comfort to Zion
Isaiah 55:   Conclusion

Spread through chapters 40–55 are the four so-called servant songs (42:1–4; 49:1–6; 50:4–9; 52:13—53:12). They may be later additions, but they generally relate to the thought and themes of their present contexts.

(See Appendix 4j for a detailed outline of the Book of Deutero-Isaiah.)

D. TORAH TRADITIONS IN DEUTERO-ISAIAH

Deutero-Isaiah is quite aware of primeval and patriarchal traditions, including Eden, the garden of Yahweh (51:3), Noah and the flood (54:9), Abraham and Sarah (41:8; 51:2), the unusual title for God, "the mighty one of Jacob" (*'abir ya'aqob*; 49:26 see Gen 49:24), God's promise of descendants to Abraham (48:18–19). He is familiar with the Exodus traditions (43:16; 51:10; 52:4), including such details like the drowning of Pharaoh's army in the sea (43:16–17; see Exod 14:21—15:21) or the rock that provided water for the Israelites in the desert (48:21; see Exod 16:6; Num 20:11). Creation is also a major theme for Deutero-Isaiah (40:26, 28; 44:24; 45:7, 12, 18; 48:13; 51:13, 16), but his descriptions of creation show few literary contacts with Genesis accounts.

Deutero-Isaiah lived in close geographical and temporal proximity to Ezekiel, who attempted so intently to reestablish the identity of Israel on the basis of cult and law—a Judaism centered on an elaborated Torah. Yet, he gives no prescription for cult, mentioning it only once as a metaphor for the death of the suffering servant (53:10). Only one text in Deutero-Isaiah refers (twice) to the Torah as the Law of God (42:21, 24), according to which Israel should walk.

This prophet is oriented far more to the future than to the past traditions (43:18–19). For Deutero-Isaiah, the reconstruction of Israel lies far more in the new things God is doing. Hence it is hard to evaluate his relative silence about the development of the Pentateuch as we know it. This period later in the Exile may well be the time when priestly circles were collecting and canonizing writings and traditions. But the prophet is little interested in a canon fixed in the past.

II. Significant Passages in Deutero-Isaiah

A. ISAIAH 40 / INTRODUCTION

40:1–11 *The announcement of salvation*

Without the usual title verse introducing the prophet and this book, this collection begins immediately with a command of

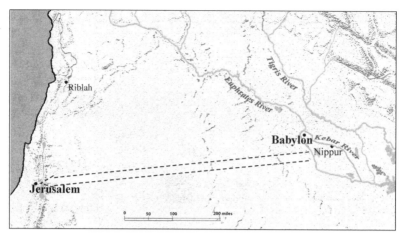

12A—Deutero-Isaiah's Highway through the Desert

God, presumably to some listening assembly. (The Hebrew imperatives here are plural.) The command is "to comfort" the exiles. The words of comfort will dominate the entire book, which are here summarized as an end to a term of service and the pardon of iniquity.

The next two subsections are introduced by "a voice," speaking about God and, therefore, apparently other than God. As though following the orders of the previous command to comfort the people, the voice first orders preparations for a journey through the desert (40:3–5), presumably due west from Babylonia to Judah through the impassible Arabian desert (see Map 12A). The image is that of the Exodus with Yahweh leading his people and revealing his glory. Like Ezekiel, Deutero-Isaiah envisions a kind of mobile glory of God (see Ezek 43:1), not so much as a cloud moving through the sky, but as a luminous presence leading his people along a highway of salvation (see Exod 13:21), a saving presence that all humanity will be able to see.

The voice then commands the prophet to cry out (40:6–8). We have in these verses something resembling the "call narrative" of a prophet. The response, "What shall I cry out?" functions here in the place of the usual prophetic-call hesitation. This word of hesitation becomes clearer if we take the next lines (vv. 6b–7) as though spoken by the prophet, "All flesh is grass."

What's the use? The response to the prophet by the heavenly voice (v. 8) contrasts this short-lived and unreliable existence of humanity with the eternal stability of the word of God. This proclamation introduces the main point and focus of the entire book (see 55:11). This is the word of comfort.

A third subsection (40:9–11) is directed to Zion, the city of Jerusalem, who is also to announce the coming of Yahweh. The perspective shifts from Babylon to Judah, to where God comes both with power and might. He comes like a shepherd feeding his flock, carrying them in his arms, leading them with care. Yahweh is the good shepherd gathering and leading his flock.

The act of announcing God's coming is called "proclaiming good news" (v. 9 Hebrew: *mebasser*, Greek: *euangelizôn*). The term *gospel* comes from this verb. Mark will use this word to introduce his collection of stories about Jesus: "The beginning of the gospel of Jesus Christ" (Mark 1:1). The conscious reference back to Deutero-Isaiah appears in Mark's adapted citation of Isaiah 40:3 (Mark 1:3), whereby the desert is the place of the voice of John the Baptist, not that of the highway to be built. In the beginning of John's Gospel, John the Baptist explicitly identifies himself as "the voice crying in the desert, 'Make straight the way of the Lord'" (John 1:23).

40:12–17 *The transcendence of God*

With a series of challenging questions as part of a dispute with another, the prophet proclaims the transcendence of Yahweh and his plans. The disputing opponent apparently is the one who later in the chapter complains, "My way is hidden from Yahweh. My right is disregarded by my God" (40:27).

In response, Deutero-Isaiah pictures God as a giant dominating the heavens and the earth, even the most massive realities, the sea, the heavens, the mountains (40:12, 22). More important, God, according to the prophet, operates by a plan far beyond the range of human knowledge (40:13–14). If the disasters that befell Israel seem incomprehensible, such a mystery is only the tip of God's iceberglike plans. In comparison to God, the achievements of the great nations are as drops of water or as dust or fine powder. They do not count (40:15, 23–24). This proclamation of God's transcendence also forms part the central thought of the book (see 55:8).

40:18–20 *Ridicule of idolatry*

The thought then turns to the gods of Babylonia. Deutero-Isaiah deals many times with Israel's temptation to worship the idols of their captors. He ridicules the making of an idol by human hands and the absurd belief that woodworkers could manufacture a god. The details of 41:6–7 continue the ridicule of idolatry. (The present placement of these last verses looks like the result of some awkward editing.)

40:21–31 *Yahweh the Creator*

By contrast, Yahweh dominates both the whole universe and the course of history. The motif of God the Creator of all things (40:26, 28) appears regularly in Deutero-Isaiah (44:24; 45:7, 12, 18; 48:13; 51:13, 16; see also Amos 4:13; 5:8–9; 9:5–6). Since the whole universe belongs to Yahweh, he can be trusted to be a savior. Since Yahweh is the Creator, then he is the only God. Deutero-Isaiah proclaims not simply that Yahweh is the only God for Israel, but rather, "There is no other God" (see 45:5–7, 18).

The discouraged Jews, however, are saying that Yahweh has abandoned Israel (40:27). This complaint of abandonment may be the setting that called forth both the earlier proclamation of God's transcendence (40:12–17) as well as the lawsuit scene in 41:21 (see also 49:14). In response to this accusation, the prophet directs his listeners to focus on God. In the praise of Yahweh, the Eternal One and the Creator of heaven and earth (40:28), Israel will find strength and hope. This almighty God "gives strength to the weary and new vigor to the exhausted" (40:29)—the divine comfort announced at the beginning of the chapter.

B. ISAIAH 41—48 / THE NEW EXODUS

41:1–5 *The God of history*

The prophet shifts focus from the creative function of Yahweh to God's control over all history. God appointed "the champion of justice," to whom the nations of the world are delivered. Deutero-Isaiah has in mind Cyrus the Great, the king of the Persians, who will be named again in 44:28 and eventually described as God's *mashiach* (45:1), God's "anointed." The Hebrew word gives us the English word "messiah." The Greek translation of the same word, *christos*, gives us the word "christ."

42:1–4 *The first servant song*

Interrupting a trial scene that began in 41:21 and seems to continue in 42:8–9—suggesting an earlier composition of the song and later insertion into the present text—these four verses focus on a person who appears to be an individual named simply as "my servant." God speaks throughout this song, first identifying this servant, "my chosen one," "with whom I am pleased," "on whom I have put my spirit" (42:1). The mission of the servant is to bring "fair judgment" (*mishpat*) to the nations (42:1, 4), and "instruction" (*torah*) to pagan lands. The servant's task has universal scope. Yet the servant fulfills his mission in a quiet and gentle way (42:2–3), a method that distinguishes him from Cyrus. The reference to the servant "not growing dim or being broken" before finishing his task (40:4) appears to hint at some form of suffering.

The words of God identifying the servant appear in the gospel account of the baptism and transfiguration of Jesus where the voice of God identifies Jesus (Matt 3:16–17 and parallels; Matt 17:5 and parallels). In another story, the Gospel of Matthew uses the description of this gentle servant to depict the work of Jesus (Matt 12:18–21).

Does Deutero-Isaiah have in mind a particular individual as he pens these words? A chapter earlier, the text names "Israel" as God's "servant" and "Jacob" as the one God "has chosen" (Isa 41:8; see also 44:1, 3). Furthermore, in the next servant song, the servant will be named "Israel" (49:3), where he is then distinguished from Jacob and Israel (49:5).

If the songs were written earlier and then inserted in these chapters of edited sermons, we might need to distinguish an original identification, which appears to be that of an individual, and a secondary identification, which appears to be collective. The superimposition of the two identifications corresponds to the ancient idea of collective personality and of an individual's power to stand for the whole.

43:11–21 *The new future*

This series of oracles begins with an identification formula, "I am Yahweh" (43:11). Two actions of God are mentioned in the same breath, "I [fore]told, I saved" (43:12). The fulfillment of past prophecies is for Deutero-Isaiah one of the signs of God's reliability (46:9–10). The name of God, "the Holy One of Israel" (43:14; see 40:25; 41:14; 43:3; 48:17), ties Deutero-Isaiah to the eighth-century Isaiah, suggesting there was something like a "school" in which the great prophet's words were studied and developed.

Deutero-Isaiah then reports a word of God that is nothing less than revolutionary: "Remember not the events of the past" (43:18–19)! The faith of Israel was based on remembering the events of the past. A prophet proclaiming "something new" with such emphasis as to blot out the past should have shocked the faithful listener.

In fact, however, Deutero-Isaiah does also proclaim the need to remember the past (see 46:8). In the prophets, typology from the past is often combined with the concept of newness—a new David, a new covenant. Actually Deutero-Isaiah clearly alludes to the past events of the Exodus (43:16–17) in his command not to remember the past. The paradox proclaimed here basically expresses the transcendence of God. Attention to "something new" means opening oneself to the mystery of God's love.

C. ISAIAH 49—54 / THE WORD OF COMFORT

49:1–6 *The second servant song*

Interrupting descriptions of a new Exodus (48:21–22; continued in 49:9b–12), a second song describes the "servant" of God. This time the servant himself is the speaker, addressing foreign lands. He starts with a description of his vocation (49:1, 5), much like that of Jeremiah (see Jer 1:10). Like a prophet, the mission of the servant involves speaking (49:2). Like Jeremiah, we hear a complaint from the servant (Isa 49:4). Although the prophet immediately adds a note of confidence in God, we detect here the element of resistance and frustration.

The servant explains his mission as a twofold development. In the past it was to gather Israel back to God (49:5), and now it is to be a "light to the nations," an instrument of God's salvation "to the ends of the earth" (49:6; see Luke 2:32), words reminiscent of Jeremiah's call to be a "prophet to the nations" (Jer 1:5).

The description of the servant's mission *to Israel* strongly suggests that the identification of the servant as "Israel" (49:3) is a later addition to the song, perhaps when it was incorporated into this collection of sermons. The references in this song to the mother of the servant and to his mouth clearly imply an original identification of the servant as an individual. Whatever the history of the text, the identification of this individual with Israel is an affirmation of the representative role of the servant. What is said of the servant can be said in some way of the people of Israel, who take on a prophet role as a nation.

49:14–18 *The comforting of Zion*

The next section begins with a lament: "Yahweh has forsaken me. My Lord has forgotten me" (49:14; see 40:27). The prophet disputes this despondent observation. The consoling response includes two feminine images. In the first, God is compared to a mother who does not forget her infant (49:15). In the second, Israel is compared to a bride adorned for the wedding (49:18).

50:4–9 *The third servant song*

The imagery of cloth in 50:3, which seems to continue in 50:9b, is interrupted by another servant song. The servant again is the speaker, describing his work as distinctly that of a prophet, one with a "well-trained tongue…to speak to the weary" (50:4). But this prophet is in constant contact—"morning after morning"—with the word of God (50:4). He encounters bitter hostility, beatings, and insults—which he accepts without protecting or defending himself (50:6). He defies his enemies to appear in court with him. He is confident that God will support him (50:7–9). This description strongly recalls the "confessions" of

Jeremiah, who suffered bitterly because of his prophetic mission yet expressed confidence in God (see Jer 20:7–13).

52:13—53:12 *The fourth servant song*

God is the speaker, alternating with a chorus of observers. The song begins and ends with the exaltation of the servant, recognized by the nations (52:13–15; 53:10b–12).

Sandwiched between these sections, the chorus describes the servant's sufferings (53:1–10). The description is like the description of a dead person, "like a lamb led to the slaughter," "cut off from the land of the living," and "assigned a grave" (53:7–9; see Jer 11:19). The chorus focuses on his wretchedness along with the contempt he received from others. He was sick, pierced, wounded, killed, whipped, imprisoned, and given a degrading burial.

Given equal insistence is the affirmation of his personal innocence. The servant was "crushed for our sins" (53:5). It was "our infirmities" and "our sufferings" that he bore (53:4). "Our guilt" was laid on him (53:6). The chorus changes its understanding of the servant's sufferings as it recognizes its own sinfulness and guilt.

The affirmation of vicarious suffering is hinted at in the story of Moses (Deut 3:26; 4:21) and Ezekiel (Ezek 4:4, 6). Here, however, it is proclaimed with unique clarity: "Upon him was the chastisement that makes us whole, by his stripes we were healed" (53:5). Thus when the servant is described as struck "for the sin of his people" (53:8), that word *for* (*min*) takes on a meaning charged with the mystery of redemptive suffering.

Like its beginning, the ending of the song describes the vindication and success of the servant. Furthermore, this vindication comes from the hand of God: "I will give him a portion with the great" (53:12). Since his suffering and humiliation seem to have ended in death, this personally experienced triumph apparently proclaims a life after death. The song is a promise of restoration, without a clear indication of what that restoration after death consists of. The descriptions regarding "seeing his descendants," "dividing spoils," and being given "his portion among the great" are taken from traditional expressions of happiness now found in psalms of thanksgiving and lamentations. This vindication and personal reward, however, provide a glimpse at personal life after death. This description might be one of the earliest texts in the Bible to express faith in life after death—the only real answer to the suffering of good people in this world.

The ending points back to the saving effect the servant has for others: "My servant will justify the many….He shall take away the sins of the many" (53:11–12). The expression, "the many," here is equivalent to "all." The word "many" (*rabim*) occurs five times in this song. The universal outlook of the song is unparalleled in the Old Testament.

The text was a favorite of New Testament authors who pondered the mystery of Jesus' death. Quotations of the song occur in different New Testament books, suggesting it was part of the common repertoire of Christian preachers (Luke 22:37; Act 8:32–33; 1 Pet 2:22–24). Matthew cites the text but changes its meaning to explain Jesus' healings (Matt 8:17). Paul alludes to the text several times (Rom 4:25; 8:3; 10:16; 15:21; 2 Cor 5:21; Gal 3:13; Phil 2:9) and perhaps built his theology of redemptive suffering upon the servant of Deutero-Isaiah.

While the New Testament use of the text provides insight into the divine reality sketched by this text, we must not lose sight of the historical intention of the author. The prophet was speaking to his people in the sixth century BC suffering great sorrow. If he intended the collective sense of the servant, then he saw in the horrors of destruction and deportation a way in which great healing and redemption will take place "for the many." If he intended to describe an individual, his description fits one person from the recent past remarkably well, Jeremiah. Chosen from the womb, given a prophet's voice, rejected and cut off from the living, like a lamb led to the slaughter, Jeremiah may well have been on the mind of the author, who could now see in the suffering of the prophet the saving action of God.

Why did not Deutero-Isaiah simply identify the servant as Jeremiah? Why the deliberate and tantalizing anonymity? Perhaps the specific person of Jeremiah was less important than the pattern of God's saving ways that Deutero-Isaiah saw looming through and behind the person of Jeremiah. That pattern could be found in others going all the way back to Moses, also named as God's servant (Exod 14:31). A later editor could see Israel as a whole fitting the role (Isa 49:3).

D. Isaiah 55 / Conclusion

55:1–13 *The conclusion*
This chapter functions as a grand finale, including a subtle reinterpretation of the Davidic covenant to now apply to the people as a whole (55:3–5). What is interesting in this chapter is the way the major themes of Deutero-Isaiah introduced in chapter 40 reappear for review.

- 55:1–2 starts the chapter with a call to approach God for nourishment and care. 40:11 described God like a shepherd who feeds his flock.
- 55:8–9 expresses the transcendence of God's ways above human ways and thoughts. 40:13–14 insisted that no one advises God or acts as his counselor.
- 55:10–11 praises the power of God's word accomplishing what it is sent to do. 40:8 proclaimed the permanence of God's word.
- 55:12–13 proclaims a new Exodus with the transformation of nature. 40:3–4 issued the command to prepare a highway for God in the wasteland.

Twice St. Paul used the text of Isaiah 55:8–9, as he grappled with the meaning of the crucifixion (1 Cor 2:16) and again as he tried to account for Israel's place in the plan of God (Rom 11:34).

Deutero-Isaiah personifies God's word as a messenger who executes God's decisions (55:11). What God has spoken through the prophet will take place. Much later, the author of Wisdom will use the same personification to describe the power of God's word (Wis 18:14–16). This figure appears as the Fourth Gospel attempts to probe the origins and nature of Jesus, "In the beginning was the Word…and the Word became flesh" (John 1:1, 14).

III. The Message of Deutero-Isaiah

A. REVIEW OF IMAGES AND THEMES

The Book of Deutero-Isaiah is filled with various images of God, the cosmic God (40:12, 22), God as mother (49:15), God shepherding his flock (40:11; see Jer 23:3; Ezek 34:12–15). The salvation of God for Israel in this book revolves especially around the images of a saving journey (49:22; 52:11–12), especially a joyful new Exodus (40:3–5; 51:10; 55:12), a highway for God (40:3–5), specifically a return from Babylon (48:20–21). Other characteristic images include Zion as mother (54:1–3), Cyrus the instrument of God (41:2; 44:28; 48:14–16), the messenger with good tidings (40:9; 52:7), and the everlasting covenant of peace (54:10; 55:3; see Ezek 16:60; 34:25; 37:26).

When we look for the more developed themes, the one that dominates is that of the unshakable love of Yahweh for Israel (54:10). This theme appears in a multitude of forms:

- Yahweh's will to care for and comfort Israel (40:1–2, 11; 52:9)
- Yahweh as the husband of Israel (54:5–8)
- Yahweh as God of Gentile nations (45:1–22)
- Yahweh as the redeemer, savior of Israel (41:14; 43:1, 3; 44:6)
- The servant of God as the instrument of God's salvation (42:1–4; 49:1–6; 50:4–10; 52:13—53:12) with a portrayal of vicarious suffering and redemption (53:5–6, 8)

These themes are then aligned with several that focus on the power and transcendence of God:

- The power of God's word (40:8; 55:11)
- The power of God giving strength to the weary (40:28–31)
- Yahweh, the Creator of all things (40:26, 28; 44:24; 45:7, 12, 18; 48:13; 51:13, 16) and therefore the only God (45:5–6, 18, 21, 22; 46:9)

- Yahweh, the master of history (40:23–24; 41:2; 47:1–15; 48:20) who can accurately predict the future (43:9; 44:7–8)
- The transcendence of God's incomprehensible plans and thoughts (40:13–14; 55:8–9)
- God's willingness to create something new (43:18–19)
- The folly of idolatry (40:18–20; 41:6–7; 44:9–20; 46:1–2, 6–7)

B. THE THEOLOGY OF DEUTERO-ISAIAH

1. *The universal God who comforts.* The tapestry woven from these themes develops the picture of an incomprehensible abyss from which echoes the command, "Comfort my people" (Isa 40:1). This is a message from a God who seems to have abandoned his people. This is a message from a God whose ways and thoughts are immeasurably beyond our ways and thoughts (55:8) so that one gazing on this God will see only darkness, a dimension that may appear to be a huge empty abyss.

Yet the message from this abyss is that of love. Although hidden, God promises salvation. To hope in this help and salvation one must forget the things of the past (43:18–19). Salvation will come from a mysterious future, something new, a future for which the person of faith can only wait. The restoration of Israel will not be simply a return to the way things were. This prophet provides no elaborate plans for rebuilding the Temple or reestablishing the Davidic monarchy. This prophet is open to the great mystery of God's creative love.

We are reminded that this God is the God who created all things (42:5) and directs all of history (41:1–5), the cosmic giant who cups in his hand the waters of the seas (40:12), the first and the last (44:6). The word of comfort that comes forth from God is thus likened to the creative word that issued from the primal abyss (Gen 1). This is the creative word by which all things arise in absolute novelty. This comforting abyss is the powerful source of the universe, the ground of all reality, the controlling hand behind all history.

Furthermore, if God is the Creator of all things, all nature and all peoples, then there is no other God but Yahweh. In that view of God, all peoples are related. Therefore, among the new things for the faith was also an attitude of openness to the Gentiles. Cyrus, the Persian king, becomes God's *mashiach*. God issues a universal call, "Turn to me and be safe, all you ends of the earth, for I am God; there is no other!" (45:22). To his own people, God offers salvation through the hands of the "pagan" Cyrus—who in fact worshiped many other gods.

2. *Redemptive suffering.* At the very depths of this mystery of God is also the message of redemption through suffering. No longer do we have promises of great warriors and kings to lead the people powerfully out of oppression. No longer do we have the hope for a wisdom like Solomon that will bedazzle the kings and queens of the earth. The promised redemption comes from a servant who is despised and crushed, who carries our infirmities, sufferings, and guilt (53:4–6). The servant stands in the midst of the abyss and gives his life in silence. And we, the onlookers, gaze at the same abyss speechless and in amazement (52:14–15).

With his portrayal of redemptive suffering in the image of the suffering servant (Isa 53), Deutero-Isaiah also provides a response to the problem posed by Ezekiel's insistence on personal responsibility. How do we understand the death or suffering of the good person? Within the ancient structures of national solidarity, good people understandably suffered with bad people because they were all "in the same boat." With the destruction of those structures and end of that sense of solidarity, suffering and death were linked by Ezekiel to an individual's sinfulness. Soon the Book of Job will arise to protest this simple association of suffering and sin. Suffering and death may not be indicative of a person's evil character.

With Isaiah 53 a new logic arises based on a deeper link of solidarity. The innocent can stand in the place of the sinner, and the suffering of the innocent takes on redemptive value for the sinner. The good person may undergo suffering and death *for the* other. The good person's suffering may become a healing power for the sinner. Solidarity is reestablished on a deeper level.

On the level of the final redaction, the suffering servant seems to be identified with the people of Israel as a whole. If this holds true, we have a theology of national suffering, which could have extreme importance given the horrific suffering of the Jewish people, particularly in the last century. By their wounds we are healed. As if Christ's crucifixion were continued in the Nazi death camps, their suffering brings redemption to "the many."

Because Deutero-Isaiah proclaims God and his ways as a truth that transcends even the prophet's mission and words, Deutero-Isaiah's historical message contains a message for every age—which in fact successive ages recognized by their rereading of this book. When the New Testament focused on the suffering servant to find some meaning in the suffering and death of Jesus, it clearly went beyond the intention of the sixth-century prophet. Yet by providing this overlay, the New Testament allows the message of this prophet to ring with new overtones concerning God's salvation. Suffering could clearly be "for" another (Rom 4:25). Suffering and death had been seen by the earlier prophets as a kind of remedial punishment for sin. Now the suffering and death of the innocent becomes the very instrument for destroying sin itself. "By his stripes we are healed." "He shall take away the sins of the many."

The glimpse at life after death in the description of the suffering servant adds the nuance that suffering and death are not the final words. Having been "cut off from the land of the living" and "given a grave with the wicked," the servant is highly exalted and sees his descendants (53:13, 10–11). Exaltation after death is now part of God's redemptive action. The deliberate lack of precision by the poet is tantalizing. We cannot see exactly what happens. Clearly, however, in the end good triumphs even over death—whether the words describing this triumph be read from the perspective of a Babylonian exile or that of a modern reader anguishing over the suffering in this world.

PART III

The Postexilic Prophets

13
Historical Background

Read Ezra 1—6; 1 Chronicles 3:17–19.

What Jeremiah foretold from afar, what Ezekiel envisioned in the resurrection of the dead bones, and what Deutero-Isaiah described as the new thing on the horizon, became fact in 539 BC when Cyrus the Great defeated the Babylonians, established the Persian Empire, and decreed the return and reestablishment of the Jews in the land of their birth.

The history of that return and resettlement is told in Ezra-Nehemiah, the last part of the Chronicler's history. The prophetic books of Trito-Isaiah, Haggai, and Zechariah fill in some of the history between 520 and 516 BC. Mal'aki gives some idea of conditions prevailing around 460–450 BC. Other than these very incomplete accounts, mostly silence covers this period down to the time of the Maccabees in the early second century.

The return to the land of Judah began shortly after Cyrus's edict of 538 BC (see Map 13B). A Jewish prince, Sheshbazzar, the son of Jehoiachin, led the first group of repatriates. Some years later, the nephew of Sheshbazzar, Zerubbabel, led another group back to Israel. The Book of Ezra-Nehemiah names both Zerubbabel and Sheshbazzar and describes their work (Ezra 1:8—3:2). Zerubbabel, son of Shealtiel, appears in both prophets Haggai and Zechariah. Their names also appear in the genealogy of 1 Chronicles 3:17–19 as descendants of Jeconiah (Jehoiachin), where Zerubbabel, however, is named a son of Pedaiah. This part of the Davidic family tree can be diagrammed as follows (see diagram 13A):

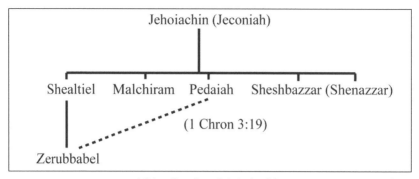

13A—Family of Jehoiachin

The information available to us shows that the exiles returned to the stark reality of a poor and devastated homeland, bristling with economic and political problems, and surrounded by hostile Samaritans to the north and unfriendly Edomites to the south. It also shows a Judaism isolating itself from the world with the mentality inspired by Ezekiel 40—48.

The first task of the repatriates was to reestablish the sacrificial cult of Yahweh, interrupted by the destruction of the Temple some fifty years earlier. Under Zerubbabel and a high priest by the name of Jeshua (named "Joshua" in Haggai and Zechariah), son of Jozadak, an altar was built for the offering of holocausts "as prescribed in the Law of Moses" (Ezra 3:2). Jeshua and Zerubbabel apparently shared leadership in Israel at this time, as reported also in the prophets Haggai and Zechariah, in an apparently priestly-Davidic power share.

Around the year 536 BC, the foundations for a new Temple were laid. When Zerubbabel, Jeshua, and the other leaders of the Jews refused the local people any part in the Temple construction, these local people, now known as Samaritans, took a hostile position toward the Jews and successfully blocked further construction of the Temple until 520. As a result of a series of political interventions to the court of the new Persian emperor, Darius I (521–485), work on the Temple was restarted and completed with a solemn dedication in 515.

Apparently the next major step some sixty years later in the reestablishment of Israel was the rebuilding of the walls around Jerusalem along with the institution of several social reforms—all under the leadership of Nehemiah, a Jewish layman with considerable political power in Persia. The work of Nehemiah should be dated from 445 to 433.

Armed also with considerable political power from the Persian court, Ezra, the Jewish priest and scribe, traveled to Judea to institute religious reforms. His work is dated from the seventh year of the Persian emperor, Artaxerxes (see Ezra 17:7), who most likely should be identified with Artaxerxes II (404–358). Most likely, then, the mission of Ezra should be dated at 398, some thirty-five years after Nehemiah. In the Book of Ezra-Nehemiah the stories of the two Jewish leaders are interwoven so as to give the impression that they were contemporaries of each other (see Map 13B).

In the stories of Ezra-Nehemiah, we see the development of Judaism as a religion of the Law. In these stories, "the book of the Law" or "the book of the Law of Moses" figures prominently, as binding not just on the king but on all Jews. Jews are now defined by their observance of the Law and by a sense of exclusivity in regard to all other nations. Mixed marriages were annulled, and non-Jewish spouses were expelled from Israel along with the children of these marriages (see Ezra 9; Neh 13:23–31).

It is in this "Persian period" of Israel that the Old Testament develops. This is probably the period when the Torah takes the form we know today. The development of the Torah and its

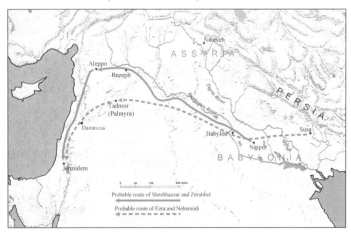

13B—The Return from Exile

movement into the center of Jewish life is dramatized by the story of Ezra bringing forth "the book of the Law of Moses" and reading it aloud to the whole assembly with all the people responding, "Amen, amen!" (Neh 8:1–12). In this period the writings of the prophets are also collected and appended to the deuteronomistic history. The early collections of psalms are gathered into a continuous book. Existing wisdom literature is also gathered and new reflections added, including protests against the exclusivity of Ezra-Nehemiah, like the books of Jonah and Ruth.

With the disappearance of the kings and the rise to political power of the priests, prophets are moved to the back burner. Apart from Trito-Isaiah, the prophets of this period are for the most part connected with the Temple and cult.

The chronology of the early postexilic period would include the following important dates:

539–333	The Persian period, extending from the conquest of Babylon by Cyrus to the conquest of Persia by Alexander the Great
538–537	Return of the first exiles to Israel
536–515	Reconstruction of the Temple; foundations laid in 536 but construction interrupted until 516
522–485	The reign of Darius I, repulsed by the Greeks at Marathon in 490
485–465	The reign of Xerxes I, defeated by the Greeks at Thermopylae and Salamis
480–350	The golden age of Greece
465–424	The reign of Artaxerxes I, patron of Nehemiah
460–450	The preaching of "Mal'aki"; a time of apathy and despair
445–433	Nehemiah's work of rebuilding the walls of Jerusalem and instituting reforms
404–358	The reign of Artaxerxes II, patron of Ezra
398	Ezra's mission with group of exiles from Babylon to Jerusalem

14
Trito-Isaiah (Isa 56—66)

I. Overview

A. THE AUTHOR

As we pass from Isaiah chapters 40–55 to Isaiah chapters 56–66, we note a subtle change in tone and orientation. The author or authors are no longer in Babylon awaiting the return from captivity but back in Israel experiencing the hardship, frustration, and pessimism of the returned exiles. The atmosphere is similar to that of the books of Haggai and Zechariah, two postexilic prophets.

The text says nothing about Cyrus or Babylon. Geographical allusions suggest the hills and valleys of Palestine rather than the flat, canal-irrigated plains of Babylon. When the prophet speaks about exiles, he seems to have in mind the Israelite brethren who have not yet returned from exile (see 57:5–7; 58:12; 61:3–4; 62:6–7; 66:18–21). The writer still looks to the future for Israel's glorification, but he is forced to explain why it is delayed (see 57:14–19; 60–62; 66:18–24). He, so it seems, is speaking to Israelites who returned to Palestine with high hopes now shattered by the grim realities of life in postexilic Judah.

The topic of the Temple appears in several places. At times, it seems already rebuilt (see 56:5–8; 58:2; 62:9; 66:6, 20). At other times, like Haggai and Zechariah, the prophet appears to be concerned with rebuilding the Temple or at least refurbishing it (see 60:7, 13; 66:1). The concern for observing the Sabbath, keeping the fasts, and offering acceptable sacrifices (56:6–7; 58:1–8; 61:1–6) reflects the concerns for cult and ritual characteristic of Ezra, Nehemiah, and Mal'aki—all postexilic books.

Because of these historical allusions and other shifts from Deutero-Isaiah, many scholars suggest that Isaiah 56—66 was written by yet another prophet or group of prophets, whom we name Trito-Isaiah. In this hypothesis we need to date these writings some time between the return from exile in 538 down perhaps to as late as 450, just before the reforms of Nehemiah. More than likely these writings consist of several parts that were progressively added, thus producing a combination of joyful promises of salvation, community lamentations, and warnings of punishment against evildoers, who are carefully distinguished from the faithful Israelites.

B. THE BOOK

The text of Trito–Isaiah has few clear dividing lines. Chapters 60–62 form a kind of nucleus containing only messages of salvation, with a consistency of theme and style attributable to one author. Furthermore, the whole text of Isaiah 56—66 seems framed by the thematic inclusion formed by Isaiah 56:1–8 and Isaiah 66:17–24. In both places we find a surprising stress on the Gentiles and their inclusion in Israel's worship. With these groupings of text we can divide the book roughly as follows:

Isaiah 56:1–8:	Introduction: Inclusive Temple worship
Isaiah 56:9—59:21:	Part one: True leadership
Isaiah 60:1—62:12:	Messages of salvation
Isaiah 63:1—66:17:	Part two: From sorrow to a new heaven and earth
Isaiah 66:18–25:	Conclusion: Gathering of the nations

(See Appendix 4k for a detailed outline of Trito-Isaiah.)

C. TORAH TRADITIONS IN TRITO-ISAIAH

It is striking that no mention at all of *torah* occurs in Trito-Isaiah at this time when the book of the Law was becoming so important. Trito–Isaiah indicates, however, familiarity with the story of Abraham (63:16) and with the story of Moses and the "dividing of the waters" (63:10–13).

The extraordinary stress of Trito-Isaiah on observing the Sabbath connects this prophet with Ezekiel and the legal traditions of the Torah (56:2–6; 58:13; see 63:23). However, Trito-Isaiah's use of the Sabbath law to override the legal traditions of exclusion of foreigners and eunuchs (56:2–6; see Lev 22:25; Deut 23:2) would put him at loggerheads with Ezekiel and the priestly legal traditions (see Ezek 44:5–9).

Overall, Trito-Isaiah seems to reflect Deutero-Isaiah's theme of forgetting the things of the past (65:17; see 43:18–19). It is the vision of "a new heavens and a new earth" (65:17; see 66:22) that captures his imagination, not that of a new Law.

II. Significant Passages in Trito-Isaiah

56:1–8 *Inclusive Temple worship*

Trito-Isaiah begins with the traditional insistence on a moral life: "Observe fair judgment (*mishpat*), do what is just" (*tz^edaqah*, 56:1). Picking up a line from Isaiah 46:13, the prophet here insists that the event of God's salvation and justice is still coming but is very near. In effect Trito-Isaiah links the arrival of God's promised salvation to individual moral life. He insists on observing the Sabbath (56:2), an important theme of Trito-Isaiah (see 58:13; 66:23). The references to the Temple ("my house"; 56:5) suggest the completion of its rebuilding and thus date the passage to sometime after 515 BC.

What is extraordinary in the sermon, however, is the openness to foreigners. Whether one is Jew, Gentile, or eunuch is not important as long as one observes the Sabbath (56:3–6). This position runs contrary to that in Ezekiel 44:5–9 and more specifically Deuteronomy 23:2–9, where the foreigner and the eunuch are explicitly excluded. The general attitude of Trito-Isaiah here is a far cry from the exclusivism that would soon arrive in the generations of Ezra and Nehemiah. For Trito-Isaiah, the Temple is a house of prayer for all people (56:7; see the use of this text in

Matthew 21:13 in combination with Jeremiah 7:11). The theme of all nations coming to the Temple of Jerusalem is repeated with even greater insistence in the inclusion formed by chapter 66:17–24.

58:1–14 *An admonition on fasting and the Sabbath*
A lamentation in the form of a question is posed calling for an instruction regarding the practice of fasting and penance (58:3). The answer stresses the importance of a humble attitude (58:5) and of caring for the needy (58:6–7). Moral attitudes and ethical practice trump religious practices like fasting. What God asks in terms of religious practice is for his people to "remove oppression from your midst" and "bestow your bread on the hungry…shelter the homeless…clothe the naked" (58:6–10; see Matt 25:31–46). Israel had known in exile what it meant to be bound and set free from oppression. Now Israel is admonished to show that liberality to other human beings. Trito-Isaiah will later describe his vocation as "proclaiming liberty to captives" (61:1). Again the prophet promises that God's blessing and salvation for his people will break forth when this social moral practice is implemented (58:8–12).

The one religious observance stressed by this prophet is the Sabbath rest, which he describes as avoiding the pursuit of self-interest (58:13–14). By associating this observance with care for the poor and doing good for others, the prophet lays the foundation for Jesus' instructions on Sabbath observance (Mark 2:23—3:6).

60:1–22 *A proclamation of glory to Zion*
Three chapters of uninterrupted promises of salvation form the core section of Trito-Isaiah (chapters 60–62). The prophet starts the section with a sermon of consolation by the prophet (60:1–9) followed by an oracle of salvation, where God speaks mostly in the first person (60:10–22). Mention of "rebuilding your walls" (60:10) places the oracle before 445 BC, when Nehemiah did just that.

Gentiles are included in the coming glory of Jerusalem. The light and glory of God, which shines on Jerusalem, is reflected to these nations, who "shall walk by your light" (60:3). Even those who despised and oppressed her will come in amazement to rebuild her and venerate her. The "gold and frankincense" (60:6; see Matt 2:1–12) along with the wealth of nations stream to Jerusalem, and with this stream come "your children from afar" brought by "the ships of Tarshish" (60:6–9). This description dramatizes both an openness to all peoples and the new glory of Jerusalem.

The geographical names here (66:6–9) indicate places mostly from the south and southeast (see Map 14A). Midian is a region in southern Arabia. Ephah is apparently the name of an Arabian tribe related to Midian (see Gen 25:4). Sheba is also a region in southern Arabia. Kedar is a tribe and a region east of Transjordan in northern Arabia. Nebaioth is an Arabian tribe related to the tribe of Kedar (see Gen 25:13). Tarshish is mentioned several time in scripture, usually in connection with ships, sometimes as indicating a place far to the west (Spain?), sometimes indicating a place near India. While the place of Tarshish is impossible to locate with any certainty, the term "ships of Tarshish" apparently became the name of large seagoing vessels.

Symbolized by the city of Jerusalem, Israel remains special and distinct, by no means absorbed into the nations. However, the source of Israel's glory and distinction is nothing she has accomplished on her own, but rather the presence of God, a sun and moon shining on her (60:19; see Rev 21:23; 22:5), a light that she can then reflect to others. Jerusalem's gates "shall stand open constantly" (60:11).

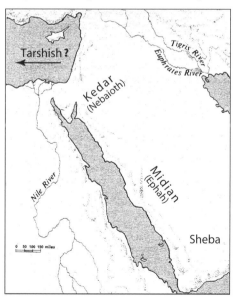

14A—The Nations Bringing
Wealth to Zion

61:1–3 *The sending of the prophet*

This text appears to function as the vocation narrative of the prophet. Like "the servant" of Isaiah 42:1, the impulse of this prophet is attributed explicitly to "the spirit of Yahweh" (61:1). Like Deutero-Isaiah, the prophet sees his mission as "to proclaim good news" (*lebasser*; see 40:9). The recipients of his gospel are the weakest members of society: the lowly, the crushed, the captives (61:1).

Luke will choose this text as the "inaugural address" of Jesus, bringing together the themes of the Spirit, the gospel, and the poor (Luke 4:18–21).

62:1–5 *Zion as bride of Yahweh*

The image of Israel as bride, now familiar in the prophets, reappears. Here it a thoroughly positive image. It describes the intense and joyful love that Yahweh has for Israel. (The expression in 62:5, "your sons" [*banayik*], in the Hebrew Massoretic text should read, "your builder" [*boneyk*].) No longer is Jerusalem the "God-forsaken" ruins that the exiles saw on their return. Now she is a precious crown in the hand of God.

63:15–16 *Yahweh as Father*

In the middle of a community lament (63:7–19), the people invoke God as "our father" (see also 64:7). The description of Yahweh as "father" is rare in pre-exilic times, although Hosea had described Israel as God's son (Hos 11:1) and Jeremiah explicitly described God as "a father to Israel" (Jer 31:9).

65:17–25 *A new heavens and a new earth*

Repeating Deutero-Isaiah's theme about forgetting the things of the past (43:18–19), the prophet introduces the apocalyptic theme of "a new heavens and a new earth" (65:17; see 66:22). Without being named as such, salvation is pictured as a radical act of God, as fundamental as the creation of the universe (see 2 Cor 5:17; Rev 21:1). Salvation consists of longevity, property ownership, fruitful harvests, and safe childbirth; these mark a new era of God's readiness to answer prayers (65:20–24). Trito-Isaiah then alludes to the prophecy of Isaiah 11:1–9 in his description of the transformation of nature into a paradise—with a resounding silence about any Davidic king, (65:25).

66:1–5 *True worship of God*

An oracle questioning the value of building a Temple contrasts with the contemporary urgings of Haggai and Zechariah (see below). The paradox of the God of the universe having a "house" in Jerusalem is not new (see 1 Kgs 8:27). Consistently in the Old Testament, the heavens are the true throne of God (see Ps 29:10; Ezek 1:26–28). The earth and the Temple are but God's footstool. The oracle may have been uttered at a time when the people were discouraged by the incomplete building of the second Temple.

Following a typical prophetic theme, Trito-Isaiah directs attention toward personal relations with God. More important than a building and ritual sacrifices is the person "who trembles at God's word" (66:2, 5).

66:6–16 *Jerusalem as mother*

Trito-Isaiah draws to a close with feminine images. Jerusalem is a woman giving birth (vv.7–12), a birthing that involves speed and multiple births beyond anything ever seen. "Can a country be brought forth in one day, or a nation be born in a single moment?" (66:8). The whole nation is the "male child" that the woman delivers (66:1; see Rev 12:5). Verse 13 shifts the image from Jerusalem to God as mother.

This beautiful picture of life and maternal care is placed in a framework describing death and punishment in the style of the classic theophanies, where God appears to annihilate his enemies (66:6, 16; see Isa 30:27–33; Jer 25:15–38).

66:18–24 *Gathering the nations*

The conclusion of the book forms an inclusion with the opening in 56:1–8. The perspective is universal. Peoples from Tarshish (?), from Put (northern Africa), Lud (western Asia Minor), Tubal (central Asia Minor), and Javan (Greece)—all will come to see God's glory and to proclaim that glory among the nations (see Map 14B). Like Israelites bringing their offerings to the Temple, so will these nations bring offerings to Jerusalem.

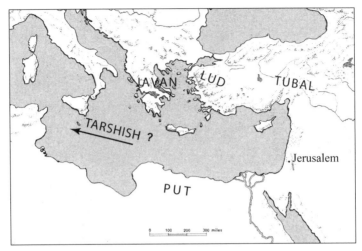

14B—The Nations to Gather in Jerusalem

Despite the ambiguity of the expression, "some of these" (66:21), Trito-Isaiah seems to propose the astounding picture of Gentiles serving as priests and Levites (66:21). The section ends with another reference to God making "the new heavens and the new earth" (66:22) and a picture of all humanity month by month, week by week worshiping God (66:23).

The last verse of the whole Book of Isaiah (66:24) describes a scene of punishment, a scene of the decaying and burning dead bodies of God's enemies, where "worm does not die or the fire go out" (66:24). In the New Testament, Mark cited this verse repeatedly to describe the eternal punishment of those who scandalize the little ones (Mark 9:42–48). In a modern Jewish Bible, this verse is followed by a repetition of 66:23 to ensure that the reading not end on such a sour note.

III. The Message of Trito-Isaiah

A. REVIEW OF IMAGES AND THEMES

Trito-Isaiah stands out by his play on images of light: the light of the glory of Yahweh shining on Zion, reflected to the Gentiles (60:1–3), replacing sun and moon (60:19–20).

God appears as a woman and mother (66:13) but is also addressed as father of Israel (63:15–16; 64:7) who announces an "everlasting covenant" (61:8) and a new heavens and a new earth (65:17; 66:22).

The images of the people are concentrated in that of the city of Jerusalem, whose gates are open (60:11). Streams of gold and frankincense come from Gentile nations to Zion (60:6) and ships of Tarshish carry Zion's children back home (60:6–9). Zion appears as a joyful bride of Yahweh (62:1–5; see Hos 2:16–19) and as mother of a multitude (66:7–13).

The characteristic themes of Trito-Isaiah that we have seen in the selected texts include the following:

- Yahweh, the savior and redeemer of Zion (60:16; 62:11)
- The importance of the future, the coming salvation of God (58:1), even if that means forgetting the things of the past (65:17)
- True worship of Yahweh that stresses the Sabbath rest (58:13–14) and the importance of personal reverence of God (66:2, 5), but perhaps not a Temple or Temple sacrifices (66:1–3)
- The inclusion of foreigners in Temple worship (56:3–7), which involves the gathering not just of Israel but also of the nations (66:18–21)
- Justice and care for the hungry, homeless, and naked (58:6–10) to the extent that Trito–Isaiah sees his mission as proclaiming good news to the oppressed (61:1–3; see 40:9–11)

B. THE THEOLOGY OF TRITO-ISAIAH

1. *A gentle God.* In Trito-Isaiah the figure of Yahweh is that of a gentle God. The image of the maternal care of God for the most part replaces the dangerous theophany. The one graphic insistence on the transcendence of God dealt with the de-emphasis on building the Temple: "The heavens are my throne; earth is my footstool" (66:1). Yahweh is greater than any temple. In effect Trito-Isaiah preaches a more spiritual God.

2. *Justice over temple building.* Religion is more about reverencing the word of God and caring for the poor than erecting a church building (58:6–7; 66:1–2). Religion is more about observing what is right and doing what is just (56:1). Zeal to build a temple can easily become a vain effort to monumentalize our own achievements. The walls of a church can easily become barriers to exclude those we consider outsiders and unworthy. Trito-Isaiah rejects these forms of idolatry (66:3) and insists that any temple must be "a house of prayer for all peoples" (56:7). If God speaks from an abyss beyond history, it is to direct Israel back to justice toward the poor and openness to others.

3. *Openness to outsiders.* Trito-Isaiah may be the prophet most open to Gentiles, who are admitted to Israelite prayer. Perhaps some are even to be priests and Levites (66:21). This is revolutionary language. Yet Trito-Isaiah is comfortable with new things. God is "creating a new heaven and a new earth. The things of the past shall not be remembered" (65:17). The future opens up as a comforting abyss from which God speaks, directing Israel to a new reality and a unity of peoples.

In many ways, Trito-Isaiah anticipates Paul in the New Testament with his openness to the Gentiles and his insistence on a reconciliation that is nothing less than a "new creation" (2 Cor 5:17). The Letter to the Ephesians also will proclaim that in the body of Christ the wall separating Jews and Gentiles is broken down (Eph 2:11–18).

4. *Hope in times of disappointment.* Trito-Isaiah had to deal with disappointment. Deutero-Isaiah's prophecies of "valleys filled" and "mountains leveled" did not occur. There was no spectacular procession through the desert led by the glory of God. How can a fervent believer in Yahweh deal with such disillusionment? The situation is very similar to that of the second generation of Christians, who were promised the return of Jesus in the previous generation (Mark 13:30).

Trito-Isaiah does not waver from his hope. Building on the words of Deutero-Isaiah, Trito-Isaiah proclaims the nearness of fulfillment: "Thus says Yahweh, 'Observe fair judgment, do what is just; for my salvation is about to come; my justice, about to be revealed'" (Isa 56:1; see 46:13). Here the prophet connects this hope with just conduct. The way to prepare for the coming of God's salvation is to act with justice toward one other. Trito-Isaiah in fact seems to suggest that social morality might even speed things up:

> This is the fast I desire…setting free the oppressed, breaking every yoke; sharing your bread with the hungry, inviting the poor into your home; clothing the naked when you see them, and not turning your back on your own kin. Then your light shall break forth like the down, and your wound shall quickly be healed. Your vindication shall go before you, and the glory of the Lord shall be your rear guard. (58:6–8)

In the New Testament, Matthew explains the need for vigilance in regard to the return of Jesus. Explaining the nature of this vigilance, Matthew climaxes Jesus' teaching on the end-times with a parable stressing care for the little ones who have needs almost identical to those mentioned by Trito-Isaiah (Matt 25:31–46). Hope for future salvation operates through just and caring engagement with the present.

Trito-Isaiah clearly avoids identifying this future salvation with any particular political event. He no longer evokes the recent return from exile or any military victory coming up as the moment of deliverance. Instead this prophet speaks of Yahweh's epiphany simply as the shining of light. The hoped for events seem more spiritual, more mysterious—or, as we would say, more eschatological.

15
Two Prophets of Reconstruction

I. Haggai

A. OVERVIEW

Haggai preached in 520 BC, the second year of Darius I (1:1). His message is direct and blunt. God wishes the Temple rebuilt without further delay. As evident from his words, times were difficult, money was short, and sacrifices were needed to complete the Temple. In his concern for the Temple and proper cult, Haggai resembles the ancient cultic prophets. In his address to Zerubbabel, he resembles a court prophet like Nathan. He is mentioned along with the prophet Zechariah in Ezra 5:1–2 and 6:14 as part of the impetus for building the Temple.

The book is divided into four short oracle sermons each introduced by a date given in terms of the reign of King Darius of Persia (522–485):

Haggai 1:1–15:	An exhortation to rebuild the Temple—dated to our August 520
Haggai 2:1–9:	An encouraging prophecy about the glory of the new Temple—our October 520
Haggai 2:10–19:	A rebuke to the people and a promise of blessings—our December 520
Haggai 2:20–23:	A promise to Zerubbabel—our December 520

Outside a brief reference to the Exodus tradition (2:5), Haggai makes no allusion to Torah traditions developing at this time.

B. Significant Passages in Haggai

1:1–15 *Exhortation to rebuild the Temple*

The first of the oracles is directed to the two leaders of the Jews, Zerubbabel, grandson of King Jehoiachin, and Joshua, the high priest (named Jeshua in Ezra). These two figures appear repeatedly in postexilic literature as messiah figures (2:20–23; see Zech 3:1; 4:9).

Whereas the Book of Ezra explained the delay of the Temple construction as based on local political opposition (Ezra 4), Haggai puts the blame on the attitude of the Jews who returned. Economic hardships apparently have discouraged the people from supporting the building project.

Haggai now addresses the people and counters that the neglect of the things of God has caused the economic hardships. While such a message sounds like the clever techniques of a "development director," the prophet here is insisting on the ancient tradition that connected God's presence with material blessings (see Prov 16:3, 9; 19:2; 21:5, and so on). Twice Haggai tells the people to "reflect with your hearts (*simu lvavkem*) on your ways" (1:7). As the faculty of understanding, the heart should be able to go beyond the physical facts to see a divine plan. The prophet points out that the real point of the construction project is that Yahweh "be glorified" (1:8).

Unlike the pre-exilic prophets in general, Haggai is quite successful in his preaching. The narrator distinguishes three distinct listeners: Zerubbabel, Joshua, and "the remnant of the people" (1:14). All three are persuaded to start building the new temple.

2:1–9 *A message of hope for the discouraged and disappointed*

On the feast of Booths ("the twenty-first day of the seventh month") some three months after his first exhortation, Haggai addresses the apparent disappointment of the people about the humble appearance of this second Temple. It does not compare to that of Solomon (see also Tob 14:5). The Temple will not be completed until 515 BC but already the foundations were begun in

536. Those who were old enough to remember the first Temple do not like what they see.

His encouragement has two elements. First, the prophet stresses the presence of God in the temple: "I am with you…my spirit continues in your midst" (2:4–5). This presence is far more important than architectural glory.

Second, the prophet directs attention to the future: "Glory" for the house of God is assured, although it must wait "a little while" (2:6). The Temple will be decorated by "the treasures of all the nations" that will come when Yahweh "shakes the heavens and the earth" (2:6). The coming glory of the Temple will be the act of God, *Yhwh tsba'oth*, the Lord of the cosmic armies (1:2, 5, 7, 9, 14; 2:6, 8, 9, 11, 23). The final result will be God's gift of "peace" (2:9).

2:20–23 *The promise to Zerubbabel*

Although the term *anointed* or *messiah* does not occur in this passage—or for that matter anywhere in Haggai—the Davidic prince, Zerubbabel, picks up messianic colors through the solemn declaration of a special relationship that God establishes with him: "I will take you…my servant," "I have chosen you," "I set you as a signet ring."

The last mentioned expression is quite striking as a blunt reversal of God's rejection of Coniah (Jehoiachin), the royal grandfather of Zerubbabel, as described by Jeremiah, "As I live, says Yahweh, if you Coniah, son of Jehoiakim, king of Judah, are a signet ring on my right hand, I will snatch you from it" (Jer 22:24). The signet ring gave the official seal to important documents. Here Haggai is alluding to God's seal on his official decrees and the way Zerubbabel will function like King Jeconiah (Jehoiachin) did before the Exile. Here also this will happen as God "shakes the heavens and the earth" (2:21).

Although never called "king," a title reserved for Darius (1:1), Zerubbabel seems to be the key for getting the Davidic dynasty back on track as God's representative. In the New Testament both Matthew and Luke will include Zerubbabel in their genealogies of Jesus (Matt 1:12; Luke 3:27).

C. The Message of Haggai

1. Review of Images and Themes

The central images in Haggai include that of Zerubbabel, the Davidic prince (1:14; 2:2, 4, 20, 23), and that of Joshua, the priestly partner of Zerubbabel (1:14; 2:2, 4). Haggai also paints a picture of the treasures of the nations filling the Temple (2:6).

The theological themes of Haggai are two:

- The rebuilding of the Temple (1:8, 14)
- The future glory for the Temple (2:6)

2. The Theology of Haggai

With his insistence on building the Temple, Haggai forms a counterpoint to Trito-Isaiah. In Haggai the divine abyss seems to be domesticated. God wants to move into the neighborhood.

In effect Haggai declares the importance for the people to have a place where they can point to God's presence. God wills that his presence appear in the skyline of the city. The Temple declares God's place among the visible social institutions of the people. The real issue, therefore, is not about a building but about a community, and how that community expresses the presence of God. That community is entrusted with reestablishing God's Temple. Haggai reminds us that now is the time to build God's house.

As for the glory of the Temple, that is God's work. On this point Haggai directs our thoughts to the future. The Temple of Zerubbabel was disappointing. However, God *will* shake the heavens and the earth. God *will* fill this house with glory. On the horizon of Haggai's vision appears a future of God's presence that will not disappoint. "Yet a moment, yet a little while" and the glory of God will appear. With this aspect, God again speaks from beyond the present flow of history.

II. Proto-Zechariah (Zech 1—8)

A. OVERVIEW

Zechariah was a contemporary of Haggai and like him was credited with bringing the Temple reconstruction to a happy conclusion (Ezra 5:1–2; 6:14). In his theme of rebuilding the Temple, Zechariah encourages his fellow Israelites. He assures them of God's favor in the present and points out to them the glories of the messianic age in the future. The year is 520 BC (1:1).

In this section we will study the first eight chapters of Zechariah. The style and subject matter of Zechariah 9–14 are so different that they suggest another author, a "Deutero-Zechariah," and therefore a text that we will treat in the next chapter.

The book has two main parts. After an introduction, Zechariah 1—6 consists of a series of eight visions with accompanying sermons. Chapters 7 and 8 stand apart as special moral teachings framed around the question of fasting:

Zechariah 1:1–6:   Introduction:
Zechariah 1:7—6:15:   Eight visions:
    The colored horses (1:7–16)
    The four horns and plowmen (2:1–4)
    The new Jerusalem—with diverse promises to the
      city (2:5–17)
    The purification of Joshua (3:1–10)
    The lampstand and the leaders—with promises to
      Zerubbabel (4:1–14)
    The flying scroll (5:1–4)
    The flying bushel container (5:5–11)
    The four chariots—with promises to Joshua
      [Zerubbabel?] (6:1–15)
Zechariah 7:1—8:23   The question of fasting and other
      moral teachings

(See Appendix 4l for a more detailed outline of Proto-Zechariah.)

With their emphasis on the visual rather than the "word of Yahweh," the eight visions of Zechariah are an important link to the development of apocalyptic literature. The particular visual symbols of Zechariah will recur again and again in later literature (Rev 1:12–20; 11:3–4).

Proto-Zechariah contains no apparent allusions to Torah traditions. The descriptions of the priestly garments (3:5) as well as of the menorah (4:2–3, 11–12) in this book have little in common with the respective descriptions in the Torah texts of Leviticus 8:6–10 and Exodus 25:31–40 and more likely are rooted in tradition and recent memory. The question of fasting raised here deals specifically with the destruction of Jerusalem not with the contexts described in the Torah. As for the development of the second part of the Hebrew Bible, we do have interesting allusions to the teachings of "the former prophets" (1:4; 7:7).

B. Significant Texts in Proto-Zechariah

1:7–17 *Vision of the four horses*

The year is 519 BC. The month would correspond to February. Zechariah's first vision is one of four different colored horses. The rider of the red horse is identified as "the angel of Yahweh." Another angel is introduced who interprets the vision, in that way leading the human being beyond the factual details to the deeper meaning. Later, Yahweh himself speaks "words of comfort" (1:13) to the interpreter angel, who then relays the oracle to the prophet Zechariah. This is the style of message relays found in later apocalyptic writing. We see here also the pattern of (1) vision details, (2) the question of the meaning of the vision, and (3) the interpretation by an angel.

In the interpreter angel's explanation of the vision, the horses are patrolling the whole earth, a horse for each of the four corners of the earth. The prophet is reporting on God's universal management of humanity.

The report is that "the whole earth is tranquil and at rest" (1:11). The report apparently refers to the victory around 520 BC of Darius over his rivals for the throne of Persia. This tranquility is not seen as a good thing, since the angel of Yahweh asks how long will God withhold his mercy from Jerusalem. Then a report comes of Yahweh's anger "with the nations at ease" (1:14–15), perhaps a reference to the countries neighboring Judah, who are putting early obstacles in Judah's reconstruction efforts (see Ezra 3:3; 4:1–24). Despite this opposition, God's Temple will be rebuilt (1:16) and Jerusalem will enjoy prosperity (1:17).

2:14–17 [2:10–13] *Zion rejoices*

Addressed as a woman, "daughter Zion" (see "daughter Babylon" in 2:11) is summoned to rejoice because "I am coming to dwell (*shakan*) among you, says Yahweh" (2:14; see also 8:3, 8). Earlier God promised his "house" will be rebuilt in Jerusalem (1:16). Here he gives the signification of such a Temple. God will dwell among his people, possess the land of Judah, and choose Jerusalem. The perspective is the future. At the time of the oracle, Jerusalem and Judea had little reason to rejoice, but Yahweh is coming.

Connected with this promise to Judah and Jerusalem is an extraordinary promise to the "many nations." They will join themselves to Yahweh and "they shall be his people" (2:15). Nowhere else in the Old Testament is this covenant formula applied to anyone outside of Israel. To all these nations God promises "to dwell among you." This universalism reminds us of the promises in Trito-Isaiah (see Isa 66:19–21).

3:1–10 *The vision of the high priest*

The fourth vision introduces Joshua the high priest. Similar to the scene in Job 1—2, Joshua appears in the divine council (*sôd*) subject to the accusations of some heavenly district attorney, *ha-satan*, the Hebrew word for "the adversary" (see Job 1:6–12). Fortunately, "the angel of Yahweh" silences the Satan and commands the investiture of Joshua for his office. The reference to the "unclean garments" perhaps deals with the way the Israelites dwelling in Babylonia would be seen in priestly circles as defiled and incapable of returning to the Temple. Joshua, the high priest, stands in the place of the people and is granted the purity needed for Temple functions. He is clothed with "festive garments" along with a "clean turban."

Interrupting the story is a brief mention of a messiah figure: "Yes, I will bring my servant, Bud" (*tzemach*, 3:8). The title apparently is taken from Jeremiah 23:5–6; 33:15–18 (see also Isa 11:1) with the repeated references to the budding of life from the stump of the Davidic dynasty. This "Bud" is presented here alongside Joshua the high priest and most likely is Zerubbabel, the Davidic governor of Jerusalem, who is called "my servant" by Haggai (Hag 2:23).

The unexplained "stone" with seven facets or eyes ('*eynaim*) is later placed in the hands of Zerubbabel (see 4:10).

4:1–14 *The vision of Zerubbabel*

In the fifth vision, Zerubbabel, the grandson of King Jehoiachin, is named as the one to build the Temple (4:9). The "two olive trees" and the "two sons of oil" (4:3, 11–14) are probably Zerubbabel and Joshua. They are the sources of the oil that flows through tubes or channels presumably to light God's menorah, or seven-branch lamp.

Reference to Zerubbabel, the Davidic prince, and Joshua, the high priest, as "sons of oil" may well be a way of designating them as "anointed" or "messiah" figures. The Jewish tradition of expecting two messiahs, a tradition that appears some four hundred years later in the community associated with the Dead Sea Scrolls (see *The Damascus Document [CD]* 12:23; 14:19; 20:1), is apparently rooted in this text. Because of their association of these two figures with the building of the Temple, Jewish theology will reserve any future rebuilding of the Temple to the Messiah (see also John 2:19).

5:5–11 *The woman in the bushel container*

In the seventh vision, wickedness is personified as a woman who eventually is placed in a temple in the land of Shinar, an old name for the city of Babylon. Like the flying scroll in the previous vision, this evil element is removed from Israel. The woman probably represents Ishtar, the Babylonian goddess. While Jerusalem will have a Temple to Yahweh, Babylon will have a temple to sin.

The literary device of personifying evil as a wicked woman will continue in apocalyptic imagery (see Rev 17).

6:9–15 *The crowning of Joshua*

After the eighth vision, the leader is given the messianic title "Bud" (6:12; see 3:8), that is, a Davidic descendant. He is identified as the authorized builder of the Temple (6:12–13). Everything in the context points to Zerubbabel, who elsewhere is explicitly identified as the builder of the Temple (4:9) and by implication is given the name "Bud" (3:8), but the text names Joshua the high priest. More than likely, the name Zerubbabel was removed by a later scribe and Joshua's name substituted when the high priest became in effect the only political ruler in Judah. Although he is remembered with admiration centuries later (see Sir 49:11), Zerubbabel now fades from view. For all his importance, we do not know what happened to him.

8:18–23 *The question about fasting*

The book concludes with an answer to the question of fasting posed in 7:1–3. Should the Jews continue the liturgical mourning over the fall of Jerusalem? As part of the answer, the prophet reminds the people of the importance of social justice (7:9–10). Then at the end of the section (chapters 7–8), the prophet declares by his own authority that the fast days are transformed into feast days. For the prophet the essential is not to fast or feast but rather "to love faithfulness and peace" (8:19). The coming of the nations to the city of God (8: 20–23) picks up on the universalism seen in 2:15[11] and reiterates the theme of Isaiah 2:2–4; 60:1–14; and Haggai 2:7.

C. THE MESSAGE OF PROTO-ZECHARIAH

1. *Review of Images and Themes*

Following the style of Amos's visions of destruction (Amos 7—9) and Ezekiel's call (Ezek 1—3), Proto-Zechariah provides us with a wealth of images. The visions of our significant texts paint the following images of things: the four horses (1:7–17); Jerusalem as "daughter Zion" (2:14); the lampstand and the oil (4:1–14); the flying scroll (5:1–4); and the four chariots (6:7). Persons are also involved in the visions: the angel interpreter (1:9–14; 3:6; 4:1–4; 5:5; 6:5); Satan (3:1–2); Joshua the high priest (3:1–9); Zerubbabel, the "Bud" and Davidic prince (3:6–10; 6:11–13; see Jer 23:5–6; 33:15–18); and the evil woman in the basket (5:5–11).

The signature themes of Proto–Zechariah include the following:

- The rebuilding the Temple through God's anointed (1:16–17; 4:9–10; 6:12–15)
- Joy from God dwelling among his people (2:14, 17; 8:3–8), involving the transformation of days of fasting into days of celebration (7:1–3; 8:18–19)

We find also the following themes common to other prophets:

- The future vindication and glory of Jerusalem among the nations of the world (1:14; see also 2:4, 9–16)
- An openness and invitation to Gentile nations (2:15; 8:22–23)
- Social justice (7:9–10)

2. The Theology of Proto-Zechariah

Like Haggai, Proto-Zechariah's God wants to be part of this world. The prophet's message focuses on the mundane task of building the Temple but then links that construction to a mysterious messiah and an inclusion of all humanity. Only God's anointed can build the temple. Zechariah's perspective is consistently future: "My house will be built…my cities will again overflow with prosperity" (1:16–17). Christians later will identify another Anointed one who would promise to build the Temple. But this new temple would not be of stones. In the New Testament, the Fourth Gospel begins with the proclamation that the Word, who was God, "became flesh and dwelt (*skênoô*) among us" (John 1:14).

Zechariah's concern for the Temple is more than a desire for a new building. The issue here is really that of the presence of God: "I am coming to dwell among you, says Yahweh" (2:14). The Fourth Gospel will see Jesus as the glorious dwelling of God among us (John 1:14).

The transcendent element in Zechariah appears in the way that this message comes through visions that give the prophet and us a divinelike view of history. Mysterious visions flash out of the heavenly abyss. As apocalyptic literature develops, the message will become more and more insistent that only a divinelike view makes sense of history. Yet this final view remains shrouded in the mystery of cryptic symbols.

16
Independent Oracles

I. Deutero-Zechariah (Zech 9—14)

A. OVERVIEW

In style and subject matter, Zechariah 9—14 differs so much from Zechariah 1—8 that the second half makes more sense if considered the work of a different author, whom we will call Deutero-Zechariah—who may in fact represent several authors in this collection of various preachings. In this section the age of Temple rebuilding is past. Nothing is said about Zerubbabel and Joshua; nothing about the Persian Empire. The center of interest is no longer the small struggling postexilic community but Israel as a whole and at times the world. For a time frame, we have a period of judgments and divine threats as well as one of promises of eschatological salvation. Instead of prose oracles dated to the time of Zechariah, we seem to have a collection of undated oracles for the most part in poetry, none of which are complete enough for us to make much sense. This incompleteness leaves the texts wide open to later reinterpretations.

The references to a return to the land (9:11–12; 10:6–9) argue to a time of composition after 539 BC. Other indications suggest pre-exilic composition.

In general the perspective of Deutero-Zechariah is future, even eschatological. The prophet looks to the great day when God will directly intervene to judge the world, bringing glory to his people and punishment to evildoers. He presents the messiah as a future royal figure but one without worldly pomp, a peaceful king in contrast to the military rulers of the time (9:9–10). The messiah may also be identified with the mysterious personage "whom they have pierced" (12:10), an innocent man killed much like the servant of Isaiah 53. It is not surprising, therefore, to see the text of Deutero-Zechariah used repeatedly by the gospels as a foreshadowing of Jesus.

The two parts of Deutero-Zechariah, chapters 9–11 and chapters 12–14, each begin with the Hebrew words *massa' d^{e}bar Yhwh*, which means "burden/oracle of the word of Yahweh." The word *massa'*, which literally means "burden," is also the word that Isaiah and Nahum use to introduce their oracles against the nations. The same three Hebrew words also introduce the Book of Mal'aki and suggest that these two parts of Deutero-Zechariah along with the Book of Mal'aki might be three independent oracles placed here by editors at the end of the collection of the prophets.

(See Appendix 4m for a detailed outline of Deutero-Zechariah.)

Like Proto-Zechariah, this section of the book contains no apparent allusions to Torah traditions.

B. SIGNIFICANT PASSAGES IN DEUTERO-ZECHARIAH

9:9–10 *The peaceful king*

Sandwiched between two descriptions of God as warrior (9:1–8 and 9:11–17) is a description of a future king, who appears as a peaceful ruler arriving in the city of Jerusalem, daughter Zion. He rides on a donkey, not a war horse. He banishes instruments of war and proclaims peace to all the nations. Indeed, his rule will be universal, "to the ends of the earth" (9:10).

The announcement of a future "king" is unprecedented in the biblical literature of the Persian period. It is difficult to see how such a prophecy could have made it by the official censors. Even descriptions of Zerubbabel in Proto-Zechariah avoided calling him a king (4:1–14). Perhaps this text stems from pre-exilic times.

Both Matthew and John saw the resemblance between this prophecy and the arrival of Jesus on "Palm Sunday" (Matt 21:5; John 12:14–15).

11:4–17 *The breaking of the covenants*

A rather confusing allegory of shepherds describes the breaking of the covenant between God and "all peoples" (11:10). The allegory begins with the prophet taking the role of an unfeeling and unsparing shepherd of the flock (11:7–9). This bleak picture of cruel and uncaring shepherds reminds us of Jeremiah's denunciation of the Judah's last kings (Jer 22:6–30).

The prophet then breaks the staff called "favor" to represent the breaking of some mysterious covenant (11:10–11). The prophet also breaks the other staff called "bond" to represent the breaking of the union of Judah and Israel (11:14). This action is a clear counteraction to the prophetic gesture of Ezekiel joining two staffs and promising the union of Israel and Judah (Ezek 37:15–28).

Before breaking this second staff, however, the prophet in Deutero-Zechariah receives his wages of "thirty pieces of silver," which are thrown into the treasury of the Temple (11:12–13). (In the Hebrew Massoritic text the word *yotzer* [potter] should probably read *'otzer* [treasury].) The prophet returns then to the role of "a foolish shepherd," with a prediction of the ascendancy of a vicious shepherd (11:15–17).

The five parts of the allegory appear to form a chiasm:

> A. The harsh shepherds (10:4–6)
> > B. Breaking the staff (10:7–11)
> > > C. The thirty pieces of silver (10:12–13)
> > B'. Breaking the staff (10:14)
> A'. The harsh shepherd (10:15–17)

The image of the "thirty pieces of silver" appears here at the heart and focus of the allegory. Why this sum of money receives such stress is not clear. The Torah specifies this amount as the proper compensation for serious injury to another's slave (Exod 21:32). In the New Testament, Matthew introduces the "thirty pieces of silver" into his account of the betrayal of Jesus, clearly alluding to this text of Deutero-Zechariah, thus covertly suggesting the theme of covenant breaking (Matt 27:3–10).

12:10–14 *Grief over an only son*

What appears to be an oracle of salvation for Jerusalem and the house of David involves the death of some person. No clue identifies this person whose death leads to bitter grief, "as for an only son." Nor do we see the connection between the "spirit of grace and petition" and this death. The prophet might be alluding to the servant of Isaiah 53. The text here actually places more stress on the grief of the mourners than on the person killed. In the New Testament the Fourth Gospel connects this text with the death of Jesus (John 19:37; see Rev 1:7).

The oracle continues comparing the mourning to that of Hadadrimmon, a reference to a storm god, possibly part of the myth of Ba'al, whose death was mourned by his sister. The "plain of Megiddo" is mentioned as the place of this mourning, the place where the good King Josiah was killed by the evil Pharaoh Neco (see 2 Chron 35:20–25). This place of conflict between good and evil may be the background for the *Ar-magedôn* mentioned in Revelation 16:16.

This great mourning will occur "on that day" (12:11). The prophet is referring to the future, not in a general way, but as envisioning a very specific event or day. The theme of "that day" has been dominant from the beginning of chapter 12 (see 12:3–4, 6, 8–9). It returns through much of the rest of this book (13:1–4; 14:1–21).

14:16–21 *Universal worship in Jerusalem*

Concluding Deutero-Zechariah is a text describing the inclusion of all nations in the worship of Yahweh in Jerusalem. Here Yahweh is identified as "the king." Jerusalem, however, is a city from which the prophets have been eliminated (13:2–6). In an earlier text, the human king has also been eliminated ("Strike the shepherd that the sheep may be dispersed," 13:7; see Matt 26:31). No mention is made of priests in this city. This is the city to which all nations come for the feast of Booths (*sukkoth*; 14:16–19), a feast celebrated outside the Temple. The horse bells of the stables and the pots of the kitchen will be placed on the same level as the truly holy objects. Buying and selling in the Temple will not be needed (14:20–21). Official public religion seems to have stopped. In effect, the distinction between sacred and profane disappears.

C. The Message of Deutero-Zechariah

1. Review of Images and Themes

The disjointed nature of Deutero-Zechariah gives rise to a wide range of images. In the selected texts above we see the peaceful king on a donkey (9:9–10), breaking the staffs and the thirty pieces of silver (11:10–15), the only son who is pierced (12:10–14), the pouring out of the spirit (12:10), and the worldwide celebration of the feast of Booths (14:16–21).

Striking themes also appear:

- "That day" (9:16; 12:3–11; 13:1–4; 14:1, 4, 6, 8–9, 13, 20–21)
- The breaking of covenants (11:10–14)
- Violence, mourning, and suffering (11:4–6, 16; 12: 10–14; 13:7)
- Openness to Gentiles (14:16–18; but see the destruction of the nations in 9:1–8)
- The messianic advent of joy for Zion (9:9–10)
- The relativization of Temple cult and "the holy" (14:20–21).

2. The Theology of Deutero-Zechariah

This part of the Book of Zechariah appears as a hodgepodge of different messages, without apparent internal connection to each other, without clear historical context. The theology of Deutero-Zechariah, therefore, is murky. We are directed to a future coming or advent of Yahweh, often in a violent context (9:14), occasionally in a saving way (10:6), apparently connected to "that day" (12:3–11). In this way Yahweh appears as beyond the current flow of history.

The New Testament gospel authors caught glimpses of this hodgepodge of images. Matthew and John interpreted the peaceful king coming to Jerusalem (9:9–10) as Jesus coming from the Mount of Olives as his death approached (Matt 21:4–5; John 12:14–15). Matthew saw the thirty pieces of silver as part of a broken covenant with Israel, replaced with one for all nations (Matt 21:43; 28:19). Deutero-Zechariah describes a mysterious person who was pierced and became the occasion for God's pouring out of a Spirit of grace and prayer (Zech 12:10–14). The author of the Fourth Gospel saw this description as pointing to Jesus on the cross (John 19:37).

These reinterpretations of Zechariah, of course, are examples of overlays from Christian faith, not necessarily indications of the prophet's faith. We may never know what the prophet believed and held by these snatches now used by the New Testament authors. Significantly, this book now ends with the revolutionary abolition of the distinction between the holy and the profane (14:16–21). Expressed in and through this fragmentary vagueness, the prophet was open to a new thing, a new way of God acting in the world.

II. Mal'aki

A. Overview

1. The Author

The Book of Mal'aki poses several literary questions. Is this a distinct prophetic book or is it the third anonymous oracle (*massa' debar Yhwh*), concluding the collection of the literary prophets, along with Zechariah 9—11 and Zechariah 12—14, which begin with the same expression? Is "Mal'aki" the name of a prophet or the designation of "my messenger," through whom the messages come (1:1)? *Mal'ak* is Hebrew for "messenger." The suffix *i* functions as the possessive adjective "my." The name is not otherwise used in the Old Testament or attested elsewhere in contemporary literature. To whom does the "my" refer? What are the relationships between "my messenger" of 1:1, the priest named "messenger of Yahweh" in 2:7, and "my messenger" of 3:1?

The book appears to be written shortly before the reforms of Nehemiah and Ezra (445–398 BC). The Temple has been rebuilt, but the days of zeal and fervor are past. A spirit of weariness and routine has set in. In fact many of the practices to which Mal'aki objects are dealt with in the reforms of Nehemiah and Ezra: lax priesthood (Mal 2:1–11; see Neh 13:1–10, 29), mixed marriages (Mal

2:1–11; see Ezra 10:1–12; Neh 13:23–31); nonsupport of the Temple (Mal 3:8–9; see Neh 13:10–14). If Mal'aki was one of the principal stimuli leading to the reforms, then we would have to place his preaching around 450 BC, a good half-century after the time of Haggai and Zechariah and the rebuilding of the Temple.

We learn of a devastation of Edom (1:3–4), probably the same as that behind the Book of Obadiah (see chapter 17 below). We do not know from history any details of this destruction except that the Arab nation of Nabataeans at this time was putting pressure on Edom as its people migrated from their original homeland westward into southern Judah.

2. The Book

The book is made up of six disputations, following more or less the same format: a provoking proclamation, reference to the words or actions of an objector to the proclamation ("but you say..."), and an extended answer to the objection. If we follow this pattern, we can break the book down into six topics:

Mal'aki 1:2–5:   God's love for his people
Mal'aki 1:6—2:9:   Duties of the priests
Mal'aki 2:10–16:   Mixed marriages
Mal'aki 2:17—3:5:   The coming of God
Mal'aki 3:6–12:   Returning to God and supporting the
                    Temple
Mal'aki 3:13–21   God and his justice

Two detached statements, 3:22 and 3:23–24, conclude the book.

(See Appendix 4n for a more detailed outline to Mal'aki.)

3. Torah Traditions in Mal'aki

Torah traditions appear to be quite strong at the time of the writing of the Book of Mal'aki. Although probably added somewhat later to the main body of this book, the most obvious allusion to the Torah traditions in this book is the text of 3:22, "Remember the law of Moses my servant, which I enjoined upon him on Horeb, the statutes and ordinances for all Israel." The use of the term *Horeb* indicates that the text reflects the Deuteronomist (D) account of the "Ten Commandments" (see Deut 5:2).

In the main body of this book, the term *torah* is not used as the basic covenant Law. In 2:6–9 the term appears to have the sense of priestly instructions for particular cases. However, the specific legal observances stressed in Mal'aki strongly suggest that Torah was recognized at the time of the writing as a law for all the people. The issue of offering only unblemished animals in sacrifice (1:7–10) seems to presuppose the cultic legislation we have now throughout Leviticus (see Lev 1:3, 10; 3:1; 22:17–30; and so on), although the basis for this position is presented here in terms of the logic of political life rather than an appeal to the Law. The issue of tithes as owed to Yahweh (Mal 3:8, 10) presupposes the legislation in Leviticus 27:30–32 or Numbers 18:21–28. The prescription against defrauding "widows, orphans, an aliens" (Mal 3:5) reflects numerous prescriptions along the same line in Deuteronomy (10:18; 14:29; 24:17–21 and so on). Seeing mixed marriages as a "profaning of the covenant of our fathers" (Mal 2:10–11) would seem to be rooted in an understanding of Deuteronomy 7:1–4 or Exodus 34:11–16.

The only allusion to the stories of the patriarchs is that of Jacob and Esau (Mal 1:3), an allusion that presupposes the text of Genesis 25:19–34. The argument against divorce seems to refer to the description of Genesis 2:24.

The reference to God's "covenant with Levi" (2:4–5), may be an allusion to the promise of an "everlasting priesthood" made by God to Phinehas, son of Eleazar, son of Aaron (Num 25:13). A late addition to the Book of Jeremiah also includes mention of a divine "covenant with the Levites" (Jer 33:21–22) and may witness to a late effort to add a foundation to priestly authority.

B. SIGNIFICANT PASSAGES IN MAL'AKI

1:6—2:9 *The duties of the priests*
The criticism against priests is twofold. The first deals with priests offering damaged goods to God (1:7–8, 13–14). Between the repeated mention of junk sacrifices by priests is the contrast

of an "incense offering" and "a pure offering" that describe the honor given God "among Gentiles" (*ba-goyim*) from East to West (1:11), an surprising expression of universalism. These words appear as the object of future hope. These words have found their way into many canons of the Christian Eucharist.

The second criticism of the priests aims at their teaching function. Again, sandwiched between repeated accusations (2:1–3, 8–9) is the contrasting "covenant with Levi" involving "true instruction (*torah*) from his mouth" (2:6, 7). A later post-exilic addition to the Book of Jeremiah also mentions a "covenant with the priests of Levi" parallel to God's covenant with David (Jer 33:21). In this period of reconstruction, the priests are assuming the central role in the covenantal relationship of the people to God. The author here in Mal'aki names the priest in his function as teacher and as "the messenger (*mal'ak*) of Yahweh" (2:7).

2:10–16 *Mixed marriages and divorce*

In the next disputation, the topic shifts to Jewish marriages. Here there seem to be two distinct topics. In the first (2:10–12), the prophet accuses Judah of "breaking faith" (*bagad*), described as "profaning the holiness of Yahweh," and "marrying an idol worshiping wife," (literally, "marrying a daughter of an alien god"; 2:11). The author describes this type of marriage as "violating the covenant with our fathers" (2:10). Nehemiah and Ezra will oppose any marriages with Gentile spouses even to the point of demanding divorces and abandonment of children (Ezra 9:2; 10:3; Neh 13:23–31). Mal'aki seems more restricted in his concern.

In the second topic, the prophet repeats the accusation of "breaking faith" but this time as doing so "with the wife of your youth" (Mal 2:14–15). The accusation aims at divorce itself (2:16). The argument follows an interpretation of Genesis 2:24, where marriage is becoming "one flesh" in intense companionship and love, much like the interpretation that appears on the lips of Jesus in Matthew 5:31–32.

If the two topics in this disputation are supposed to clarify each other, then the abuse here apparently involves the practice of divorcing one's wife to marry a more "modern" idol-worshiping wife.

2:17—3:5 *Preparing the way before God*

In the fourth topic, the words of the objector seem to indicate the problem of the hiddenness of God in the world. Where is God? Why do evildoers prosper?

The answer lies in a description of an apocalyptic figure who comes like a purifying fire (see 3:2–3). The figure prepares for the coming of God, who then draws near as judge and witness against a list of sins (3:5). Dominating this list is a warning against oppressing the weak and vulnerable. To the traditional enumeration of the weak and vulnerable—widows, orphans, strangers—Mal'aki adds "the hired worker."

"Mal'aki" here insists on the messenger to prepare the way before God. "The lord" (*ha-'adon*) will then come suddenly to the temple, and the desired "messenger of the covenant" will come (3:1). The expression for "the lord" is *not* the usual way of referring to God ('*Adonay* or *Yhwh*). It is not clear who this "lord" and this "messenger" are. The parallelism suggests that they are the same. Earlier the author identified a priest figure as "the messenger of Yahweh" (2:7). Perhaps the author had a hint of the coming work of Ezra. In any case, it will constitute the "day of Yahweh" (3:23).

On the other hand, an appendix to this biblical book identifies the one sent by God—and by implication the messenger—as Elijah, apparently coming from heaven (3:23). This identification will contribute an element to Jewish messianic expectations. According to one expectation, Elijah will come first (see Matt 17:10 and parallels; John 1:21).

In the Synoptic Gospels, John the Baptist is identified as Elijah, the coming messenger (see Mark 1:2; Matt 11:14; 17:11–13 and parallels; Luke 7:27; also 1:17, 76). John's announcement of one coming to baptize with fire may well rest on Mal'aki 3:1–3.

C. THE MESSAGE OF MAL'AKI

1. Review of Images and Themes

Like those of Deutero-Zechariah, the images from the above selected passages are striking but disjointed: the pure offerings and incense among the Gentiles (1:11); the covenant with Levi

(2:4); the covenant of our fathers (2:10); the messenger of God (2:7; 3:1); Elijah (3:23); and the day of Yahweh (3:23).

We have seen in the selected passages the following sometimes conflicting themes:

- The sin of junk offerings to Yahweh (1:6–8)
- The role of Gentiles in the "pure" worship of Yahweh (1:11)
- The evil of marriage with Gentiles (2:10–12)
- The importance of the bond of marriage (2:11–16)
- The role of priests and their "torah" (2:1–9)
- The coming of God's messenger who prepares the way of God (3:1–5)
- Social justice (3:5)

2. The Theology of Mal'aki

The God of Mal'aki is a relatively domestic God. The book, for the most part, consists of a series of discussions concerning moral imperatives especially as regards priests. Among these duties Mal'aki reminds the readers of the serious duty to worship Yahweh. God deserves the best—a matter that could be of real concern to liturgical planning today. The book insists on the covenantal duties of priests and of married people, and it returns again to the fundamental duties toward the weak and vulnerable.

Contact with Yahweh is here and now in the Temple, but the book also directs our attention to a future coming of Yahweh and "the messenger." God is sending his messenger to prepare God's "way" (*derek*, 3:1). This coming will constitute "the great and terrible day of Yahweh" (3:23). The messenger will act like fire and lye, purifying and refining the priests (3:2–3). Yahweh himself, however, does not threaten a catastrophic theophany. He simply "draws near for judgment" (3:5).

These are details that will be used by New Testament writers to link the gospel to the Old Testament. Linking up to the identification of that messenger as Elijah (3:21), Jesus will declare John the Baptizer to be the Elijah to come (Matt 17:10–13).

17

Two Prophets on the Occasion of Disasters

I. Obadiah

A. OVERVIEW

Like Nahum, Obadiah's whole book consists of a single oracle against one nation—Edom. Since Obadiah refers to the destruction of Jerusalem (vv. 10–11), 587 BC would be the date after which the book was written. Since it celebrates in prediction form the downfall of Edom, the book could be from the same time as Mal'aki, which also celebrates some destruction of Edom (Mal 1:3; compare also Obad 18 with Mal 3:19). In the fifth century BC, the Nabataeans warred against the Edomites and pushed them out of their ancestral homeland and into southern Judah, where they became known as Idumeans (see Map 17A). This time period is most likely the setting of this book.

The enmity between Judah and Edom had ancient roots. Despite the fact that the Edomites were descended from Jacob's brother, Esau, they had refused passage to the Israelites on their way to the promised land (Num 20:14–21). David subdued the Edomites in the tenth century (2 Sam 8:13). Joram did the same in the ninth century (2 Kgs 3:20–22). Not only Obadiah, but Amos (1:11–12), Jeremiah (49:7–22), Ezekiel (24:12–14; 35:1–15), the author of Lamentations (4:21–23), and a psalmist (Ps 137) inveigh against them. Ironically, King Herod the Great (37–4 BC), who rebuilt the Temple in Roman times, was an Idumaean.

The book begins with a prediction of Edom's downfall and a condemnation of her pride (vv. 2–9). Then, with glances back at the fateful summer of 587 BC, the prophet explains the reason for Edom's downfall. He excoriates the Edomites for exulting over and assisting in the destruction of Judah by the Babylonians (vv. 10–14). Parallels to Jeremiah 49:7–22 suggest that Obadiah knew this text of Jeremiah (Obad 1–4 // Jer 49:14–16; Obad 5 // Jer 49:9; Obad 8 // Jer 49:7).

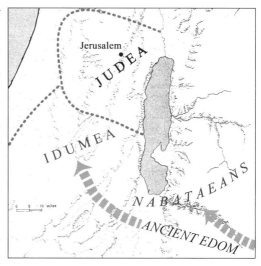

17A—Edom and Idumea

Apart from the Jacob-Esau rivalry (Gen 25:19–34), no apparent allusion to Torah traditions occur in this book.

B. Significant Passage in Obadiah

15–21 *The day of Yahweh*

For their crime against their brother nation, "the day of Yahweh" is coming upon Edom as well as on other nations (vv. 15–16, see also v. 8). "The day" is a day of destruction but it is not the eschatological "day." Rather, it seems to be the very early sense of "the day of Yahweh" as a day of military victory in holy war. Judah (the house of Jacob) as well as Israel (the house of Joseph) will be restored, and Yahweh will again reign as king on Mount Zion, which will provide security and refuge (vv. 17–21).

This day will be a day when "the captives of the children of Israel" will gather and occupy the Negeb in the south, the land of the Philistines in the west, the lands of Ephraim and Samaria, Gilead in the east, even the city of Zarephath in the north. These captives will come from as far away as Sepharad, an Aramaic name for the city of Sardis (vv. 19–20; see Maps 17B).

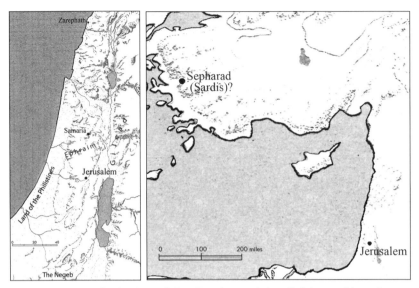

17B—The Gathering of the Captives of the Children of Israel

C. THE MESSAGE OF OBADIAH

1. Review of Images and Themes

Obadiah plays especially with images of the patriarchs: Jacob and Joseph, consuming fires (v. 18), Benjamin (v. 19) and Esau (vv. 6, 19, 21), as well as images of destructive fire (v. 18) and seizure of lands (vv. 19–21).

The dominating themes include the following:

- War and vengeance (vv. 15–18)
- The day of Yahweh (vv. 8, 15)

Connected with these themes are the following:

- Israel destroying and dispossessing others (vv. 19–21)
- Israel occupying and dwelling in the land (vv. 19–21)

2. The Theology of Obadiah

The theme of Obadiah gives rise to profound questions concerning the relations God expects to exist among nations.

Obadiah presumes the existence of obligations on the part of one nation toward another and the just anger of God when these obligations are not fulfilled.

The God of Obadiah is in effect the national God who is the master of military history. Peoples are punished because they are the enemy of Israel, because they cooperated with the Babylonian destruction (vv. 10–14), not specifically because of their ethical failures.

Yet Obadiah draws the message from a deeply felt sense of justice. The vengeful joy of Obadiah is a cry for justice, the cry found in later apocalyptic writings. If uttered in the mouth of a powerful majority, this cry appears grotesque. In the Bible, however, this cry is found consistently in the mouth of an oppressed and often helpless minority. The vengeance expressed here is a cry of anguish. God must do something! Why? Because by his nature God is Justice itself. From our weak human perspective, justice often looks like vengeance. The gospels of the New Testament will correct this.

II. Joel

A. Overview

1. The Prophet

The Book of Joel is a prophetic response to a disaster. An invasion of locusts has ravaged Judah. Joel describes the suffering and interprets the scourge as part of the day of Yahweh, calling for repentance and prayer. He then predicts the recovery from the plague as a day of great joy. The recovery will demonstrate that Yahweh dwells in Zion.

Except for 4:4–8, which is a later addition, the book appears to be a literary unity, moving from a local disaster to a cosmic vision of judgment. The smaller sections appear as coordinated scenes. The book may well have been planned and composed as a unit by Joel himself. Unlike most of the earlier "literary" prophets whose works appear more as collections of isolated preachings, Joel is a literary artist.

The circumstances described in the account point to a time between 400 and 350 BC. The Temple seems presupposed (see 4:18). However, Joel does not mention any cultic abuses or problems. All this points to a period after the reforms of Nehemiah and Ezra (445–398 BC). On the other hand, Tyre and Sidon seem to be still standing. They were destroyed in 332 and 343 BC respectively. An early fourth century dating would explain some expressions in Joel that seem to be copied from Mal'aki (Joel 2:11 // Mal 3:2; Joel 3:4 // Mal 3:23) and Obadiah (Joel 4:2–3 // Obad 11; Joel 4:19 // Obad 10; Joel 3:5 // Obad 17).

2. The Book

What makes Joel interesting for the study of ancient Jewish literature is the way this book combines the old style of prophetic literature with the new style of apocalyptic literature. The linkage of the two styles runs right down the middle of the book. In the first two chapters, Joel speaks like the old style prophet. He addresses the people, the priests, and the elders and calls them to conversion, "Even now, says Yahweh, return to me with your whole heart" (2:12), calling for a change of the interior not just the outward display (2:13). In the last two chapters, however, Joel moves into the literary milieu of apocalyptic. In visual tableaus of cosmic dimensions, he portrays "the day of Yahweh" (chapter 3). With images of harvest and vintage he describes the judgment of all nations (chapter 4). The shift comes after a transitional section from 2:18–27.

The book should be read with the following parts in mind:

Joel 1:1—2:17:	The locust plague
Joel 2:18–27:	Transition: God pities his people
Joel 3:1[2:28]—4:21[3:21]:	The day of Yahweh

(See Appendix 4o for a more detailed outline of Joel.)

When it introduced chapter divisions, the medieval Hebrew text of Joel ended chapter 2 with what we today identify as verse 27. However, also in the Middle Ages, several translations included the next five verses as part of chapter 2 (2:28–32). This leads to confusion in modern translations trying to identify verses after 2:27. We will follow the chapters and verses of the Hebrew texts, indicating other versifications by brackets.

3. Torah Traditions in Joel

Torah traditions in Joel appear in the reference to the Garden of Eden (2:3), in the covenant formula (2:27), and in the description of God as "gracious and merciful, slow to anger and abounding in steadfast love" (2:13; see Exod 34:6; Num 14:18). The general call to solemn prayer as a cultic "assembly" (2:16; *qahal*) recalls the frequent use of that term in Exodus (12:6; 16:3), Leviticus (4:13–17, 21; and so on), Numbers (10:7; 14:5; and so on) and Deuteronomy (23:2–4, 9).

B. Significant Passages in Joel

1:2—2:17 *The locust plague*

Even today swarms of locusts periodically attack regions of the Middle East. The swarms darken the sun with clouds of locusts reaching from one horizon to the other (2:2). They blanket the ground and cover walls sometimes several inches thick in a crawling, chewing mass. In futile gestures farmers beat them with brooms, knowing that soon all plant life will look as if it had been burnt by a massive firestorm (1:19–20). In a land where survival depends on each year's harvest, such a swarm is as deadly as an army of invading warriors (2:4–10).

Joel describes this disaster beginning in the countryside (1:2–18). After summoning and admonishing various named groups, he ends in a prayer (1:19–20). The prophet then describes the disaster in the city (2:1–11) ending in an intense call to assemble as a people for prayer and penance (2:12–17).

By identifying such a disaster as "the day of Yahweh" along with a call to repentance, Joel is seeing an analogy between this natural disaster and the terrible invasions about which prophets like Amos, Isaiah, and Jeremiah preached. Joel's call to prayer in effect skips over natural causes to acknowledge God's transcendent control and mysterious plan for all events of the universe.

2:18–27 *God's merciful response*

The end of the plague is announced from 2:18 where God is "stirred to concern" for his people, presumably as a result of the prayer of the people. In the part of this discourse directed to "the land" (2:21–22), Joel predicts the healing of nature. For the prophet, rescue from the locusts and restoration to prosperity is above all a sign that God is with his people (2:27). This too is part of "the day of Yahweh."

3:1–5 [2:28–32] *The day of Yahweh*

The end of the plague, however, is only a small stone in a mosaic ultimately depicting the whole universe. In the big picture, the rescue by God transforms the universe and brings an end to the history of sin. In modern theological terms, we call this perspective "eschatological" because it describes the last things (*eschata*).

Joel's eschatological description has become standard for later descriptions, especially by associating the spirit of God with the end-times. Joel here is borrowing from a theme that reaches back to Isaiah, where the "pouring out" of the spirit was the sign and the backbone of God's future rescue (Isa 32:15; see 44:3). Joel adds the universalist note of all humanity (*kol-basar*)—men and women, young and old, servants and masters—receiving this spirit (3:1). Here Joel links prophetic speech with the gift of the spirit, much like the account in Numbers 11:24–25. In fact, behind the universalist note lies perhaps a memory of Moses' prayer, "Would that Yahweh bestow his spirit on them all" (Num 11:29).

The earthly scenes of war, "blood, fire, and columns of smoke," and those of heavenly catastrophes, "the sun will be turned to darkness," express the "terrible" side of the day of Yahweh (3:3–4). These scenes are drawn from traditional statements of the prophets (see Amos 8:9; Isa 13:9–10; 24:21–23; Ezek 32:7) and become literary stage props for apocalyptic writers in their attempt to depict visually the last days (see Matt 24:29; Rev 6:12; 8:7; 9:2–3).

In the New Testament, when Christians will fret about the delay of the expected end of the world (see 2 Pet 3:3–10), Luke will draw upon this text of Joel to understand how the end-times in some way did come in the generation of Jesus (Acts 2:14–21). If for Joel the pouring out of the spirit is the constitutive element of the end-time, then a community "infused" with this Spirit is an eschatological community. As Paul would put it, "life in the Spirit" is a life of eschatological freedom, the first step in the elimination of death and corruption in the created universe (Rom 8:14–27).

4[3]:1–21 *The assembly of nations*
in the Valley of Jehoshaphat

The last section describes the great reversal of fortunes. In his enthusiasm to describe the final "holy war" between good and evil, Joel irreverently reverses the great hope for peace on the part of the eighth-century prophets (Isa 2:4; Mic 4:3). Now it is "plowshares into swords…pruning hooks into spears" (Joel 4:10).

The events include a great assembly of all nations on this "day of Yahweh" (4:14). The assembly will occur in "the Valley of Jehoshaphat" (4:2, 12), a place named for one of the Judean kings (1 Kgs 22:41–51; 2 Chron 17—18) and identified in a much later tradition as the Kidron Valley, which runs just east of the Temple and Jerusalem (4:2). More than likely the prophet had no specific valley in mind. The name Jeho-shaphat, "Yahweh is judge," is just a great name for the place of the final harvest and vintage (4:13).

The symbol of the "grim reaper" appears to be inspired by the figure of Joel 4:13. The combined use of the "harvest" (see Jer 51:33) and the "vintage" (see Isa 63:3) as symbols of divine judgment likewise seems to be rooted in this text of Joel.

C. The Message of Joel

1. Review of Images and Themes

We can distinguish the images of the earthly disaster—the swarm of locusts (1:4; 2:25); fire (1:19; 2:3); an attacking army (2:4–9); famine (1:15–18); the call to repentance (2:12)—from the eschatological scenario—the pouring out of the spirit (3:1); the darkened sun and the blood-red moon (3:4); the final harvest and vintage (4:13).

So likewise, we can distinguish the themes relating to an earthly disaster:

- The day of Yahweh as an earthly disaster (1:15; 2:1–2; 2:11)
- Yahweh stirred to pity and merciful restoring of food (2:19–26)
- Knowledge that Yahweh is in the midst of his people (2:27)

And those relating to the end-times:

- The day of Yahweh as a day of cosmic disaster (3:4; 4:14, 18)
- The pouring out of God's spirit of prophecy (3:1)
- All humanity receiving the divine spirit (3:1)
- The final judgment of the nations (4:2–3, 12–14)

2. The Theology of Joel

The God of Joel combines the God of our world and the God of the great abyss. At first the message of Joel concentrates on prayer and penance as the appropriate way of dealing with worldly suffering and distress. Joel calls for community prayer and penance as a way of dealing with such distress. He calls on all the leaders and the different groups to join in this prayer and penance. The merciful response of God shows the effectiveness of such prayer. Joel calls for a faith that can observe natural events with all their natural causes—so important in our scientific mentality—and see the hand of God. The prophet calls for a recognition of God as a person, gracious and merciful, to whom we can pray, to whom we can address a cry of anguish.

Joel provides us with a vision that links people, nature, and God. At the same time he proclaims the absolute sovereignty of God and thus avoids the "fertility cult" mentality—a mentality according to which God can be manipulated by rituals and prayer formulas. From chapter three on, we meet the God of the great abyss.

In effect then Joel provides us with a profound yet delicate theology of the power of prayer. The prayer of petition is not a magical ritual that automatically produces results. Yahweh is a God of mercy whose entire plan and will for his creation is geared toward salvation, eschatological salvation. Joel invites us to see how the daily favors we ask of God are in effect anticipations of the day of Yahweh. This balance will appear in the New Testament's account of the Lord's Prayer, especially as Luke remembered it, "Father…thy kingdom come, give us each day our daily bread" (Luke 11:2–3).

Joel's confidence rests ultimately on eschatological salvation. However, he sees how God can anticipate that eschatological salvation with a very worldly material rescue that transforms our time of distress into joy. The rescue from the locusts and the final pouring out of the spirit are two aspects of the same picture for Joel.

PART IV

Prophetic-sounding Midrash

18
Introduction to Midrash

I. The Development of Midrashic Literature

Rabbinic literature uses the term *midrash* (plural: *midrashim*) to describe commentaries on Scripture. This Hebrew word is the noun form of the verb *darash*, which means "to search" or "to scrutinize." Commentaries that dealt with biblical stories or narrations were called haggadic midrash, from the Hebrew word *haggadah*, which means "narration."

Midrashic literature is essentially a literature about another piece of literature, a reflection on, a meditation of, or a searching into a sacred text. This literary practice testifies to a great love and veneration for the written stories of Israel, considered inspired and the revelation of God's word. The practice also testifies to a sense of religious tradition as a living voice, expressing the changing life of the people of God, adapting the inspired words into contemporary expressions of Israel's teaching.

It was apparently during the Babylonian Exile that the synagogue service developed during which Israel's Book could be examined and treasured. Typical of a synagogue service—which needed no Temple, no priest, no king—was the practice of reading from the Torah and the prophets. The practice of respected teachers explaining or discoursing on the texts also developed (see Luke 4:14–30). In the postexilic period, these biblical expositions or homilies became collected and written as learned leaders devoted their lives to the study and explanation of scripture (see Ezra 7:6, 10). We now understand that sometimes whole biblical books fit into the literary form of haggadic midrash.

The main purpose of the writer of this literature was practical rather than speculative, seeking to adapt the sense and teaching of the sacred text to the immediate spiritual needs of the audience. To accomplish this purpose, the author allowed himself great latitude, even to the point of inventing an entire story around a detail in the text in order to make it relevant and meaningful. Thus these stories graphically illustrate some aspect of life that God expects of every good Israelite. In these stories the characters appear and speak in a way to keep the story moving and dramatic. Prayers and speeches serve as vehicles for expressing the author's teaching. Thus the historical nucleus upon which the story is based is relatively unimportant.

II. Jonah and Daniel as Midrash

In this study we are treating the books of Jonah and Daniel as midrash. In doing so we perhaps reluctantly forgo reading these stories for historical information. However, seeing these stories as midrash allows us to concentrate on this literature as saying something important about our faith. As such they underline the fully human nature of that faith. They do this in two ways, first by the narrative form of these books and secondly by their very existence as later pseudonymous writing.

A. NARRATIVE FORM

In their narrative form, these writings remind us that our faith is not primarily a faith of abstract dogmas and creeds—although dogma and creed can enrich that faith. Our faith is not a faith based just on complex historical knowledge—although the action of God in history is a foundation of that faith. Ours is a faith of people living in families and cultures where concrete experience is the fundamental principle.

Concrete experience is often best captured in story, not philosophy. Story allows us to portray and celebrate the person and his or her challenge in all his or her uniqueness. Yet story also allows us to see the patterns of existence that bind us to that unique event and person, patterns that illumine our own unique person and challenges. Story allows us to engage our imagination as well as our intellect and will in the attempt to grasp truth.

People will object, "But these stories are made up! They are fictional!" Good fiction, however, represents more than creative imagination. In and through the characters and actions it describes, good fiction allows a deeper dimension of reality to shine forth. As in all great art, a dimension of reality is present in and through the medium. We recognize that reality when we are captivated by a story. We recognize that the story ultimately is about ourselves. We may not be able to present that reality in any way outside of that story—although scholars continue trying to analyze and dissect. We make attempts to articulate that deeper dimension, but ultimately understanding requires returning to the medium in its concreteness in simple, joyful appreciation. Good fiction does that, as Jesus knew when he told parables.

So it is with Jonah and Daniel. We will attempt to analyze the stories. In the end, however, we must return to the stories as stories and rejoice in the concrete presentation of characters who demonstrate their faith by living out the unique situations of their contingent existence. In some strange way, by this aesthetic experience we touch the eternal essence of God.

B. Pseudonymous Writings

Secondly, by their late pseudonymous existence, the stories of Jonah and Daniel remind us of the continued presence of God's revelation among his people. The large body of midrashic writings that emerged after the time of Ezra and Nehemiah appears to have come about because "the authorities" wanted to close the canon of scripture. Jonah made it into "the prophets" section of the Bible because it purported to be from a little-known prophet of the eighth century, Jonah ben Amittai (2 Kgs 14:25). Daniel snuck into "the writings" because it described itself as revelation to a sixth-century exile in Babylon, like Ezekiel. When "the writings" were finally closed, a massive body of pseudonymous writings appeared in the Judaism of late antiquity, all presented as long-lost writings of great past heroes.

Although the norms of our faith are now found in the historical documents of scripture, we read scripture not just to know about history. We read it to find God in the present. The scriptures must be interpreted and applied in such a way that they can speak to the present. One way of accomplishing that interpretation and application is to retell the ancient story so that it speaks to the present. Such seems to have been the historical purpose of Jewish midrash.

The Jewish writers of course understood the importance of the permanence of the ancient texts whose meaning was captured in the writing, and whose writing was to be passed on as *copies* of an original. Without such permanence there could be no norm by which to measure the faith of successive generations. Yardsticks and miles have to remain fixed if they are to be used as measures. If we attempt to bring two cities closer together by simply changing the standard used to measure their distance, we end up destroying meaning, and the cities remain the same distance apart. Thus, canons are fixed. They are then capable of measuring the possible revelation and inspiration of other later expressions of faith.

Ironically, both Jonah and Daniel were incorporated into the canon of scripture. Thus their very attempt to adapt the faith becomes a canon or norm of faith. In effect these writings *authoritatively* proclaim that God's revelation does not stop at some watershed moment determined by human authority. From the canon of scripture, we get the impression that God feels good about a fixed tradition of faith, something that would insert later believers into a historical community, something that would allow us to have ancestors in the faith, and thus something that would compel us to continue the process of passing down the faith. But from that same canon of scripture, we get the impression that God delights also in creativity and growth, a creativity and growth that allows us to adapt the faith to new challenges, one that turns us to the future, one that allows our children to assimilate the faith into their lives.

The books of Jonah and Daniel thus assure us that God's revelation continues to give us life. The books also strongly suggest that prophets remain among us, mediating the word of God to us and interceding before God on our behalf. Their form is different from the ancient prophets of Israel. We are not even sure what to name these people or how we can identify them clearly. But for sure, God continues to reveal his word and to raise up men and women who stand in his council and in some way announce the will of God to the world.

19
The Book of Jonah

I. Overview

When the Jewish authorities drew up the collection of the "Twelve Prophets" sometime before the second century BC, they apparently identified the Book of Jonah as the collection of preachings from a historical prophet, like the collection of preachings of Hosea or Joel. The Book of Jonah begins like Hosea and Joel, "This is the word of the Lord that came to…" (1:1). The name "Jonah son of Amittai" recalls the mention of the prophet of the same name associated with the events of Jeroboam II back in the eighth century (2 Kgs 14:25).

Literary indications, however, abound in this book to signal the reader that this work is not like the other books of the prophets but rather consists of a midrashic story made up to teach an important lesson. For one thing, Jonah "the prophet" succeeds in his preaching—with hardly any effort—a rather suspicious fact for those who are familiar with the work of the great prophets in Israel. Furthermore, the Hebrew of this book has more the characteristics of fifth-century than of eighth-century Hebrew.

The story line itself suggests the same conclusion. Little effort is made to state names and specific times. The narration is fast moving and concentrates on the main events. The characters are boldly drawn without complications, although ironically reversed in terms of "villain" and "good guys"—much like the story of the Good Samaritan. The pagan Gentiles of this story are insightful, compassionate, and deeply reverent. Jonah on the other hand is disobedient to God, easily irritated, and full of hatred for others. Events are narrated, like those in 1:16, after

Jonah has been removed from the scene, and no one else is around to record the events.

Furthermore, a number of unrealistic details argue to the fictional character of this book. The size of Nineveh in the story is exaggerated. Nineveh was a big city for its day. Its outer walls still visible today run about eight miles around the city—not a three day's walk (see 3:3). Perhaps most important, history records no evidence of a massive conversion of the Assyrian Empire's capital to Yahwism. Such a conversion would have changed the course of history! (We need not deal at all with the issue of the possibility of a human surviving the gastric juices of a "large fish.")

These details are literary indications by which an author signals to the reader the literary form in which the author is working. The option for an interpreter today is whether or not to accept these literary indications as evidence of midrashic literary form or to stick by a preconceived identification of the literary form as classic prophecy. This is not a matter of faith but of literary analysis.

As a fictional story, the Book of Jonah has a griping message—even if colored with dry humor. The book appears to be from the fifth century BC. This would be the time when Ezra and Nehemiah were insisting on religious separatism—no association with nonbelievers (see Ezra 9:1–15). The universalism proposed by Isaiah 56:1–8 or 66:18–21 appears to have fallen into the shadows. Into that historical context, the Book of Jonah would have blared an important message.

If we follow the scenes or settings of the story, the book falls into two major parts, each with parallel developments:

Jonah 1:1–3:	Introduction
Jonah 1:4—2:11:	Part I: At sea
Jonah 3:1–10:	Part II: At Nineveh
Jonah 4:1–11:	Conclusion: Jonah and God

One faint echo of Torah traditions can be heard from 4:2 with its description of "a gracious and merciful God, slow to anger, rich in clemency, renouncing punishment" (see Exod 34:6–7).

II. Significant Passages in Jonah

1:1–3 *The mission of Jonah*

Told to go east to Nineveh, Jonah sails as far west as he can—to Tarshish, possibly some city or district as far away as Spain.

1:4–16 *Jonah and the sailors*

The good dispositions of the "pagans" appear in sharp relief. They immediately cry out to their gods for help while Jonah sleeps and has to be awakened by the captain and told to pray. The sailors are horrified at Jonah's disobedience yet row hard to save him. Only with great reluctance do they cast him into the sea—a sharp contrast to Jonah's attitude toward nonbelievers in 4:1–3. After Jonah is gone, the men are filled with reverent fear offering sacrifices and vows to Yahweh!

2:1–11 [1:17—2:10] *Jonah and the great fish*

Although it appears a bit of a literary "lump" in its present context, the psalm of thanksgiving placed in the mouth of Jonah furthers the story line. From this psalm it is clear that the "great fish" is an instrument of God's rescue of Jonah from the depths of the sea. Jonah remains in the belly of the fish "three days and three nights." Since the expression "three days" is often used in both biblical and nonbiblical stories to describe the duration of a journey, the author here is probably thinking of the "great fish" as the divinely ordained means of transporting Jonah from the "depths" (like Sheol) back to life. (See Matt 12:40 where this detail of the story of Jonah is related to the resurrection of Jesus.)

3:1–10 *Jonah and the Ninevites*

The second time around, Jonah shows a lot more docility. The whole prophetic preaching of Jonah is given in one verse (see 3:4). His success is astonishing. Just as the author had contrasted the moral character of the sailors with that of Jonah, so here too we see a striking contrast between the faith and promptness of the Ninevites and the attitudes of Jonah. Even the king joins in—with all the animals! As a result, God "repented of the evil that he had threatened to do them" (3:10). The author may well be thinking of the oracle of God found in Jeremiah 18:7–8.

4:1–11 *Dialogues with God*

The first dialogue with God captures the meaning of the book. Jonah did not want God to be "gracious and merciful." He wanted the Ninevites to get blasted! He would rather die than see the hated Ninevites forgiven! God responds with a sense of perplexity, "Have you reason to be angry?"

In a second dialogue between Jonah and God, the author makes his point. God provides shade for Jonah by a miraculously fast-growing vine and then produces a worm to destroy the vine. Jonah is intensely angry. God asks Jonah to use this experience to understand the divine concern for Nineveh.

III. The Message of Jonah

A. REVIEW OF THEMES

The themes Jonah are simple:

- God's love for all peoples, Jews and Gentiles (1:2; 3:10; 4:9–11)
- The folly of exclusive nationalism (1:3–16; 4:1–4)
- The persistence of God's call and the folly of resisting it (1:2—3:5)

B. THE THEOLOGY OF JONAH

In the Book of Jonah, we also have an extraordinary portrayal of God. Besides insisting on God's love for all peoples, this book also dramatizes the disparity between human thoughts and divine thoughts. God breaks into Jonah's world and in effect destroys it. God comes as a threat to Jonah's religious views. We have here a hint of that great divine abyss found in the great prophets.

This short story also offers its readers a mirror to see themselves as they are—petty, selfish, unreasonable, unwilling to admit that God's love extends to all persons not just to his chosen people. The book is a satire on the narrow nationalism and malignant intolerance of the fifth-century Jews who were pushing Ezekiel's monastic concept of Israel to unreasonable lengths. The Book of Jonah is the author's protest against Israel's refusal to take up the mission to be "a light to the Gentiles" (Isa 49:6).

The temptation to arrogance is one of the constant hazards of religion. With its necessary visible structures, religion tends to obscure the mystery of God, the incomprehensible goodness and graciousness of a Love we will never fathom. Jesus told a parable about workers in a vineyard who are angry that the master was prodigal to those who did not work as hard as they did. The master responds, "Are you envious because I am generous" (Matt 20:1–16).

20
The Book of Daniel

I. Overview

A. THE BOOK

The Book of Daniel at first seems like two books in one. In its first part (chapters 1–6), the author culls from tradition a number of stories dealing with an upper-class Jewish exile named Daniel and his friends during the Babylonian captivity. In typical midrashic style, this author elaborates the stories freely and skillfully in order to encourage the faithful of his time and culture to resist anti-Jewish forces just as Daniel and his friends resisted Nebuchadnezzar and Babylonian idolatry.

In the second part of the book (chapters 7–12), the author, now assuming the identity of Daniel, unreels and interprets the history of the great world empires from the time of Nebuchadnezzar down to the time of the reigning persecutor of the Jews, Antiochus. Daniel foretells the downfall of the persecutor and the advent of the kingdom that God will set up on behalf of his people.

The literary style of this second part conforms to what we today call apocalyptic literature. This is a style rooted in the visions of Ezekiel and Proto-Zechariah. The immediate forerunner of this literature appears to be Joel 3—4, where the day of Yahweh appears in cosmic proportions, involving heavenly upheavals and earthly judgment. In the later apocalyptic literature visions, symbolic animals, colors, numbers, and other elements are presented and then often interpreted by an angel. We are given a glimpse into God's plans for the world, especially God's plans for dealing with evil forces in this world.

A third part of the Book of Daniel, found only in the Greek Old Testament (chapters 13–14), contains additional midrashic stories about Daniel in Babylon and about the unjustly accused Susanna, saved from execution by the forensic wisdom of Daniel.

Probably written for people suffering unrelenting persecution and actual martyrdom, the purpose of the book most likely was to encourage the faithful to put their faith in the age-old promises of the prophets and to persevere patiently under the trials of the persecution in the certain expectation of the fulfillment of these promises in the imminent future. This purpose appears clearly in both the midrashic and the apocalyptic sections of the book. The basic unity of the book appears likewise in the connection between the dream of Nebuchadnezzar of chapter 2 and the visions of chapters 7–12, both concerned with the history of empires as determined by God's plan.

Apart from the stories of chapters 13 and 14, which we have only in the Greek version, the Book of Daniel combines both Hebrew and Aramaic texts, without any clear reason for the shift from one to the other. Daniel 1:1 to 2:4a is in Hebrew. This section includes an introductory story, perhaps added later to the collection, and the beginning of the story of Nebuchadnezzar's mysterious dream. The Aramaic then appropriately begins with the quoted words of the "Chaldeans" at 2:4a but then continues with the narration of this story and the next four stories along with the first apocalyptic vision (7:1–28). The remaining three apocalyptic visions (8:1—12:13) are narrated in Hebrew. Given a thematic unity between the story of chapter 2 and the vision of chapter 7, we can speculate that the Aramaic section was an earlier shorter version of Daniel, to which a later Hebrew speaking-author wrote the introductory story (chapter 1) and the three additional visions (chapters 8–12).

(See Appendix 4p for a more detailed outline of Daniel.)

B. HISTORICAL CHRONOLOGY

The historical setting that sheds light on both the story line and the writing of the Book of Daniel embraces the rise and fall of the great empires from the sixth to the second century BC as appears in II Kings, Ezra-Nehemiah, and 1–2 Maccabees. The following chronological outline indicates the actual personages and dates that form the historical background of this book:

605–562   Reign of Nebuchadnezzar; the active period of Ezekiel, the father of apocalyptic literature

555–539   Nabonidus, the last king of Babylon, and Belshazzar, crown prince and coregent in the last years of Babylon

539–530   Cyrus the Great and the beginning of the Persian Empire

522–485   Darius I, third emperor of Persia, after Cambyses and Smerdis (the Usurper), followed by Xerxes I, Artaxerxes I, Darius II, Artaxerxes II, and Artaxerxes III

356–323   Alexander the Great, who conquers Persia in 331 BC; his empire was then divided after his death in 323 among his generals

323–198   Israel and Palestine under the domination of the Ptolemies (or Lagids), the line of rulers from Alexander who controlled Egypt

198–143   Israel and Palestine under the domination of the Seleucids, the line of rulers from Alexander who controlled Syria

170–164   The persecution of Israel by the Seleucid king, Antiochus IV Epiphanes, starting with the assassination of Onias the high priest in 170 BC, culminating in the erection of the altar of Zeus in the Jerusalem Temple in 167

C. Dating the Book of Daniel

When it is read as a historical and prophetic book written in the sixth century BC, the Book of Daniel swarms with difficulties. Why, for instance, was this book placed among the Hagiographa ("the Writings") in the Hebrew Bible (after Esther rather than after Ezekiel)? Why was the Book of Sirach, written about the year 200 BC, silent concerning the very existence of the Book of

Daniel? Why were the authors of Job, Ecclesiastes, and Sirach, authors who struggled with the issues of life and death, apparently ignorant of the teaching of Daniel 12 on future life? Why does the author seem so confused when dealing with matters of the Babylonian Empire, such as his treatment of Belshazzar, Nebuchadnezzar, and Nabonidus—to say nothing of his descriptions of an otherwise unknown Darius the Mede—and yet is remarkably on target in his descriptions of the Hellenistic kings of the third century BC? Why the combination of Hebrew and Aramaic?

These difficulties disappear for the most part if we treat the book as a midrashic and apocalyptic work written in the early second century. As written during the persecution of Antiochus IV, the book quite naturally finds its place among the Hagiographa, the last section of the Hebrew Bible, rather than among the prophets, a section closed before the year 200 BC. The authors writing after the Exile down to the second century BC would be ignorant of Daniel and its teachings for the simple reason that it had not as yet been written. The apparent historical inaccuracies in this book regarding the Babylonian period are explained partly by the ignorance of the author regarding events some four hundred years before his time. The combination of languages suggests a succession of redactions.

The Book of Daniel betrays its youth also by its language. In its vocabulary and syntax, the Aramaic language used from 2:4b—3:23 and 3:91—7:28 reflects the Aramaic of the Hellenistic age far more than the Aramaic of the older empires. For instance, when the list of musical instruments appears repeatedly in chapter 3, three of them have transliterated Greek names, the *kitaros* (a lyre), the *pesanterin* (a kind of harp), and the *symphonya* (often translated "bagpipes"!).

In its veiled account of the struggles between the Ptolemies of Egypt and the Seleucids of Syria, chapter 11 is quite detailed and accurate in its description of the Hellenistic wars up to a certain date. The events narrated up to Daniel 11:39 correlate well with the disastrous actions of Antiochus IV and correspond with events up to 167 BC (see Appendix 5). From 11:40 on we find descriptions that do not appear to have taken place. The author is also inexact as to the place of Antiochus's death (11:45), who actually died in Persia in 164 BC. This shift away from accurate descriptions would strongly suggest the year 167 BC as the date of composition.

D. Torah Traditions in Daniel

Daniel is a person devoted to the Law of Moses (9:10–13). The very first story of Daniel takes place against the Jewish food laws found in Leviticus 11 and 19 (Dan 1:8–16).

II. Significant Passages in Daniel

A. Part One / Daniel 1—6 / Midrashic Section

1:1–21 *Introduction of Daniel*

Chapter 1 introduces Daniel as a young Jewish nobleman deported to Babylon in 605 BC (1:1–7) and explains Daniel's rise to prominence in the Babylonian court (1:17–21). In this way, chapter 1 sets the scene for the subsequent stories about Daniel as a state official in a pagan empire. On the one hand, the successes of Daniel show the possibilities of the Israelites to coexist with nonbelieving neighbors in a pagan empire. On the other hand, we see Daniel and his friends here observing their Jewish dietary laws without compromise. The scene is meant to speak to Jews living under the terror of Antiochus IV, a setting also presented in 1 Maccabees 1 and 2 Maccabees 6—7.

2:1–49 *The emperor's dream*

The story of Nebuchadnezzar's dream shares many of the themes of the apocalyptic section of Daniel and helps to bring the whole book together. Daniel professes his faith in a God "who reveals mysteries" (2:28). The word *mysteries* here clearly means God's secret plan of salvation working through history.

Daniel interprets Nebuchadnezzar's dream of a statue composed of four kinds of metal—in descending order of value—gold, silver, bronze, and iron with some ceramic tile (2:31–35), as

symbolic of four great empires, each inferior to the preceding—
a rather pessimistic view of history. The first is that of
Nebuchadnezzar, the Babylonian Empire, followed by two lesser-
quality empires. The details of the last empire (2:40–43) identify
it with that of Alexander the Great, divided in great part between
the Seleucids of Syria and the Ptolemies of Egypt. This last
empire—and all the empires—will disintegrate before the kingdom that God will set up "that shall never be destroyed." This
kingdom of God is symbolized by the great stone, "not hewn by
hand" (2:44–45). The great stone imagery is rooted in that of the
cornerstone of Psalm 118:22 or Isaiah 28:16, an image of God's key
action on earth beyond the understanding of human beings.

The early Christians used the image of the great stone to
identify Jesus (Mark 12:10–11 and parallels; Rom 9:32–33; 1 Pet
2:6–8). When Luke describes how this wonderful stone will also
destroy and crush (Luke 20:18), he is probably linking this early
Christology to the text of Daniel, seeing the coming of this final
kingdom of God in the person of Jesus.

5:1–30 *The writing on the wall*
Brought in to interpret mysterious writing on the wall
(5:5–13), Daniel explains the words as indicating the impending
end of Belshazzar's kingdom. His rule has been *numbered* and
weighed and found wanting, and so his kingdom is to be *divided*
among the Medes and the Persians, as Daniel interprets the three
mysterious words on the wall, *mᵉne*, *tᵉkel*, and *parsin* (5:25–28).
The story illustrates "that the Most High God rules over the
kingdom of men and appoints over it whomever he wills" (5:21).
The setting of the desecration of the Temple vessels (5:1–4) recalls
the desecration of the Jerusalem sanctuary by Antiochus IV (1 Macc
1:44–50). Daniel here insists that God punishes the proud, who
misuse God-given power, by taking away from them their power
and glory (5:18–23). The Jewish faithful can be assured that the
kingdom of Antiochus IV will likewise be taken from him.

6:1–29 [5:31—6:28] *Daniel in the lions' den*
Perhaps more than any other midrash of this book, the best
known is that of Daniel in the lions' den. In order to destroy

Daniel's power, jealous Babylonian politicians have the king pass a law making it unlawful to pray to anyone but to the king for thirty days (6:1–10). As expected, Daniel continues his prayerful devotion to God and when discovered is condemned to death (6:11–18). God, however, delivers Daniel from the mouth of the lions, and when the king discovers this miracle, Daniel's enemies are destroyed with poetic justice (6:19–25).

When Antiochus IV prohibited sacrifice and prayers to God under pain of death (1 Macc 1:44–50), this story would remind faithful Jews that God is "a deliverer and a savior" (6:28). Governments on earth may rail against him, but "his kingdom shall not be destroyed, and his dominion shall be without end" (6:27). The story ends with Daniel's prosperity.

B. PART II / DANIEL 7—12 / APOCALYPTIC SECTION

Written in apocalyptic style, chapters 7–12 develop the theme of the coming kingdom of God, which according to the author will follow after the end of the Syrian persecution. This theme was introduced earlier in chapter 2 by the stone that destroys and replaces the composite statue representing the kingdoms or empires of earth. This theme then appears in four different tableaus: (a) the beasts in chapter 7, (b) the ram and billy goat in chapter 8, (c) the seventy weeks of years in chapter 9, and (d) the conflict of the kingdoms in chapters 10–12.

This type of repetition is characteristic of apocalyptic literature and is based upon the Hebrew method of developing a theme by means of different independent tableaus, where each tableau emphasizes a different aspect of the same subject. Thus chapter 7 concentrates on the opposition between the kingdoms of this world and the kingdom of God that supplants them. Chapter 8 describes the persecution and death of the persecutor, Antiochus IV. Chapter 9 concentrates on the timing of the eschatological kingdom. Chapters 10–12 describe at length the history of the Seleucids and the persecution of the Jews by Antiochus IV, ending in the promise of resurrection and eternal life for the martyrs of the persecution.

Prophetic-sounding Midrash

7:1–28 *The vision of the four beasts*

The first tableau falls into two parts: (a) the details of the vision (7:2–14) and (b) the heavenly interpretation of the details (7:15–27). The details of the vision likewise consist of two parts: (a) an earthly scene of four beasts arising from the primal sea of chaos in an atmosphere of violence and arrogance, and (b) a heavenly scene of the divine throne room in an atmosphere of serene power where matters on earth are determined. The angelic interpretation identifies the four beasts as symbols of four great kingdoms of the earth.

Hints of divine control of these kingdoms appear already in the passive verbs by which at least the first three kingdoms are described. Curiously, the fearsome teeth normally associated with a lion and the feet supporting an upright posture normally associated with a bear (see Rev 13:1–2) are transposed. In any case, the tableau thus far follows the description in chapter 2 of the four kingdoms. The description of the fourth beast moves its focus to "the little horn" who speaks arrogantly (Dan 7:8). Mention of "the little horn" brings the scene down to the reign of Antiochus IV, whose persecution is explained by the angel (7:24–25).

In a sudden shift—which itself expresses the transcendence of the divine level—we are moved to the heavenly war room. God, "the Ancient One," appears like the God of Ezekiel (7:9–10; see Ezek 1:26). The arrogant beast is quickly neutralized according to "the books," the predetermined script according to which God determines history (7:11–12). Most important, "kingship" (*malkû*; 7:14) is given to one like a "son of Man" (*bar 'enosh*; 7:13). The expression "son of man" could be simply a way of saying a human being (as we see in Ezek 1:26). Yet this one "like a son of man" has angelic features: on the clouds of heaven, in the presence of God, given great power by God (7:13–14).

In the heavenly interpretation, what is said of the "one like a son of man" is said now of "the holy people of the Most High" (7:27). The eternal kingdom and power is given to Israel, God's people, who for a temporary period (32 years, see 7:25) must suffer the oppression of Antiochus IV. The heavenly "son of man" who starts out clearly as an angel thus also represents Israel, perhaps the way that the guardian angels of nations in this literature represented the people (see 10:20–21).

The descriptions throughout chapter 7 revolve around the great contrast between the earthly level and the divine level, between the earthly kingdoms and the heavenly one. The earthly kingdoms are connected to beasts. The kingdom of the holy ones is connected to one "like a human being." The earthly kingdoms are from below and from the sea; the kingdom of the holy ones is from above. The earthly kingdoms are successive and limited temporally; the kingdom of the holy ones is universal and eternal.

After Daniel a Jewish tradition arose about a heavenly human being who would be God's instrument of salvation, intervening at the end-times, sitting on God's glorious throne, and judging the world. This figure, named also the "Elect One," appears intermittently in 1 *Enoch* 37—71 (see especially 45:3–5; 48:2–7; 51:3; 61:8; 62:9). In the Synoptic Gospels, Jesus consistently identifies himself as the "son of man" (Mark 2:10, 28; 10:45; and so on). The identification seems at once rooted in the "one like a son of man" in Daniel 7:13 (see especially Mark 13:26) but also tied into the later tradition as it moved from an angelic figure with collective significance to a human individual with divine power and glory. Jesus, however, adds to this figure the role of suffering (Mark 8:31; 9:12, 10:33).

8:1–27 *The vision of the ram and billy goat*

Imitating Ezekiel 1:1 with its mention of Babylonian cities and rivers, the author of Daniel begins another tableau. Like chapter 7 in theme and form, this tableau consists of a vision of a heavenly battle in which a ram is destroyed by a billy goat (8:3–7). In the second part of the vision, the angel Gabriel interprets the ram as representing the kings of the Medes and Persians and the billy goat as representing the king of the Greeks (8:15–21). The author may be relying on contemporary astrology where Aries (the ram) was a sign of Persia and Capricorn (the goat) a sign of Greece.

Although mentioned in some ancient literature, modern history knows of no dominant empire of the Medes like that named in this text of Daniel (8:20) and probably presupposed in the earlier stories of the emperor's dream (2:38–40), the lions' den (6:1, 29), the vision of the four beasts (7:17)—which all seem to present a repeated schema of four empires: (a) Babylonian, (b) Mede, (c) Persian, and (d) Greco-Syrian. While the Medes were a force at one time allied with the Babylonians against the Assyrians, Cyrus the Great of Persia had conquered this people and subsumed their authority and power into his empire before he rolled against the Babylonians.

Gabriel, whose name combines *geber* (strong man or hero) and *'El* (God), appears in the Old Testament only in these chapters of Daniel (8:16; 9:21; and probably also 10:5–6), where he is always described as a "man" or "like a man." Gabriel thus becomes the apocalyptic angel, revealing the eschatological realities.

As in the preceding chapter, Antiochus IV appears as a "little horn" on the billy goat and persecutes the holy ones, the faithful of Israel. He interrupts the daily sacrifice (see 1 Macc 1:45–54; 4:38–39), rises up against God himself, and is powerful enough to cast down even some of the stars from heaven. (Dan 8:9–13, 23–25).

The vision, however, is clear about the ultimate victory of God (8:25). This rage of evil is to last only three and a half years ("two thousand three hundred evenings and mornings," 8:14). This number, half of seven, signifies the idea of incompleteness and therefore a provisional reality. In fact the desecration of the temple by Antiochus IV is dated by 1 Maccabees from Chislev (November–December) 167 to Chislev 164 BC (1 Macc 1:54; 5:52)—almost exactly three years.

As in chapter 7, the author insists that the struggle on earth between good and evil people has its roots in a heavenly realm. The real forces of good and evil are more than human. All hope therefore lies in the heavenly victory by the forces of God over the forces of evil, a victory that is assured.

This story of hope is presented in the form of a dramatic myth of a heavenly battle against evil monsters and kings who presume divine glory. Variations of this story were well known in the ancient Middle East and evidenced in the Bible (see Isa 14:12–15; 27:1; 51:9–10).

* * *

The third tableau (9:1–27) is different. It is less about visual symbols than about the details of scripture. The text at point is Jeremiah 25:11–12 or 29:10, where the prophet foretells a period of exile for Israel in Babylon lasting some seventy years. Daniel searches for a way to have this text of scripture speak to the present.

9:24–27 *Gabriel's reinterpretation*
In response to Daniel's prayer, Gabriel the archangel reinterprets the seventy years of Jeremiah to mean seventy weeks of years or some 490 years (see Lev 25:8) as the time of distress, calculated from the prophecy of Jeremiah in 605 BC (see Jer 25:1–13)—after which "the end will come like a torrent" (9:26), a time of "everlasting justice" and the "anointing of the most holy" (9:24). The sequence of events cryptically described leads up to the desecration of the Temple by Antiochus the IV (9:27), which took place in 167 BC—actually 438 years later.

* * *

The fourth tableau spans chapters 10–12. Chapters 10:1–11:1 describe Daniel's meeting with the revealing angel. In 11:2–45 this angel tells Daniel about the succession of kings from those of Persia and Alexander the Great, including a detailed account of his successors. Here the interpreter angel recounts the history of the Seleucid kings from Seleucus I to Antiochus IV and his persecution of the Jews. (See Appendix 5b for a table of the Seleucid kings of Syria.) Daniel 12:1–13 describes the resurrection and eternal life that await as rewards those who persevere to the end of the persecutions.

10:1—11:1 *The vision of heavenly conflicts*
After describing the place and time of Daniel as well as his personal preparation for the revelation (10:1–4), the account of the vision begins with the description of the messenger from heaven (10:5–6). Although unnamed, this person parallels the figure of Gabriel, who appeared in chapters 8 and 9. This angelic

figure will impart to Daniel the "truth" (*'emet* 11:2; see 10:1), which here means God's saving plan worked out in the conflicts of history.

The scene echoes many motifs found in the text of Ezekiel 1. The description of a heavenly person in verse 6 draws directly on the text of Ezekiel 1:24. This description of the appearance will be used again by Revelation 1:13–14 to indicate the risen Christ.

This angel himself is involved in a heavenly conflict, but he is helped by the angel Michael (10:13, 20–21), later identified as the guardian angel of Israel (12:1). The conflict is with the angels ("princes") of Persia and Greece. Thus the conflict of good and evil on earth appears rooted in a transcendent conflict of angelic proportions. God is above this conflict, but forces far greater than human are at the root of the horrors appearing on earth.

12:1–13 *The end-time*

The author's description of the end-time involves one of the earliest unequivocal statements of faith in the resurrection of the dead:

> Many of those who sleep in the dust of the earth will awake; some to everlasting life; others to everlasting horror and disgrace. But the wise shall shine like the splendor of the firmament, and those who lead the many to justice, like the stars forever. (12:2–3)

Close literary connections link this text with that of Isaiah 26:19, a very late addition to the Book of Isaiah:

> Your dead will live, your corpses arise.
> Awake and shout for joy, you who dwell in the dust.
> For your dew is a dew of light, and the land of shades
> give birth.

This faith in a life after death arose with considerable emphasis at the time of the Maccabees, when the martyrdom of those loyal to God's law almost demanded a vindication after death of their sacrifice (see 2 Macc 7:9–14, 23–36; 12:43–46). In the

Jewish anthropology of the time not yet influenced by Platonic dualism, picturing such life after death required picturing a resurrection of the dead body.

The command to "seal the book until the end-time" is part of the author's explanation why a book supposedly written in the sixth century would not be read until the second. Thus the readers of the book would understand themselves as living in "the end-time" (*'et qetz*; 12:4).

The conclusion of the vision turns to the question of timing: "How long shall it be until the end?" (12:5). The answer, "three and a half years" (12:7), becomes the symbolic duration of evil times. The numbers of days mentioned in verses 11 and 12—1,290 or 1,335—are inexplicably different, but both come to about three and a half years, the duration more or less in fact during which the Temple lay desecrated.

III. The Message of Daniel

A. REVIEW OF THEMES

The nature of apocalyptic appears in its variety of themes revolving around the conflict of good and evil and the divine view in which that conflict can be understood. We see this variety in Daniel:

- The challenge of faithful life in the Diaspora (1:1–21; 6:2–18)
- Divine protection of the faithful outside of Israel (1:9, 17–20; 2:19–30; 6:1–29)
- God's plan of history, revealed to special people (2:27–30; 2:47; 7—12)
- God's power over the worldly authorities (2:31–45; 5:18–28; 7—12)
- The kingdom of God (2:44–45; 6:27–28; 7:14, 18)
- The parallel worlds of heaven and earth with angelic mediators (7—12)

- The conflict of good and evil powers with its great distress on earth (7:7–8, 19–25; 8:8–14, 23–25; 9:25–27; 10:13, 20–21)
- The ultimate victory of God over evil (7:11–12, 26–27; 8:25; 9:24; 12:12–13)
- The end of time (8:17; 9:26; 12:1–13)
- The fulfillment of prophecy as a precise prediction of the future (9:24–27)
- Life after death (12:2–3, 13)

B. THE THEOLOGY OF DANIEL

1. *Fidelity in a hostile culture.* The Book of Daniel assures the faithful that the promises of the ancient prophets are worthy of belief. This message is important for a religious people living their faith in a culture that does not share that faith. How do you maintain fidelity to a religious tradition when the very structures of society run counter to the basic elements of your faith?

The midrashic stories of Daniel include the idea of some accommodation with that culture. Neither Daniel nor his friends long to go back to Israel. Like Joseph in Egypt, Daniel in Babylonia evokes respect from the highest circles of power. He beats the magicians at their own game yet shows compassion for them. The midrashic part concludes with the prosperity of Daniel and the Persian kings proclaiming the kingdom of God (6:26–29).

On the other hand, Daniel in these stories draws a clear line beyond which he will not step, standing firm even under the threat of a horrible death. He refuses to bow to the gods of Babylon. For all ages to come, Daniel in the lions' den (chapter 6) portrays the faithful person who has made his or her decision in faith at a great cost. Daniel took his stand on principle. The divine protection of Daniel and others portrayed in this story provides for the reader a satisfying assurance that Daniel and his friends were right and did not need to fear the frightful dangers that surrounded them.

2. *A divine view of the world.* For those who are not protected by divine miracle, for those whom the reader might personally know who died with no protecting angel sheltering them from

beast or fire, the Book of Daniel suggests another form of divine protection, one that begins after death (12:2). The visions of Daniel thus propose a divinelike perspective of the great global "distress" and what otherwise remains the black veil of death. Those destroyed by the flames of a furnace, those ripped apart by the claws and teeth of beasts are also shown to be right in their firm stance opposing society.

Such a conclusion can only be drawn from a divinelike perspective of the global "distress." To perceive the true significance of world history, Daniel must have dreams and visions. He must converse with angelic interpreters. Apocalyptic form sees history like a woven rug. From underneath, the fabric looks like a mess, loose strings, mixed colors, incomplete figures. But on the top side, the weaving displays its perfect order. History is under God's control, following God's plan—whatever the appearances from below suggest. Above the conflict, acting in his own time, God remains in control and will in the end establish his kingdom.

In apocalyptic literature, God belongs to another realm. To some degree the visions are disturbing contacts with a mysterious abyss. Yet the message is clear. God has things under control. The earth might be chaotic but heaven is in order and eventually that order will spill over to earth.

3. *The end-time.* Part of the message of Daniel deals with the timing of the end. This is always the part that causes perplexity. Daniel's approach seems clear. The end is coming in the generation of the readers—a message that Jesus himself echoes (Mark 9:1; 13:30; Matt 10:23). After all, the book was to be sealed and kept secret until the end (12:9). The end was to come like a torrent once seventy weeks of years had passed from 605 BC as the starting point (9:24–27).

But the end did not come. The temple was rededicated after the last "half week" of years (1 Macc 4:36–61; 2 Macc 10:1–8)—an event that apparently was still part of the future for the writer of Daniel. As it now stands in history, the Book of Daniel reminds us that the future must remain future—the great mystery coming to us, before which we stand with reverent docility, over which we have no control, that timing of which we cannot calculate (see 1 Thess 5:1–3). We still stand before the future as mystery. We remain confident that the mystery of the future coincides with the mystery of God's grace and redemption.

About two hundred years later when Jesus began preaching, his message was clear: "The kingdom of God is at hand" (Mark 1:15; Matt 4:17). He taught his disciples to pray, "Thy kingdom come" (Matt 6:10; Luke 11:2). Of all the titles and descriptions used to address him, Jesus seemed to prefer "Son of Man." He apparently spoke of himself as a glorious Son of Man "coming with the clouds of heaven" (Mark 13:26) but also as a Son of Man who must suffer much (Mark 8:31). The angel Gabriel, who in Luke's Gospel announces the births of both John the Baptist and Jesus the Christ (Luke 1:19, 26), can now in the light of Daniel be seen not just as any "messenger" between God and humanity, but as the one commissioned for the eschatological message.

When John of Patmos reflected on the horrors of the Roman persecutions, he again drew many of his images from the visions of Daniel in order to make sense of the evil in his contemporary world. Among the many apparently borrowed from Daniel are the visions of grotesque beasts (Dan 7:3–8; Rev 13:1–2), of the angelic son of man (Dan 7:13; Rev 1:13–16), of the evil beast powerful enough to cast down stars from heaven (Dan 8:10; Rev 12:4) but who would ultimately be thrown into the fire to be destroyed (Dan 7:11; Rev 20:10), and of Michael "and his angels" who battle Satan (Dan 10:13, 21; 12:1; Rev 12:7). John of Patmos develops Daniel's final word of hope into an elaborate scenario of a new heavens and a new earth with a new heavenly Jerusalem coming down from heaven (Rev 21). The point is the same. In the end goodness triumphs over evil.

Conclusion

21

The Message of the Prophets

In our Bible, the books of the prophets now follow a fully developed Torah, according to which Israel began with its encounter with God at Sinai, where it was formed by a covenant with God. Israel was to worship the one God and to deal justly with one another. As presented in this order, the message of the prophets is a call to Israel to return to a more faithful following of the Law. This message may well be the view seen in the postexilic perspective, when reconstruction was centered on the rules of religion and ethics.

If we look at the work of the literary prophets, however, as earlier than the Torah, as we have in this study, then the message of these prophets appears with richer theological colors. It is centered on the very being and presence of Yahweh, the God of Israel and the prophets.

But who is this God of the prophets? If we review the images and themes in the literary prophets, we see the difficulty of answering that question. We recall the bundle of contradictions that appear in the descriptions of the prophets. The God of the prophets is a destructive force yet a caring person; a jealous and vengeful ruler yet a loving parent and spouse. This God appears serenely independent of this world yet deeply involved in this world, distant yet near, cosmic yet dwelling among us, uncontrollable yet listening to our prayers. This God appears silent and inactive in the light of human suffering yet dependable and saving, condemning yet never giving up on his creatures. In the end this God of the prophets appears totally beyond our thoughts and comprehension yet speaking to us, sharing his plans and counsels.

Can we find a consistent theology in the prophets? Our task is to return to these images and themes of God—with a view to the reality of the God we know—and find a theology that the prophets would recognize. I suggest six angles from which we can view this God of the prophets.

I. God Will Not Be Denied

Often we hear the critique that religion and faith are simply human means to deal with the painful and uncontrollable aspects of life. In this view, God is the great pain reliever in the sky. In the view of the prophets, such a God is an idol, the work of human hands, or some other projection of human need. These divinities are nice gods.

The God of the prophets is anything but pleasant. He breaks into human existence often to say that he is going to destroy it. He is usually portrayed as angry, a God of doom. This is not a God anybody wants. This God is not a projection of human needs, and this God blows away the illusory comforts of religion.

Neither is the job of the prophets something anybody wants. When God calls the prophet, the first reaction is reluctance. Amos says he did not choose this role (Amos 7:14–15). At his call Isaiah worries about his very life (Isa 6:5). Jeremiah immediately protests his inability to do the job (Jer 1:6). They do not want this call. They do not want this encounter with God.

The message of the prophets is often a bitter message and usually rejected by the people. They accuse priest, king, and people of sin. They threaten terrible disasters.

Yet, here we have the books of the prophets. They did their jobs. So who is in charge? The very existence of the prophets and the literature they left behind is a testimony to a higher force, active in the lives of human beings and in the universe, often against the desires and inclinations of human beings. The existence of the prophets and their literature is a powerful testimony that human life is not the center of reality and the origin of meaning. Rather, the prophets testify to an undeniable force that human beings must seek to discover and reverence for what it is.

The encounter with this higher force is an encounter with the abyss. God appears ready to destroy all sinful human efforts and products, human illusions made to provide comfort and security—even if it is "the Temple of the Lord." We encounter God surrounded by the uncontrollable. Ultimately we encounter God in death. At any time, the encounter demands unconditional surrender. This is the "fear of the Lord [*yirat YHWH*]" described by Isaiah (11:2–3) and later preached by the wisdom teachers (Prov 5:7; Eccles 12:13).

Only by accepting this abyss, by accepting God as God, does the human being begin to hear the words of love and care coming from this unpleasant dimension. Isaiah preached trust in God's reliability (7:9). Troubled by the disturbing plan of God, Habakkuk eventually saw the need to wait in vigilance. The just person will live by his or her "fidelity [*'emunah*]" (2:1–4), not by creating gods of security.

II. God Deals with Sin

In his faithfulness, God does not just walk away from his disappointments. He refuses to use the ultimate option of returning creation to nothingness—despite the threat of Zephaniah 1. Like the parent of a rebellious adolescent, God seems stuck with human idiocy. Because he has chosen his children, the sins of his children are his problems.

Thus according to the prophets across the board, God becomes angry. Anger is the reaction toward an evil or harm that hits home. Fury is a reaction to a serious evil. We are angry when someone we love is harmed. We are outraged when someone we love is doing the harm. God's anger is his reaction to an evil that strikes at his own heart.

In the prophets the anger of God is an image of God dealing with sin. In Amos we hear the roar of God's anger throughout the book. Because God cares so much for Israel, he is angry at her failures. Because he loves the poor, he is livid at the oppression by Israel of its helpless members. God deals severely with sin. The punishing anger becomes worse and worse. Eleventh-hour rescues (Isa 10:27–34) cease until all that is left is a field of dry bones (Ezek 37:1). Death is the result and the sign of God's dealing with sin. As threatened by God, death is being cut off prematurely from life as an individual or being utterly destroyed as a nation.

In the prophets, however, the punishing justice of God does not take place simply to make God feel better by inflicting suffering. More like the disappointed parent than the vindictive ruler, God reacts with heartfelt turmoil as he punishes Israel. Like a mother, God remembers the baby she held to her cheeks, the nursling she nourished (Hos 11:4). The obnoxious adult and the clinging baby blend in one history—dominated by love and compassion. This is the God who cries out, "What am I to do with you, Ephraim and Judah?" (Hos 5:4). This is the God who is personally involved in his anger and punishment: "My heart is overwhelmed; my pity stirred" (Hos 11:8). What God has built, he must tear down. What he has planted he must uproot (Jer 45:4). In these images the prophets portray God as suffering the punishment he must inflict on Israel. God in fact goes into exile with Israel (Ezek 10:18–19). In the New Testament, God eventually dies (John 19:30).

Death, however, is not the final word addressed to human beings. And so the dry bones come alive (Ezek 37:2–14). A new heart and new spirit enter the people (Ezek 36:26). The law of Sinai is written in their hearts (Jer 31:33).

Eternal death or condemnation is not a concept in the prophets. Hosea began the extraordinary imagery of God's conjugal love of Israel. Jeremiah and Ezekiel continued it. When Deutero-Isaiah came on the scene, the words started with comfort. There is no eternal condemnation in the prophets because the final word is love and comfort. In the end God remembers his love.

III. God Is Faithful

The prophets of the Exile provide another theological color. Unlike human society that withers like grass (Isa 40:6–7), God remains firm (Isa 7:9). The God who formed Israel at Sinai remains with Israel during the prosperity of the eighth century, during the Assyrian invasions, during the Babylonian destruction, and during the post-exile reconstruction. This history is a history of human failing, but it is also a history of God's presence and his persistent call to repentance. From the time of David with Nathan and Gad to the Persian period with Joel and others, God returned over and over again to his people. On God's side, nothing changes.

When human frailty and fickleness seemed to have destroyed God's plan for Israel, Deutero-Isaiah preached that the word of Yahweh endures forever (Isa 40:8). Our hope is not in the contingencies of human history where weak human freedom shifts with unpredictable contradictions. Our hope is in the fidelity of God, who can cup the entire universe of human history in the palm of his hand (Isa 40:12). In this human history, the future can be discouraging or even frightening, but God predicts the future (Isa 43:9). He is above the contradictions of this age as the ageless Creator.

Committing his spirit to God's hands (Luke) or simply accepting God's will (Mark and Matthew), Jesus in the Synoptic Gospels dramatizes the trust one can have in the fidelity of God. This was an act of trust in the darkest moment of human history. It is a trust that is opened to the power of the resurrection to dramatize God's fidelity.

IV. God Is Foolishness

As God deals with sin, divine pathos appears in pathetic human history. Thus God reveals something of his foolishness. The world of the prophets is clearly not the best possible world. The councils of God do not follow some preestablished reason. God does it all wrong. But then, God never promises intelligibility, only love.

This great "foolishness" of God in the story of the prophets lies in the ambiguity of prophecy. Presented as a divine word, as a divine perception of human reality, these words appear not only in human form but amidst many other human voices purporting to announce divine truth (Jer 28). Without a decent roll of thunder and a trumpet blast from heaven, how is the boyish voice of Jeremiah supposed to command respect? With an army of sycophants praising the powerful institutions of the day, how is one voice supposed to rouse a nation from the numbness of prosperity and power? Even if a prophet has a marvelous story about divine robes in the sanctuary and seraphim brandishing burning coals (Isa 6), how can the objective listener determine the validity of this self-serving story?

Furthermore, the words of the prophets were hard sayings. These were words meant to oppose the numbness and deafness that come from the most ingenious method of blocking different perceptions—social institutions. Government and church are developed usually by good people for good purposes, as complex social institutions or culture allow us to relate to one another. However, the culture and social institutions that envelop us like the air we breathe can numb us. Amos's message to Amaziah was a hard message (Amos 7:10–17). Isaiah's message to Ahaz disturbed the king (Isa 7:1–16). The prophet brought a divine perspective to these rigid institutions.

If God really expects these human institutions to be like soft wet clay in a potter's hands (Jer 18:1–4), he is foolish. We crucify our prophets. From their death God brings forth life. An economist would suggest a more efficient use of energy. A canon lawyer would complain of such a revolutionary style. But as Paul will put it centuries later, "The foolishness of God is wiser than human wisdom, and the weakness of God is stronger than human strength" (1 Cor 1:25).

V. God Deals with Our Freedom

In effect the prophets describe God's dealings with radical contingency. God deals with human freedom. He confronts the world of human beings the way a parent confronts the freedom and contingency in the family. God expresses his justice (*tz^edaqah*), an absolute and necessary quality of his being, to persuade his children and change a sinful situation. Yet in love, the love that expresses God's tender kindness (*chesed*), the love that is also an absolute and necessary quality of his being, God enters the contingency of the sinful situation and maintains the freedom of his children. While maintaining their radical contingency and fallibility, God moves his children toward the life and fidelity that is absolute and necessary for humanity. Only love can accomplish this.

It is in this dialectic between necessity and contingency that the law of covenantal entropy appears so powerful. This law is a spin-off of the one describing the gradual loss of energy and vitality of every living thing and every institution, eventually leading to death. In Israel failure follows on failure. Words of restoration are followed by words of more threats and punishments. The continued existence of one prophet after another, over and over again, suggests that there is not much hope for a triumph of justice over injustice, love over oppression—at least in this world. The call to return, to repent, to come back goes largely unheeded in the lifetime of the prophet. Unlike Elijah and Elisha, who overwhelmed evil by miracles, the literary prophets appear weak. Only in retrospect does the message now written down appear compelling—often after disaster. And the cycle goes on.

Rather than a successful issue of the struggle over evil, perhaps the very process of the struggle forms the message of the prophets. The prophets thus call us to struggle, to suffer and die before the forces of sin, and—in this apparent failure—to open the world to God's act of raising the dead to new life.

VI. God Will Return

Human freedom and sinfulness in effect create the darkness of the great abyss from which God must speak. We distract ourselves from God by various amusements, instruments of security. Then we sense the superficiality and illusion of any earthly security and amusement. We realize the reality of our future death and the collective suffering and pain of humanity. We discover the hiddenness of God. In the New Testament the image of Christ carrying his cross and then being crucified epitomizes this discovery.

The prophets, however, insist on the importance of gazing into that abyss and seeing a loving God, a God who calls us to justice and life. The great abyss presupposed in the preaching of the prophets' world is not an abyss of chaos. It is the abyss from which God is speaking to us, calling us to repentance, comforting us, sharing our suffering.

This God is a God of "justice" (*tzedeq*). That justice remains as a firm reference point outside the radical contingency and chaos of history. When something is wrong, God calls to repentance. When repentance is real, God promises comfort and mercy (*chesed*). In the end, the real order and governance of the world is found, less in a well defined law and reason and more in divine anguish and joy, a law of love.

Such principles result in an order that looks beyond the disorder of human contingency to some divine kingdom that is coming. Deutero-Isaiah tells Israel to look to the future. God is doing something new (Isa 43:18–19). Past disappointments may be forgotten. Ezekiel promises a new heart and a new spirit (Ezek 36:26). All these promises of newness direct us to a mysterious future. These prophetic words are not precise predictions of coming events. These words give us no power over the future. They simply direct us to what is coming in incomprehensible mystery.

Over and over again with his formulas of fulfillment, Matthew will point to Jesus as the reality to whom the prophets were pointing (Matt 1:18—2:23). Like the prophets, Jesus is crucified. Like most of the prophets, he fails to convince many in his lifetime and promises a new future. He too points to the future, a new future in which he too will return.

22
Reflections on Old Testament Theology

Do the prophets and histories of the Old Testament speak to believers today? The question is not the same as whether readers today can think religious and inspiring thoughts while reading the Old Testament or whether we can find examples or paradigms of good moral living in the stories. The question asks whether the historical writers and editors with their messages to their ancient audiences really summon readers today to understand the truth of God and his salvation. Can we preserve the real historical nature of ancient texts and understand their theology for today?

Our expectation was to find a connection between our faith and the faith of these historical authors. To probe this possibility our study aimed at the faith-filled intentions of the authors of the Old Testament texts, which we hope could guide modern readers to a faith-filled insight.

No doubt the Old Testaments texts—as we now have them—come to us from the collaboration of a multitude of storytellers, writers, and editors. In this study our aim, therefore, was a type of collective intentionality of many strata. To speak of "the author" of any biblical text is to use a form of shorthand for the multitude of people involved as "the author" to the degree they contributed to the final product.

I. The Historical Intentions of the Authors

Focusing on the intentions of the authors, however, brings along a slough of problems, raised recently by several scholars. First and foremost, the criticism of our approach arises from a deep theological concern. The intentions of ancient authors are inevitably buried in the historical perspectives and limits of that author, addressing their contemporaries about issues of their times. As he described Immanuel, Isaiah most probably intended to describe Prince Hezekiah or other some child knowable to his eighth-century audience. Yet this identification seems to bury the word of God in a world long gone, having little to say to our world. Any key to a method for grasping the theology of scripture will involve finding the way we can work through those historical intentions without discarding the message the text has for believers today.

Second, from the point of view of feasibility, some scholars have claimed that the intention of the authors is now irretrievably lost in the passing of time. All we have are the written words left for us to read. However, as we have attempted in this study, an understanding of the words leads beyond the page to real persons who wanted to say something. The editorializing in texts often leads us to a sense of what the authors and editors aimed to say. Archeology gives us an access to the cultures of these writers. History itself gives us a sense of the limits of the pool of information available to ancient writers and thus allows us to rule out certain intentions. If we are willing to work with probabilities, the broad lines of the historical intentions can at least function like a kind of North Star to guide our investigations.

Third, from a philosophical point of view, the criticism of any search for authors' intentions often arises in a view of language itself as the ultimate source of truth. Once spoken or written down, language statements become independent of the speaker or author. Making a parallel with art, this criticism points out that an artist may not be the best judge and critic of his or her work.

Certainly the written word takes on a kind of independent existence once it is produced. And some documents like instruction manuals or rule books leave little reason to search for the authors' intentions. However, a writing of poetic character, a struggle to articulate contact with life as a whole, or a personal letter will always remain the expression of some authors. When we fail to understand such a document, the first question that pops into our heads is often "Why did she write that?"

Of course writers have at times come to rue the words they once wrote. However, like old photographs frozen in time, our works of the past are still connected to us and cannot be fully understood apart from our personal concerns and historical circumstances guiding our writing. The person responsible for the work remains such, however much time may change that person. It is true that an objective art critic may be able to evaluate a work of art better than the artist, but I do not know of any student of art who would not drool at the prospect of interviewing the artist behind an important work.

We speak of the power of words. However, a word has power only if it is a true word. When recognized as such, the lying word moves no one. Words have power because they allow realities and their meanings to enter our lives as truth. It is the truth that has a power to summon us to take a stand.

II. The Deeper Intentionality of the Authors

A philosophy of moderate realism is behind this study. In this philosophy truth exists independent of our grasp and is a synonym for reality itself. Our struggle to understand is aimed at this reality that has a meaning in and by itself, although we view this reality only through human lenses and limited perspectives. Reality in its fullness is always beyond our conceptualization and language. Yet this reality in its fullness may be contacted as a heartfelt Presence, which measures our understanding and allows us to experience the limits of that understanding.

Such a philosophy of knowledge is supported by a variety of experiences. First, we do *understand the limits* of our grasp—if we are wise. The human and socially constructed concepts we use to grasp any reality inevitable "distort" the reality. We inevitably approach things from our biases and particular experiences. The important thing is to recognize and acknowledge these limits of our knowledge. Secondly, such a philosophy also explains a sense of continuity from one perspective to another that enables us *to translate* from one language to another—however much elegance and nuances are lost in translation. If we understand what the author was trying to say, we can say "pretty much the same thing" in different words although the different words might appear much more clumsy than the original. Thirdly, such a philosophy explains *the power of words and ideas*, seeing that power not so much as coming from sounds or images but ultimately as from Reality, which grasps us long before we grasp it.

As applied to the understanding of texts and of the Bible in particular, this philosophy views authorial intentions as more than psychological perspectives and motives through which authors speak and write. Unless the author is a liar, such intentions are also dynamic openings to a reality beyond human speech and writing. We can call this opening to reality the "intentionality" of the author.

The language and culture of any biblical statements becomes the first important context for understanding the author's intention and the meaning of that statement. Without that context we cannot get started. However, understanding the text means reaching beyond that historical context and concrete motivation of the author for the reality the author attempted to express. The focus remains on the reality that the ancient writer intended and that we also presume to see.

This focus also allows us to see the limits of the author's intention—formed within restricted perspectives, human weakness, and inherited biases—as we compare the original intention with other accesses to the truth of the matter. Modern astronomy gave us a better understanding of the restricted perspectives and biases of biblical creation accounts. Understanding these limits allows us to understand better the reality intended and to translate that reality into better language—all the while sensing that our intentions too are formed by similar limits.

In a philosophy of moderate realism, God and his actions are realities, not "language events." The historical intentions of the biblical authors and editors direct us to these divine realities, which may be present to us as they were to the historical authors. Embedded in the limited historical intentions of the biblical authors is a deeper intention or intentionality: to speak the truth, to articulate the reality that they knew in their hearts would enlighten their limited historical world. Their intentionality involved finding and expressing hope in the fidelity of God, finding and expressing faith in God's saving activity on earth, and proclaiming the absolute summons to believe in that fidelity and salvation. This intentionality becomes the arrows that lead from the textual expression in its historical context to the subject matter in its reality. This reality is the presumed truth by which the text summons *us* to a response and a decision. Riding the historical intentions of the authors, we can come in contact with those realities, even though those realities lie beyond human understanding. For all their linguistic and cultural limitations, these historical intentions open to the divine mystery, which we then with our own literary forms and our cultural perspectives can attempt to touch.

The fictional character of many of the stories warns us that this divine reality on earth cannot be understood by a one-to-one relationship between the details of the story and the reality. Rather, the stories as wholes and the stories taken together provide patterns of that divine reality. The poetic character of many of the didactic texts also warns us against the same search for a one-to-one relationship. Yet for all their metaphorical and exaggerated imagery, these prophetic texts intended to speak of the God who in one respect is present with saving power in all times and in all issues yet in another respect withdraws his obvious presence leaving a frightful abyss of failure and collapse.

III. Theology beyond the Bible

As we touch these mysterious dimensions through the perceptions and perspectives of the ancient writers, something of a dialectic takes place. We step back into the historical perspective of the authors without losing our own view. Returning to our modern perspective, we are better able to understand the limits of the perceptions and perspectives of the historical writers—as well as our own. At this point we are able to translate the reality intended by the authors into language more adequate for our understanding.

Conclusion

If several perspectives are aiming at the same reality, an observer should be able to shift from one perspective to another with a sense of continuity as one perspective blends into the other. As we walk around a cube some sides come into view as others disappear. The observer should be able to sense the limits of each perspective as it is measured by the more adequate sense of the reality arising from the shift itself. By walking around it, we come to know that the cube has six sides even though we can only see at most three at any one time. Ezekiel wrote of excluding Gentiles from the new Temple as he touched the importance of preserving the faith from outside contamination. Trito-Isaiah gives us another perspective as he wrote of foreigners and eunuchs worshiping God in the Temple. We may need the Epistle to the Ephesians of the New Testament to see any continuity here.

Even the Bible as a whole provides us with an initial perspective, but a limited one. It does not give us a divinelike view—although it is assisted by a divine Spirit. The Bible thus gives us the first word on the matter, but not the last word. The Bible thus functions as a "canon" of theology by providing us with a perspective with which all future perspectives should be in continuity. However, theology can and must proceed beyond the biblical formulations.

If we proceed in this way, we can understand better the faith presuppositions involved in the historical intentions. We repeatedly focused on the presence and absence of God, with which many of the authors struggled. Such faith presuppositions can carry the message of the text to us today. Thus the biblical texts can address the modern anguish of life appearing as a gaping, apparently meaningless abyss—once the superficial illusions of wealth and power are removed. Lurking in those presuppositions is the question, "Where is God?" These presuppositions may or may not have been part of the conscious motivation of the biblical authors, but they seem to be part and parcel of their intentionality.

Appendices

Appendix 1
Ancient Prophecy outside of Israel

Unless otherwise indicated, citations are from James B. Pritchard, ed., *Ancient Near Eastern Texts (ANET)*, Princeton, NJ: Princeton University Press, 1969.

Appendix 1a—Prophecy

An Egyptian story, "The Journey of Wen-Amon," from the eleventh century BC, includes a scene where the prince of Byblos makes an offering to his gods and "the god seized one of his youth and made him possessed." Then a message is relayed to the prince from the god, without an explanation of how the message was generated (*ANET*, 26). The scene depicts a type of frenzy or mania associated with a divine message to a political leader. The matter-of-fact tone of the story suggests that such prophetic mania was normal, at least when the king needed guidance.

In the "Moabite Stone Inscription," a ninth-century stele from the Transjordan area with interesting allusions to King Omri of Israel, King Mesha of Moab describes how the god Chemosh spoke to him instructing him on military campaigns: "And Chemosh said to me, 'Go, take Nebo from Israel!'" (*ANET*, 320). The text mentions no prophetic medium, but we see the depiction of a close communication between the god of the nation and the king.

An early eighth-century inscription from Aleppo in northern Syria speaks of "seers" and "diviners" who communicate a divine message to Zakir, king of Hamat:

I lifted up my hand to Be'elshamayn, and Be'elshamayn heard me. Be'elshamayn [spoke] to me through seers and through diviners. Be'elshamayn [said to me]: do not fear, for I made you king, and I shall stand by you and deliver you. (*ANET*, 655)

In the "Mari Letters," we see an elaborate description of various forms of prophetic speech. These are letters from the time of the patriarchs (c. 1750–1700 BC). Some of the prophets of Mari are cultic professionals; some are laypeople. Some receive messages by way of dreams. Others receive and mediate messages by a type of ecstatic mania. Some messages are written out by the prophets themselves. The prophecies seem mostly to be instructions to kings and royal administrations, sometimes with a high moral tone:

Am I not Addu, Yahweh of Halab, who has raised you…and made you regain the throne of your father's house?…When a man or woman who has suffered an injustice addresses himself to you, respond to his appeal and give him a ver[dict] (A.2925).

(The text as translated can be found in Herbert B. Huffmon, "Prophecy in the Mari Letters," *The Biblical Archaeologist*, 31/4 [December 1968], 102–24.)

Appendix 1b—The Divine Assembly and Messengers

We can see the proceedings of a divine *sôd* in the myth *Enuma Elish*:

> They erected for him [the god, Marduk,] a princely throne. Facing his fathers, he sat down, presiding. "Thou art the most honored of the great gods....When in Assembly thou sittest, thy word shall be supreme....Marduk summoned the great gods to Assembly. Presiding graciously, he issues instructions. To his utterance the gods pay heed." (*ANET*, 66A, 68A)

In the same myth, the high god Anshar sends a "living letter" to the gods Lahmu and Lahamu via a lesser god, his vizier, Gaga.

> Anshar opened his mouth and to Gaga, his vizier, a word he addressed: "O Gaga, my vizier, who gladdenest my spirit, to Lahmu and Lahamu I will dispatch thee. Thou knowest discernment, art adept at fine talk....Be on thy way Gaga, take the stand before them, and that which I shall tell thee repeat thou unto them." (*ANET*, 64B)

Appendix 2
A Synopsis of the Kings of the Divided Kingdom

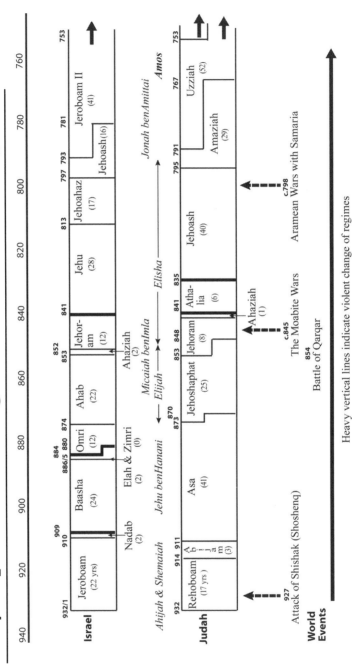

| 940 | 920 | 900 | 880 | 860 | 840 | 820 | 800 | 780 | 760 |

Israel

932/1 Jeroboam (22 yrs) | 910 909 Nadab (2) | Baasha (24) | 884 886/5 880 874 Omri (12) Elah & Zimri (0) | Ahab (22) | 852 853 841 Jehor-am (12) | Jehu (28) | 813 Jehoahaz (17) | 797 793 Jehoash(16) | 781 Jeroboam II (41) | 753

Ahijah & Shemaiah *Jehu benHanani*

— Elijah — *Micaiah benImla* — Elisha —

Ahaziah (2)

Jonah benAmittai

Amos

Judah

932 Rehoboam (17 yrs) | 914 911 A b i j a m (3) | Asa (41) | 873 870 Jehoshaphat (25) | 853 848 Jehoram (8) | 841 Atha-lia (6) | 835 Jehoash (40) | 795 791 Amaziah (29) | 767 Uzziah (52) | 753

Ahaziah (1)

World Events

927 Attack of Shishak (Shoshenq)

c.845 The Moabite Wars

c.798 Aramean Wars with Samaria

854 Battle of Qarqar

Heavy vertical lines indicate violent change of regimes

A Synopsis of the Kings of the Divided Kingdom *continued*

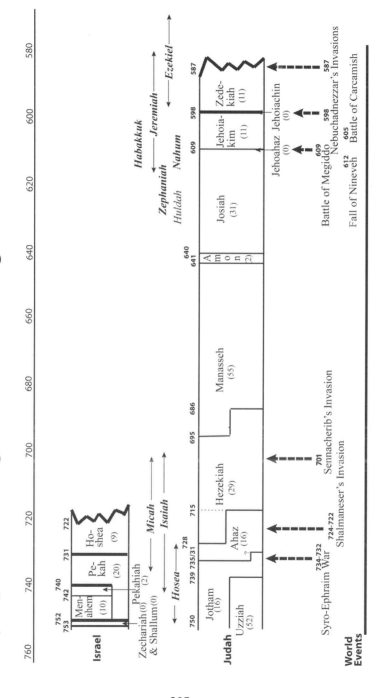

Appendix 3
Assyrian Annals

Appendix 3a—The Annals of Tiglath-Pileser III

1. THE WAR OF 744 BC

"I received tribute from Kushtashpi of Commagene, Rezon of Damascus, Menahem of Samaria, Hiram of Tyre...." (*ANET*, p. 283)

2. THE WAR OF C. 731 BC

"[As for Menahem I ov]erwhelmed him [like a snow-storm] and he...fled like a bird, alone, [and bowed to my feet (?)]. I returned him to his place [and imposed tribute upon him, to wit:] gold, silver, linen garments with multicolored trimmings,...great....[I re]ceived from him. Israel (lit.: "Omri-Land")...and all its inhabitants (and) their possessions I led to Assyria. They overthrew their king Pekah and I placed Hoshea as king over them. I received from them 10 talents of good, 1,000(?) talents of silver as their [tri]bute and brought them to Assyria." (*ANET*, pp. 283–84)

Appendix 3b—Fragments from the Annals and Inscriptions of Sargon II

"[Sargon] conqueror of Samaria and of the entire (country of) Israel...."

"I besieged and conquered Samaria, let away as booty 27,290 inhabitants of it. I formed from among them a contingent of 50 chariots and made remaining (inhabitants) assume their (social) positions..."

"I conquered and sacked the towns Shinuhtu (and) Samaria, and all Israel (lit.: "Omri-Land")."

"I crushed the tribes of Tamud, Ibabidi, Marsimanu, and Haiapa, the Arabs who live, far away, in the desert (and) who know neither overseers nor official(s) and who had not (yet) brought their tribute to the king. I deported their survivors and settled (them) in Samaria." (*ANET*, pp. 284–85)

Appendix 3c—Inscriptions from Sennacherib

"In my third campaign I marched against Hatti....As to Hezekiah, the Jew, he did not submit to my yoke, I laid siege to 46 of his strong cities, walled forts and to the countless small villages in their vicinity, and conquered (them) by means of well-stamped (earth-)ramps, and battering-rams....Himself I made a prisoner in Jerusalem, his royal residence, like a bird in a cage. I surrounded him with earthwork in order to molest those who were leaving his city's gate....Hezekiah himself, whom the terror-inspiring splendor of my lordship had overwhelmed and whose irregular and elite troops which he had brought into Jerusalem, his royal residence, in order to strengthen (it), had deserted him, did send me, later, to Nineveh, my lordly city, together with 30 talents of gold, 800 talents of silver, precious stones, antimony, large cuts of red stone, couches (inlaid) with ivory, *nimedu*-chairs (inlaid) with ivory, elephant-hides, ebony-wood, box-wood (and) all kinds of valuable treasures, his (own) daughters, concubines, male and female musicians. In order to deliver the tribute and to do obeisance as a slave he sent his (personal) messenger." (*ANET*, pp. 287–88)

Appendix 4
Detailed Outlines of the Books of the Prophets

*Passages treated in the commentary.
Alternate versification is indicated by [brackets].
{Braces} indicate passages treated as later additions.

Appendix 4a—Detailed Outline of Amos

Introduction (1:1–2)*

I. Indictments of surrounding nations and Israel for their crimes
(1:3—2:16)
   A. Against Damascus (Aram) (1:3–5)
   B. Against Philistia (1:6–8)
   C. Against Tyre (1:9–10)
   D. Against Edom (1:11–12)
   E. Against the Ammonites (1:13–15)
   F. Against Moab (2:1–3)
   {G. Against Judah (2:4–5)}
   H. Against Israel (2:6–16)*

II. "Hear the Word" and "Alas" Sermons (3:1—6:14)
   A. First "Hear the Word" (3:1–15)—to "men of Israel"*
   B. Second "Hear the Word" (4:1–13)—to "women of Samaria"*
      refrain "Yet you returned not to me, says Yahweh"
         (4:6, 8, 9, 10, 11)
      judgment (*laken*) (4:12)
      –creation hymn (4:13; see 5:8–9; 9:5–6)*

C. Third "Hear the Word" (5:1–17)*
   a. lament (5:1–3)*
      b. religion (5:4–6)*
      –creation hymn (5:8–9)*
         c. social injustice (5:7–13)*
      b' religion (5:14–15)
   a' lament (5:16–17)*
D. First "Alas" (5:18–27)*
   –hypocritical religion (5:21–25)*
E. Second "Alas" (6:1–14)—for the wealthy and complacent
   in Zion and Samaria
   expressions of wealth and complacency (6:1–6)
   judgment (*laken*) (6:7–14)

III. Visions of Destruction (7:1—9:8a)*
   A. The locusts (7:1–3)*
   B. The fire (7:4–6)*
   C. The plumb line (7:7–9)*
      –The opposition of Amaziah (7:10–17)*
   D. The ripe fruit basket (8:1–14)*
      1. The vision (8:1–2)*
      2. "On that day" refrain
         a. First "on that day" (8:3)*
            –sermon against social injustice (8:4–8)*
         b. Second "on that day" (8:9–12)*
         c. Third "on that day" (8:13–14)*
   E. Vision of Yahweh beside the altar (9:1–8a)*
      –creation hymn (9:5–6)

Conclusion—restoration (9:8b–15)*
   {Restoration of the "hut of David" 9:11–15}*

Appendix 4b—Detailed Outline of Hosea

Introduction (1:1)

I. Hosea and his family symbols of Yahweh and Israel (1:2—3:5)
   A. First account (1:2—2:25)* [1:2—2:23]
   B. Second account (3:1–5)*

II. Sermons (4:1—14:9)
   A. "Hear the Word of Yahweh"; a legal process (*rîb*) against priests and prophets (4:1–19)*
   B. "Hear this"; against priests and king and Ephraim (5:1–7)
   C. "Blow the trumpet"; predictions of disaster for Ephraim and Judah (5:8–14)
   D. "Let us return"; insincere conversion (5:15—6:3)*
   E. The divine response (6:4—7:2)*
   F. Failure of kings and princes (7:3–7)
   G. Evil foreign alliances (7:8–12)*
   H. "Alas" for perverse Israel (7:13–16)
   I. "Put the trumpet to the mouth"; the sins of making false kings and gods (8:1–14)
   J. "Do not rejoice"; threat of exile (9:1–6)
   K. Hostility toward the prophet (9:7–9)
   L. "Like grapes in the desert"; Israel's history of sin (9:10–17)
   M. "Israel is a vine pouring out "; her faithlessness and punishment (10:1–10)*
   N. "Israel is a trained calf"; her faithlessness and punishment (10:11–15)
   O. "Israel is a child" exile and failure to repent (11:1–7)*
   P. "How could I give you us"; restoration (11:8–11)*
   Q. Legal process (*rîb*) against Israel (12:1—14:1)* [11:12—13:16]
   R. Call to conversion (14:2–9)* [14:1–8]

Conclusion (14:10) [14:9]

Appendix 4c—Detailed Outline of First Isaiah (1—39)

I. Isaiah 1: The introduction to the collection:
   A. Superscript (1:1)*
   B. Accusations, appeals, and threats regarding Israel's sinfulness (1:2–31)*

II. Isaiah 2—5: The indictment of Judah and Jerusalem, possibly from the time of Jotham and perhaps Ahaz before the Syro-Ephraimite war
   A. The mountain of Zion (2:1–5)*
   B. Judgment against wealth, pride and idolatry (2:6–22)*
   C. Judgment against the leaders (3:1–15)
   D. Against haughty women (3:16—4:1)
   E. Salvation (4:2–6)
   F. Song of the vineyard (5:1–7)*
   G. "Alas" sermons—chiastic parts A, B, C, B' (5:8–23)*
   H. "Outstretched hand" speech—part 4 (5:24–25)

III. Isaiah 6: The commissioning of Isaiah (6:1–13)*

IV. Isaiah 7—12: The Immanuel prophecies, during the reign of Ahaz in the context of the Syro-Ephraimite war
   A. Outbreak of the Syro-Ephraim war and call to faith (7:1–9)*
   B. The offering of the sign of Immanuel (7:10–16)*
   C. Threat of invasion "on that day" (7:17–25)*
   D. The birth of the son of Isaiah (8:1–10)*
   E. False and true alliances (8:11–15)
   G. The written and sealed record (8:16–22)*
      {–The great distress of someone (8:21–22)}
   H. The birth of a Davidic prince (8:23—9:6)* [9:1–7]
   I. "Outstretched hand" speech—parts 1–3 (9:7–20) [9:8–21]
   J. "Alas" sermon—part A' (10:1–4)
   K. "Alas" to Assyria (10:5–19)
   L. Promises for "the remnant" (10:20–27a)
   M. Invasion—Zion schema (10:27b–34)*

N. Rule of the "shoot" from Jesse (11:1–9)*
O. "The signal to the nations" assembling the remnant
(11:10–16)
P. Song of praise to God as savior (12:1–6)

V. Isaiah 13—23: Oracles against the nations,
A. Against Babylon (13:1—14:23)
B. Against Assyria (14:24–27)
C. Against Philistia (14:28–32)
D. Against Moab (15:1—16:14)
E. Against Damascus (17:1–14)
   –Zion schema? (17:12–14)*
F. Against Cush [Ethiopia] (18:1–7)
G. Against Egypt (19:1–24)
H. The Assyrian war against Egypt and Ethiopia [711 BC]
(20:1–6)
I. Against the wastelands by the sea [Babylonia] (21:1–10)
J. Against Dumah/Seir [Edom] (21:11–12)
K. Against Arabia (21:13–17)
L. Oracle of the Valley of Vision—destruction of Jerusalem
(22:1–14)
M. Replacement of Shebna with Eliakim as master of the
palace (22:15–25)
N. Against Tyre and Sidon (23:1–17)

{VI. Isaiah 24—27: "The apocalypse of Isaiah," probably from
the postexilic period
A. Devastation of the world (24:1–20)
B. God's triumph (24:21—25:12)
C. Song in praise of God "On that Day" (26:1—27:13)}

VII. Isaiah 28—33: Prophecies against foreign alliances, against
the background of King Hezekiah's anti-Assyrian policies to
which Isaiah was strongly opposed
A. "Alas" for Samaria (28:1–6)
B. Indictment against Jerusalem (28:7–29)*
   –Yahweh the wise farmer (28:23–29)
C. The attack on Jerusalem and rescue (29:1–8)*

D. Against the blindness and perversity of the people (29:9–16)
E. Salvation (29:17–24)
F. "Alas" for rebellious sons (30:1–5)
G. Against the beasts of the Negev (30:6–7)
H. Writing the prophecy (30:8–18)*
I. Salvation (30:19–26)
J. Theophany against Assyria (30:27–33)
K. Against an alliance with Egypt (31:1–3)
L. Against Assyria (31:4–9)
   –Zion schema (31:4–5)*
M. The ideal kingdom (32:1–8)
N. Against the women of Jerusalem (32:9–14)
O. The reversal of conditions from the Spirit (32:15–20)
P. Miscellaneous (33:1–24)
   –Alas to the destroyer (33:1)
   –Prayer (33:2–9)
   –Yahweh's exaltation (33:10–12)
   –Moral instruction (33:13–16)
   –The restoration of Jerusalem (33:17–24)

{VIII. Isaiah 34—35: An oracle against Edom, probably the work of a later disciple, added around the time of the Nabataean destruction of Edom in the fifth century BC.
   A. Against Edom (34:1–17)
   B. Israel's deliverance—from II Isaiah (35:1–10)}

{IX. Isaiah 36—39: A historical appendix, a copy of 2 Kings 18—20 plus an account of Judah's collusion with emissaries from Babylon, obviously added by the later editor of the book.}

Appendix 4d—Detailed Outline of Micah

Superscript (1:1)

Part I: Judgment of Israel and Judah (1—3)
    A. Theophany and judgment (1:2–7)*
    B. Lamentation (1:8–16)*
    C. Crimes against the poor (2:1–11)*
    {D. Gathering of the remnant (2:12–13)}
    E. Against the leaders (3:1–12)*

Part II. Promises of salvation and threats (4—5)
    A. Exaltation of Mount Zion (4:1–5)*
    {B. Gathering of the remnant (4:6–8)}*
    C. Devastation of daughter Zion (4:9–14) [4:9—5:1]
    D. A leader from Bethlehem (5:1–4a)* [5:2–5a]
    E. The invasion of Assyria (5:4b–14) [5:5b–15]

Part III. Accusations and prayers (6—7)
    A. Prophetic instruction (6:1–8)*
    B. Accusations (6:9—7:7)
    {C. Psalm of confidence (7:8–10)}
    {D. Psalm of confidence (7:11–20)}

Appendix 4e—Detailed Outline of Zephaniah

Introductory superscript (1:1)

I. The Day of Yahweh (1:2—2:3)*
  A. The day of universal destruction (1:2–13)*
  B. The day of wrath (1:14–18)*
  C. Exhortation to seek Yahweh (2:1–3)*

II. Oracles against the nations and Jerusalem (2:4—3:8)
  A. Against the Philistines to the west (2:4–7)
  B. Against Moab and Ammon to the east (2:8–11)
  C. Against Cush to the south (2:12)
  D. Against Assyria to the north (2:13–15)
  E. Against "the rebellious city" (3:1–8)

III. Promises of Salvation (3:9–20)
  A. Oracle for the nations (3:9–10)*
  B. Oracle for Jerusalem (3:11–13)*
  C. Exhortation to rejoice (3:14–18a)*
  {D. Oracle for the restoration of Jerusalem (3:18b–20)}

Appendix 4f—Detailed Outline of Nahum

Introductory superscript (1:1)

I. Alphabetic psalm: the coming of Yahweh (1:2–8)

II. Dialogue addressed alternately to Nineveh and Judah (1:9—2:3)
    A. To Nineveh (1:9–11)
    B. To Judah (1: 12–13)
    A'. To Nineveh (1:14)
    B' To Judah (2:1, 3) [1:15, 2]
    A" To Nineveh (2:2) [2:1]
    B" To Judah (2:3) [2:2]

III. Description of the fall of Nineveh (2:4—3:19) [2:3—3:19]
    A. Descriptions from inside the city (2:4–10) [2:3–9]
    B. The fate of the lion (2:11–14) [2:10–13]
    C. Woe to the bloody city (3:1–7)*
    D. Comparisons (3:8–17)
        1. To No-amon (3:8–11)
        2. To a ripe fig tree (3:12–15)
        3. To a locust swarm (3:16–17)
    E. Final desolation (3:18–19)

Appendix 4g—Detailed Outline of Habakkuk

Introductory superscript (1:1)

I. Habakkuk's dialogues with God (1:2—2:4)★
    A. First dialogue (1:2–11)★
        1. The prophet (1:2–4)★
        2. God (1:5–11)★
    B. Second dialogue (1:12—2:4)★
        1. The prophet (1:12—2:1)★
        2. God (2:2–4)★

II. Five woes (2:5–20)
    A. Introduction? (2:5–6)
    B. First woe—against greed (2:7–8)
    C. Second woe—against presumption (2:9–11)
    D. Third woe—against violence (2:12–14)
    E. Fourth woe—against human abuse (2:15–17)
    F. Fifth woe—against idolatry (2:[18] 19–20)

III. The Canticle of Habakkuk (3:1–19)★
    Psalm title (3:1)
    A. Fear and prayer for salvation (3:2)★
    B. Theophany from Teman (3:3–7)★
    B'. Yahweh's rage against the waters (3:8–15)★
    A'. Fear and salvation (3:16–19)★

Appendix 4h—Detailed Outline of Jeremiah

-Superscript (1:1–3)

I. First collection of sermons (1:1—25:15)
  A. From the time of Josiah (1—6)
    1. Jeremiah's call (1:4–19)*
    2. The sins of Israel (2:1—4:2)*
    3. Against Judah and Jerusalem (4:3—6:30)*
  B. From the time of Jehoiakim (7—20)
    1. The Temple sermon (7:1—8:3)*
    2. Judgment and grief (8:4—9:21 [22])
      a. Judgment against "my people" (8:4–17)
      b. The grief of the prophet (8:18–23)* [8:18—9:11]
      a'. Judgment against "my people" (9:1–8) [9:2–9]
      b'. Lamentation over Jerusalem and Judah (9:9–21)
        [9:10–22]
    {3. Additions (9:22[23]—10:25)
      a. True wisdom (9:22–25) [9:23–26]
      b. Postexilic instruction against idols (10:1–16)
      c. Postexilic oracle and prayer (10:17–25)}
    4. Decree against Judah and Jerusalem for breaking the
      covenant (11:1–17)
    5. Plots against Jeremiah and the first confession of
      Jeremiah (11:18—12:6)*
    6. Oracle of God abandoning his house (12:7–13)
    {7. Exilic oracle against neighboring nations (12:14–17)}
    8. Prophetic symbols (13:1–27)
      a. God's underwear (13:1–11)*
      b. The people and leaders as God's wine flasks (13:12–14)
    9. Warnings of exile (13:15–27)
    10. The drought (14:1–10)
    11. Against lying prophets (14:11–16)
    12. Jeremiah's lament and God's answer (14:17—15:4)
    13. God's punishment of Jerusalem (15:5–9)
    14. Second confession of Jeremiah (15:10–21)*

15. Jeremiah's celibacy as a warning (16:1–18)*
    {Exilic promise of return from exile (16:14–15)}
16. Promise for the nations (16:19–21)
17. The engraving of the sin of Judah and her punishment
    (17:1–4)
{18. Wisdom psalm (17:5–13)}
19. Third confession of Jeremiah (17:14–18)*
{20. Postexilic instruction to observe the Sabbath (17:19–27)}
21. Images of clay pots (18:1—19:15)
    a. The parable of the potter (18:1–17)*
    b. Fourth confession of Jeremiah (18:18–23)*
    c. Gesture of breaking the flask in the valley of Topheth
       (19:1–15)*
22. The scourging of Jeremiah and the fifth confession
    (20:1–18)*
C. Chapters 21—25 mostly from the time of Zedekiah
1. The message of doom to Zedekiah (21:1–10)
2. Instruction and exhortations to "the king of Judah"
    (21:11—22:9)
3. Instructions to and regarding specific kings (22:10—23:8)
    a. Shallum [a.k.a. Jehoahaz] (22:10–12)
    b. Jehoiakim (22:13–19)
    c. Coniah [a.k.a. Jehoiachin] (22:20–30)
    d. *Yahweh Tzid^eqenu* [Zedekiah?] (23:1–8)*
4. Judgment against prophets of lies (23:9–40)
5. The two baskets of figs (24:1–10)*
6. The seventy years of exile (25:1–14)

IV. Beginning of Oracles against the Nations (25:15–38) [In Greek
Bible, ch. 32]

II. Second Collection of sermons (26:1—35:19) [In Greek Bible,
chs. 33—42]
    A. The Temple sermon and the persecution of Jeremiah
       (26:1–24)
    B. Messages about submission to Babylonia and the Exile
       (27:1—29:32)
    1. Messages about serving the king of Babylonia (27:1–22)*

a. To the foreign ambassadors meeting in Jerusalem (27:1–11)*

b. To king Zedekiah (27:12–15)*

c. To the priests and all the people (27:16–22)*

2. Confrontation with the prophet Hananiah—the two yokes (28:1–17)*

3. Letter to the exiles in Babylon (29:1–32)*

C. Messages of consolation (30:1—31:40)

–Introduction (30:1–3)*

1. Addressed to Judah and Israel (30:4—31:22)*

a. Distress at an end "on that day" (30:1–24)*

b. Restoration by Yahweh (31:1–6)*

c. The gathering of all Israel (31:7–14)*

d. Call to Rachel to cease morning as Israel returns home (31:15–22)*

2. Addressed to Judah and Jerusalem (31:23–40)*

a. The new covenant (31:23–34)*

b. The reliability of Yahweh the Creator (31:35–37)

[c. Postexilic promise to rebuild Jerusalem (31:38–40)]

D. Additions (32:1—35:19)

1. Jeremiah's purchase of the field in Anathoth (32:1–44)*

2. Yahweh's promise of restoration (33:1–13)

{3. Promises of "a just shoot" for David (33:14–26)}

4. Message to Zedekiah to submit to Nebuchadnezzar (34:1–7)

5. Zedekiah's edict of emancipation of slaves and its violation (34:8–22)

6. The contrasting fidelity of the Rechabites (35:1–19)

III. Narrative of the last years of Jeremiah (36:1—45:5) [In Greek Bible, chs. 43—51]

A. The scroll of Jeremiah—time of Jehoiakim (36:1–32)

B. Jeremiah and King Zedekiah (37:1—38:28)

1. Zedekiah consults Jeremiah (37:1–10)

2. Jeremiah's attempt to acquire land and his arrest (37:11–16)

3. Zedekiah's consultation with Jeremiah (37:17–21)

4. Jeremiah placed into cistern and rescued (38:1–13)

5. Zedekiah's consultation with Jeremiah (38:14–28)

Appendix 4i—Detailed Outline of Ezekiel

I. Call of Ezekiel (1—3)*
  A. The visions of the living ones, the wheels, and the glory of God (1:1–28)*
  B. The eating of the scroll (2:1—3:11)*
  C. The commission as watchman (3:12–21)*
  D. The speechlessness of the prophet (3:22–27)*

II. Before the fall of Jerusalem (4—24)
  A. Actions and oracles (4:1—7:27)
    1. Three actions (4:1—5:4)
      a. The clay tablet and Ezekiel's lying on the ground (4:1–8)*
      b. Baking the loaves (4:9–17)
      c. Shaving his face and head (5:1–4)
    2. Oracles of judgment (5:5—7:27)
      a. Against Jerusalem (5:5–17)
      b. Against the mountains of Israel (6:1—7:27)
  B. Visions of Jerusalem (8:1—11:21)
    1. Beginning of the vision of the glory of God (8:1–4)*
    2. The sins of Jerusalem (8:5–18)
    3. The angel of judgment and the saving mark (9:1–11)*
    4. The movement of God's glory (10:1–22)*
    5. The princes of the people (11:1–13)
    6. Promise for exiles of restoration (11:14–21)*
    7. Conclusion of the vision of the glory of God (11:22–23)*
  C. Actions and oracles (12:1—14:23)
    1. Escape in the night (12:1–28)
    2. Against the false prophets (13:1–21)
    3. Against idolaters (14:1–11)
    4. Personal responsibility (14:12–23)
  D. Parables and allegories (15:1—19:14)
    1. The vine wood (15:1–8)*
    2. The faithless woman (16:1–58)*
    3. The everlasting covenant (16:59–63)*
    4. The eagles and the vine (17:1–24)*
    5. Instruction on personal responsibility (18:1–32)*

B. The new cult (43—46)
   1. The return of God to the Temple (43:1–12)*
   2. The altar (43:13–27)
   3. The closed gate and exclusion of Gentiles (44:1–9)*
   4. Levites and priests (44:10–31)
   5. The sacred land (45:1–8)
   6. Princes and offerings (45:9–17)
   7. Feasts (45:18—46:6)
   8. Rituals, the prince, and the kitchens (46:8–24)
C. The restoration of Israel (47—48)
   1. The life-giving stream (47:1–12)*
   2. The boundaries and apportionments (47:13—48:29)
   3. Conclusion: the gates of the city (48:30–35)

Appendix 4j—Detailed Outline of Deutero-Isaiah

I. Introduction (40)
  A. The promise of salvation (40:1–11)*
  B. The power of Yahweh to save his people (40:12–31)*

II. Part one: The new exodus of Israel (41—48)
  A. Israel's salvation (41:1—42:13)
    1. The champion of justice (41:1–20)*
    2. The lawsuit indictment against Babylonian gods (41:21–29)
    3. First servant song (42:1–4)*
    4. Yahweh identifies himself (42:5–9)
    5. Hymn to Yahweh (42:10–13)
  B. Yahweh as redeemer and re-creator (42:14—44:23)
    1. Yahweh identifies himself (42:14–17)
    2. Yahweh as responsible for the terrible events (42:18–25)
    3. Yahweh as creator, redeemer, savior (43:1–15)
    4. Yahweh promising something new (43:16–21)*
    5. Israel's sin and redemption (43:22—44:5
    6. Yahweh identifies himself (44:6–8)
    7. Ridicule of idols (44:9–20)
    8. Reassurance to Israel the servant (44:21–23)
  C. Yahweh's absolute power over the earth (44:24—47:15)
    1. The commissioning of Cyrus by Yahweh the Creator (44:24—45:13)
    2. Yahweh's decree (45:14–25)
    3. Indictment against idols (46:1–13)
    4. Taunt against Babylon (47:1–15)
  D. Conclusion (48:1–22)

III. Part two: The word of comfort to Zion (49—54)
  A. From sorrow to redemption (49:1—51:8)
    1. Second servant song (49:1–6)*
    2. Announcement of salvation (49:7–26)*
    3. Yahweh reproaches Israel for not seeking his help (50:1–3)
    4. Third servant song (50:4–9a)*

5. Contrast of Yahweh the Creator with men like cloth
   wearing out (50:9b—51:8)
B. Comforting the mourners (51:9—52:12)
   1. Prayer (51:9–11)
   2. Yahweh's oracle of comfort (51:12—52:6)
   3. Message of salvation (52:7–12)
C. Fourth servant song (52:13—53:12)★
D. The new Zion (54:1–17)

IV. Conclusion (55)★

Appendix 4k—Detailed Outline of Trito-Isaiah

I. Introduction: Inclusive Temple worship (56:1–8)★

II. True leadership (56:9—59:21)
   A. Accusation (56:7—57:13)
   B. Comfort (57:14–21)
   C. True and false fasting (58:1–14)★
   D. Community lament (59:1–21)

III. Messages of salvation (60:1—62:12)
   A. Consolation (60:1–22)★
   B. Call of the prophet (61:1–3)★
   C. Glory of the new Zion (61:4—62:9)
      1. The reward of Israel (61:4–11)
      2. Zion as bride of Yahweh (62:1–5)★
      3. The restoration of Zion (62:6–12)
   D. Final reflection (62:10–12)

IV. From sorrow to a new heaven and earth (63:1—66:16)
   A. The punishment of Edom (63:1–6)
   B. Confession of sin and prayer for God's favor (63:7—64:11)★
   C. True and false servants (65:1–25)
      1. Punishment and reward (65:1–16)
      2. A new heavens and a new earth (65:17–25)★
   D. True and false worship (66:1–6)★
   E. Jerusalem as mother (66:7–16)
   F. Faithless people (66:17)

V. Conclusion: Gathering of the nations (66:18–24)★

Appendix 4l—Detailed Outline of Proto-Zechariah

I. Superscript and Introduction (1:1–6)

II. Eight visions (1:7—6:15)
1. The colored horses (1:7–17)*
2. The four horns and plowmen (2:1–4) [1:18–21]
3. The new Jerusalem (2:5–17)* [2:1–13]
  —collection of diverse oracles on Zion (2:10–17)* [2:6–13]
4. The purification of Joshua (3:1–10)*
5. The lampstand and the leaders (4:1–14)*
6. The flying scroll (5:1–4)
7. The flying bushel container (5:5–11)*
8. The four chariots (6:1–15)
  —the coronation of Joshua [Zerubbabel] (6:9–15)*

III. The question of fasting and other moral teachings (7:1—8:23)
  A. Question posed (7:1–3)
  B. Assessment of the past (7:1–10)
  C. Promises for the future (8:1–17)
  A'. Answer to the question of fasting (8:18–23)*

Appendix 4m—Detailed Outline of Deutero-Zechariah

I. Part one: chapters 9—11
    A. The warrior God (9:1–8)
    B. The peaceful king (9:9–10)*
    C. The warrior God (9:11–17)
    D. God the provider of rain (10:1–3)
    E. The warrior God (10:4—11:3)
    F. The allegory of the shepherds (11:4–17)*

II. Part two: chapters 12—14
    A. Oracle concerning Israel and Jerusalem (12:1–9)
    B. Mourning (12:10–14)*
    C. "On that day" sermons (13:1–6)
    D. Striking the shepherd (13:7–9)
    E. Oracles concerning Jerusalem (14:1–15)
    F. Universal worship in Jerusalem (14:16–21)*

Appendix 4n—Detailed Outline of Mal'aki

Superscript (1:1)

I. Disputation 1: God's love for his people (1:2–5)

II. Disputation 2: Duties of the priests (1:6—2:9)*
  A. Sacrificing defective offerings (1:6–14)*
  B. Failure to instruct (2:1–9)*

III. Disputation 3: Marriages (2:10–16)*
  A. Mixed marriages (2:10–12)*
  B. Divorce (2:13–16)*

IV. Disputation 4: The coming of God (2:17—3:5)*

V. Disputation 5: Returning to God and supporting the Temple (3:6–12)

VI. Disputation 6: God and his justice (3:13–21) [3:13—4:3]

Appendix (3:22–24) [4:4–5]

Appendix 4o—Detailed Outline of Joel

Superscript (1:1)

Part I: The locust plague (1:2—2:17)★
  A. The countryside (1:2–20)★
  B. The city (2:1–17)★

Transition: God pities his people (2:18–27)★
  A. Addressed to "his people" (2:18–20)★
  B. Addressed to the "land" (2:21–22)★
  C. Addressed to the "children of Zion" (2:23–27)★

Part II: The day of Yahweh (3:1[2:28]—4:21[3:21])★ [2:28—3:21]
  A. The coming of the day of Yahweh (3:1–5) [2:28–32]★
  B. The reversal of fortunes (4[3]:1–21)★
    {–later addition: oracle on Tyre, Sidon, Philistia (4[3]:4–8)}

Appendix 4p—Detailed Outline of Daniel

Part I: The stories of Daniel (1—6)
    A. The food test (1)*
    B. Nebuchadnezzar's dream (2)*
    C. The fiery furnace (3:1–30) [3:1–97]
    D. The vision of the great tree (3:31[98]—4:34) [4:1–37]
    E. The writing on the wall (5)*
    F. The lions' den (6)*

Part II: The visions of Daniel (7—12)
    A. The four beasts (7)*
    B. The ram and the billy goat (8)*
    D. The seventy weeks (9)*
    E. The Hellenistic wars (10—12)*

{Appendices (13—14)
    A. The story of Susanna (13)
    B. The story of Bel and the dragon (14)}

Appendix 5
Historical Wars in Daniel 11

Appendix 5a—The Hellenistic Wars Cryptically Described in Daniel 11

316–282   Seleucus I was at first a vassal of Ptolemy I, first Hellenistic ruler of Egypt, "king of the south." Seleucus then broke from Ptolemy and originated the Seleucid kingdom (301–63), making Antioch in Syria his capital. See Dan 11:5.

c. 250   Ptolemy II of Egypt gave his daughter Bernice in marriage to Antiochus II of Syria. Bernice along with her infant son, however, were murdered by Ptolemy's jealous divorced wife. See Dan 11:6.

246–221   Ptolemy III of Egypt, in revenge for the murder of his sister, Bernice, invaded and devastated Syria. See Dan 11:7–8. The counteroffensive of Seleucus II of Syria in 242 was a disaster. See Dan 11:9.

217   Ptolemy IV of Egypt (221–203) defeated Antiochus III "the Great" of Syria in the battle of Raphia. See Dan 11:11.

223–187   Antiochus III of Syria eventually defeated Ptolemy V of Egypt (203–181), taking control in 198 BC of Palestine and Israel. See Dan 11:13–16.

193   The marriage of Antiochus's daughter, Cleopatra, in 193 may have been part of a peace agreement. See Daniel 11:17.

190   The defeat of Antiochus by L. Cornelius Scipio, the Roman, at the Battle of Magnesia in 190 BC ended Syrian expansionism. See Dan 11:18–19.

187–175   Seleucus IV sent his finance minister, Heliodorus, to seize the treasury of the Jerusalem Temple. See Dan 11:20; 2 Macc 3.

175–164   Antiochus IV (175–164), "Epiphanes," came to power by supplanting Demetrius, "the prince of the covenant," the son and heir of Seleucus IV. See Dan 11:21–24. In Jerusalem in 170 Onias the Jewish high priest was assassinated. Antiochus's two campaigns against Egypt in 169 and 168 were successful until the intervention of the Romans ("Kittim"), under the legate G. Popilius Laenas. See Dan 11:25–30.

167   Returning from Egypt in 167, Antiochus plunders the Temple and begins his official persecution of the Jews. See Dan 11:30–39.

164   After a series of defeats inflicted on his armies by the Jewish insurgent, Antiochus withdrew to the East and apparently died there in 164.

Appendix 5b—The Seleucid Kings of Syria

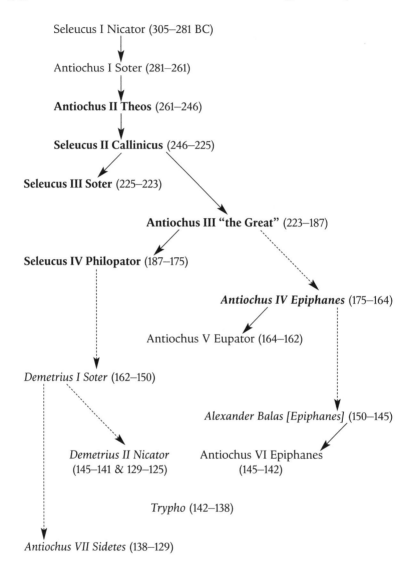

Seleucus I Nicator (305–281 BC)

Antiochus I Soter (281–261)

Antiochus II Theos (261–246)

Seleucus II Callinicus (246–225)

Seleucus III Soter (225–223)

Antiochus III "the Great" (223–187)

Seleucus IV Philopator (187–175)

Antiochus IV Epiphanes (175–164)

Antiochus V Eupator (164–162)

Demetrius I Soter (162–150)

Alexander Balas [Epiphanes] (150–145)

Demetrius II Nicator
(145–141 & 129–125)

Antiochus VI Epiphanes
(145–142)

Trypho (142–138)

Antiochus VII Sidetes (138–129)

Names in **bold print** indicate kings alluded to in Daniel 11; see also 1 and 2 Maccabees.
A solid arrow indicates succession by filiation.
A dotted arrow indicates filiation.
Names in *italics* indicate kings who seized power.

Appendix 6
Further Readings

Chapter 1

Leclerc, Thomas L. *Introduction to the Prophets: Their Stories, Sayings, and Scrolls.* New York: Paulist Press, 2007.

Petersen, David. "Introduction to Prophetic Literature," *The New Interpreter's Bible.* 12 vols. [hereafter *NIB*]. Nashville: Abingdon, 2001, VI, 1–23.

Wilson, Robert. *Prophecy and Society in Ancient Israel.* Philadelphia: Fortress Press, 1984.

Zucker, David. *Israel's Prophets: An Introduction for Christians and Jews.* New York: Paulist Press, 1994.

Chapter 3 and 8

Branick, Vincent. *Understanding the Historical Books of the Old Testament.* New York: Paulist Press, 2012.

Brueggemann, Walter. *1 & 2 Kings.* Macon, GA: Smyth & Helwys, 2000.

Gray, John. *I & II Kings: A Commentary.* 2nd ed. Philadelphia: Westminster Press, 1970.

Chapter 4

Gowan, Donald. "The Book of Amos," *NIB*, VII, 337–431.

Martin-Achard, Robert. *A Commentary on the Book of Amos.* International Theological Commentary. Grand Rapids: Eerdmans, 1984.

Shalom, Paul. *Amos.* Hermeneia. Philadelphia: Fortress, 1991.

Chapter 5

Andersen, Francis, and David Freedman. *Hosea*. Anchor Bible [hereafter: AB] 24. Garden City, NY: Doubleday, 1980.

Wolff, Hans W. *Hosea*. Trans. G. Stansell. Hermeneia. Philadelphia: Fortress, 1974.

Yee, Gale. "The Book of Hosea," *NIB*, VII, 195–310.

Chapter 6

Blenkinsopp, J. *Isaiah 1—39*. AB 19; Garden City: Doubleday, 2000.

Brueggemann, Walter. *Isaiah 1—39*. Westminster Bible Companion. Louisville: Westminster John Knox, 1998.

Tucker, Gene. "The Book of Isaiah 1—39," *NIB*, VI, 25–305.

Chapter 7

Andersen, Francis, and David N. Freedman. *Micah*. AB 24E. New York: Doubleday, 2000.

Hillers, Delbert. *Micah: A Commentary on the Book of the Prophet Micah*. Hermeneia., Philadelphia: Fortress, 1984.

Simundson, Daniel. "The Book of Micah," *NIB*, VII, 531–89.

Wolff, Hans W. *Micah: A Commentary*. Minneapolis: Augsburg, 1990.

Chapter 9

Andersen, Francis. *Habakkuk*. AB 25. New York: Doubleday, 2001.

Berlin, Adele. *Zephaniah*. AB 25A. New York: Doubleday, 1994.

Ben Zvi, Ehud. *A Historical-Critical Study of the Book of Zephaniah*. BZAW. 198. Berlin: DeGruyter, 1991.

Christensen, Duane. *Nahum*. AB 24F. New Haven: Yale University Press, 2009.

Garcia-Treto, Francisco. "The Book of Nahum," *NIB*, VII, 591–619.

Haak, Robert. *Habakkuk*. Supplements to Vetus Testamentum, 44. Leiden: Brill, 1991.

Chapter 10

Brueggemann, Walter. *The Theology of the Book of Jeremiah*. New York: Cambridge University Press, 2007

Holladay, William L. *Jeremiah 1: A Commentary on the Book of the Prophet Jeremiah, Chapters 1–25*. Hermeneia. Philadelphia: Fortress, 1986; and *Jeremiah 2: A Commentary on the Book of the Prophet Jeremiah, Chapters 26–52*. 1989.

Lundbom, Jack. *Jeremiah 1—20*. AB 21A. Garden City: Doubleday, 1999; and *Jeremiah 21—36*. AB 21B. 2004; and *Jeremiah 37—52*. AB 21C. 2004.

Chapter 11

Blenkinsopp, Joseph. *Ezekiel*. Interpretation. Louisville: John Knox, 1990.

Darr, Katheryn Pfisterer. "The Book of Ezekiel," *NIB*, VI, 1073–1607.

Greenberg, Moshe. *Ezekiel 1—20*. AB 22. Garden City: Doubleday, 1983; and *Ezekiel 21—37*. AB 221. 1997.

Chapter 12 and 14

Blenkinsopp, J. *Isaiah 40—55*. AB 19A. Garden City: Doubleday, 2002, and *Isaiah 56—66*. AB 19B. 2003.

Hanson, P. D. *Isaiah 40—66*. Interpretation. Louisville: Westminster John Knox, 2001.

Seitz, Christopher. "The Book of Isaiah 40—66," *NIB*, VI, 307–552.

Westermann, C. *Isaiah 40—66*. Trans. D. Stalker. Old Testament Library. Philadelphia: Westminster, 1969.

Chapter 13

Blenkinsopp, Joseph. *Ezra-Nehemiah*. Old Testament Library. Philadelphia: Westminster, 1988.

Klein, Ralph. "The Books of Ezra & Nehemiah," *NIB*, III, 661–851.

Myers, Jacob M. *Ezra Nehemiah*. AB 14. Garden City, NY: Doubleday, 1965.

Chapter 15

March, W. Eugene. "The Book of Haggai," *NIB*, VII, 705–32.

Meyers, Carol L., and Eric M. Meyers. *Haggai, Zechariah 1—8*. AB, 25B. Garden City, NY: Doubleday, 1987.

Petersen David L. *Haggai and Zechariah 1—8*. Old Testament Library. Philadelphia: Westminster, 1984.

Stuhlmueller, Carroll. *Rebuilding with Hope: A Commentary on the Books of Haggai and Zechariah*. International Theological Commentary. Grand Rapids: Eerdmans, 1988.

Chapter 16

Hill, Andrew. *Malachi*. AB 25D, New York: Doubleday, 1998.

Meyers, Carol L., and Eric M. Meyers. *Zechariah 9—14*. AB 25c. New York: Doubleday, 1993

Petersen David L. *Zechariah 9—14 and Malachi*. Louisville: Westminster John Knox, 1995.

Schuller, Eileen. "The Book of Malachi," *NIB*, VII, 841–77.

Chapter 17

Achtemeier, Elizabeth. "The Book of Joel," *NIB*, VII, 299–336.

Crenshaw, James. *Joel*. AB 24C. New York: Doubleday, 1995.

Pagan, Samuel. "The Book of Obadiah," *NIB*, VII, 433–59.

Raabe, Paul. *Obadiah*. AB 24D. New York: Doubleday, 1996.

Watts, J. D. W. *Obadiah: A Critical Exegetical Commentary*. Grand Rapids: Eerdmans, 1969.

Chapter 18

Neusner, Jacob. *Invitation to Midrash: The Workings of Rabbinic Bible Interpretation, a Teaching Book*. San Francisco: Harper & Row, 1989.

———. *What Is Midrash?* New Testament Series. Philadelphia: Fortress Press, 1987.

Wright, Addison G. *The Literary Genre Midrash.* Staten Island, NY: Alba House, 1967.

Chapter 19

Sasson, Jack M. *Jonah.* AB 24B. New York: Doubleday, 1990.
Trible, Phyllis. "The Book of Jonah," *NIB*, VII, 461–529.

Chapter 20

Collins, John. *Daniel.* Hermeneia. Minneapolis: Fortress, 1993.
Hartman, Louis, and Alexander A. DeLella. *The Book of Daniel.* AB, 23. Garden City, NY: Doubleday, 1978.
Smith-Christopher, Daniel. "The Book of Daniel," *NIB*, VII, 17–152.

Chapter 21

Brueggemann, Walter. *The Prophetic Imagination.* Minneapolis: Fortress Press, 2001.
Heschel, Abraham. *The Prophets: An Introduction.* 2 vols. New York: Harper & Row, 1962.
Von Rad, G. *The Message of the Prophets.* New York: Harper and Bros., 1965.